COURTNEY CRUMRIN AND THE NIGHT THINGS™

COURTNEY CRUMRIN AND THE NIGHT THINGS™

By Ted Naifeh

Design by
Ted Naifeh
with assistance from Steven Birch @ Servo

Edited by
James Lucas Jones

Published by Oni Press, Inc.
Joe Nozemack, publisher
Jamie S. Rich, editor in chief
James Lucas Jones, associate editor

This collects issues 1-4 of the Oni Press
comics series *Courtney Crumrin and the Night Things*.

ONI PRESS, INC.
6336 SE Milwaukie Avenue, PMB 30
Portland, OR 97202
USA

www.onipress.com
www.tednaifeh.com

Second edition: June 2003
ISBN 1-929998-60-0

5 7 9 10 8 6
PRINTED IN CANADA.

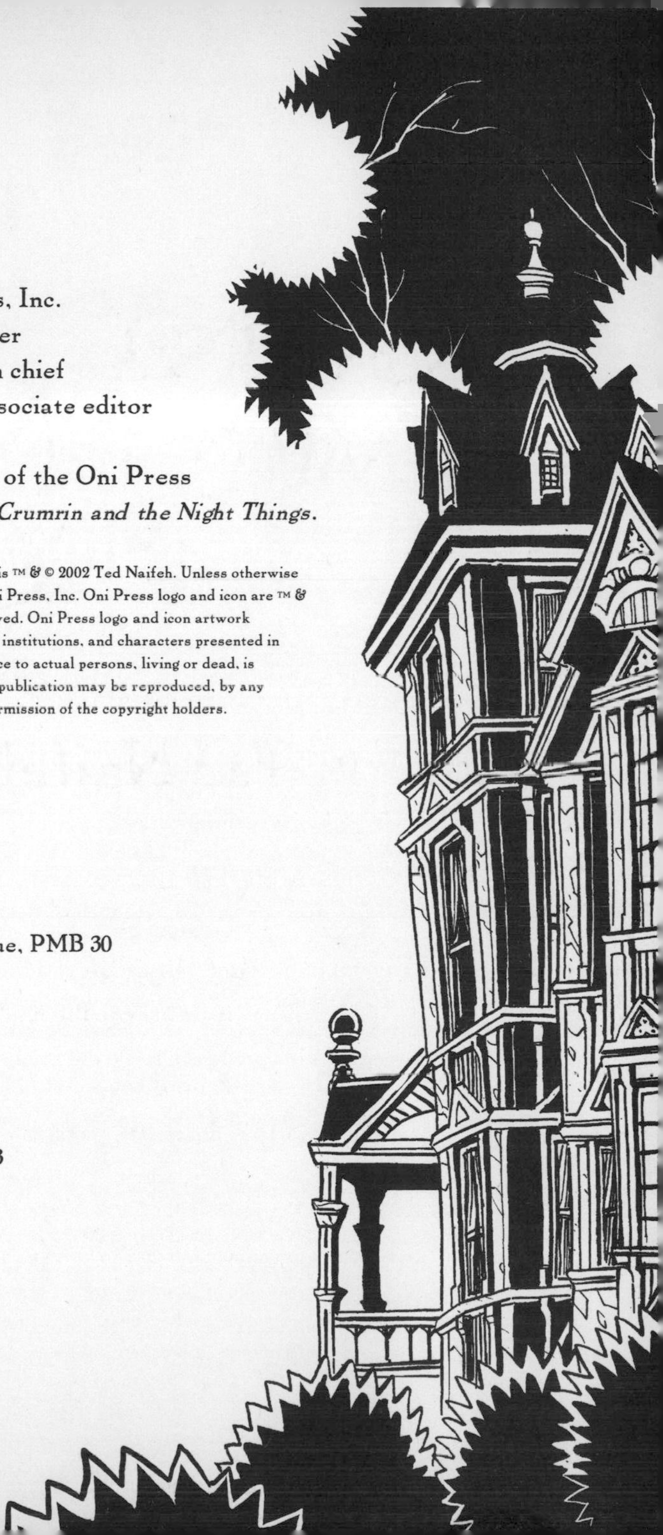

A FEW WORDS ABOUT CHILDREN, NIGHTMARES, AND OUTCASTS

Childhood is a much darker world than most adults care to remember. If anything, childhood is even more full of terror and passion than life becomes after a few decades spent killing off pesky brain cells. Small children are straight outta nature, all id, tribal survivalists to the core. They drive the weak away from the village, instinctively hating those who are different, ugly, or slow. Sure, they're preoccupied with stockpiling toys instead of guns, but the principle is the same. Behind the big shiny eyes and dimples is *The Lord of the Flies*, ticking and buzzing. We learn sweetness and the ability to sit still later on in order to fit into society and get grown-up things like jobs and apartments and girl- or boyfriends, things that seem yucky and boring until the moment we're ready for them. Among the byproducts that boil off and are lost in the process of growing up are simplicity, lots of dreams, and a huge amount of fear.

Children understand fear. But there are also childhood terrors that go even deeper than the social torture experienced daily in every grammar school in the world. One of the worst nightmares I ever had seemed to be trying to explain the bedtime fears that all kids go through. While I was asleep, my brain told me a story about children and their common, silly childhood fears: the dark, the bogeyman, the creature in the closet, the monster under the bed. The stuff we learn to laugh at and later humor and comfort in our own children. Then I saw the human predators, the real-life monsters such as serial killers and child murderers, and their helpless prey. My mind suggested that it was the terror suffered by these victims that, via some kind of collective consciousness, shows up as the Thing at the Foot of the Bed. That even the most sheltered kid lovingly tucked in every night somehow knows about these very real bogeymen and feels the horror of the unlucky ones, the ones who got caught. At 4 a.m. I woke up screaming and sat with all the lights on and my back to the wall until the watery winter sun came up. I'd never been so glad to be an adult before.

Strangely enough, despite all of the more or less real terrors they contend with on a daily and nightly basis, children love to be scared, love to be grossed out, love, above all, to be shocked.

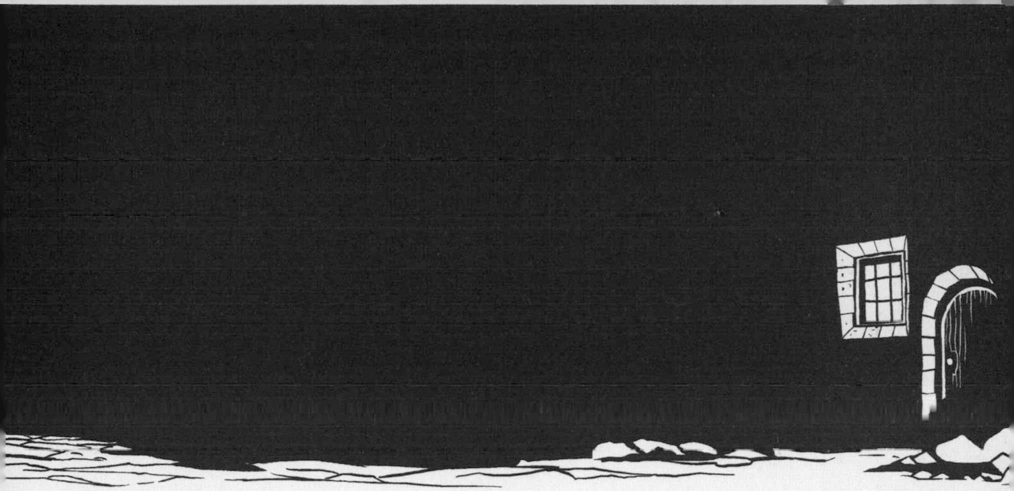

The only children's stories that are truly classic, timeless, and beloved are also subversively honest about life's ugliness. Kids experience reality on a much simpler level than adults, and don't buy stories that are too sugary. They're realists in the sense that they know there's much more to reality than what we see around us every day or what we learn in school. There almost has to be a tragic, a bitter or a vicious edge to a story, or they know it for the load of bull it is. Mark Twain, Roald Dahl, and Judy Blume, three of the all-time best-beloved children's authors, knew this. Their books are often banned from schools and libraries because of parents' need to believe that children are innocent of pain and cruelty and can be protected from knowledge about the darkness of human nature.

I grew up on those and other great authors, whose books gave me a glimpse at life's beautiful and horrible truths. Now that I'm an adult, at least in the sense that I have to pay taxes and worry about gingivitis, I see that I'm a part of the diaspora of kids that was driven from the village, for various reasons, and spent adolescence observing it all from the outside. We've formed our own tribes, and as far as I can see, we, the geeks, won. We're smarter, we're independent, we're more courageous, and we value each other more than the kids who fit in without effort, blending in and never really getting to know themselves. I only wish I could tell my little sister, who's about Courtney's age, and rapidly moving from the unicorn stage to the moody poetry stage and reading everything she can get her hands on, to hang in there. Sure, it'll be a rough eight or ten years, but at the end of it, she'll be a conscious, brilliant, confident woman with a loving, like-minded community and her own unique style. It's worth the pain you feel now. Trust me. And grown-up geekboys do make the best partners. I should know.

Actually, come to think of it, that doesn't sound particularly comforting — eight years is a lifetime to a kid. And of course, you can't tell kids anything.

- Kelly Crumrin

Kelly Crumrin is a freelance writer who lives in San Francisco and would head the campaign to elect Emperor Norton as president if only he weren't so dead.

To Magic, for helping
awaken my imagination,
and to Ron, for telling me
of the Night Things.

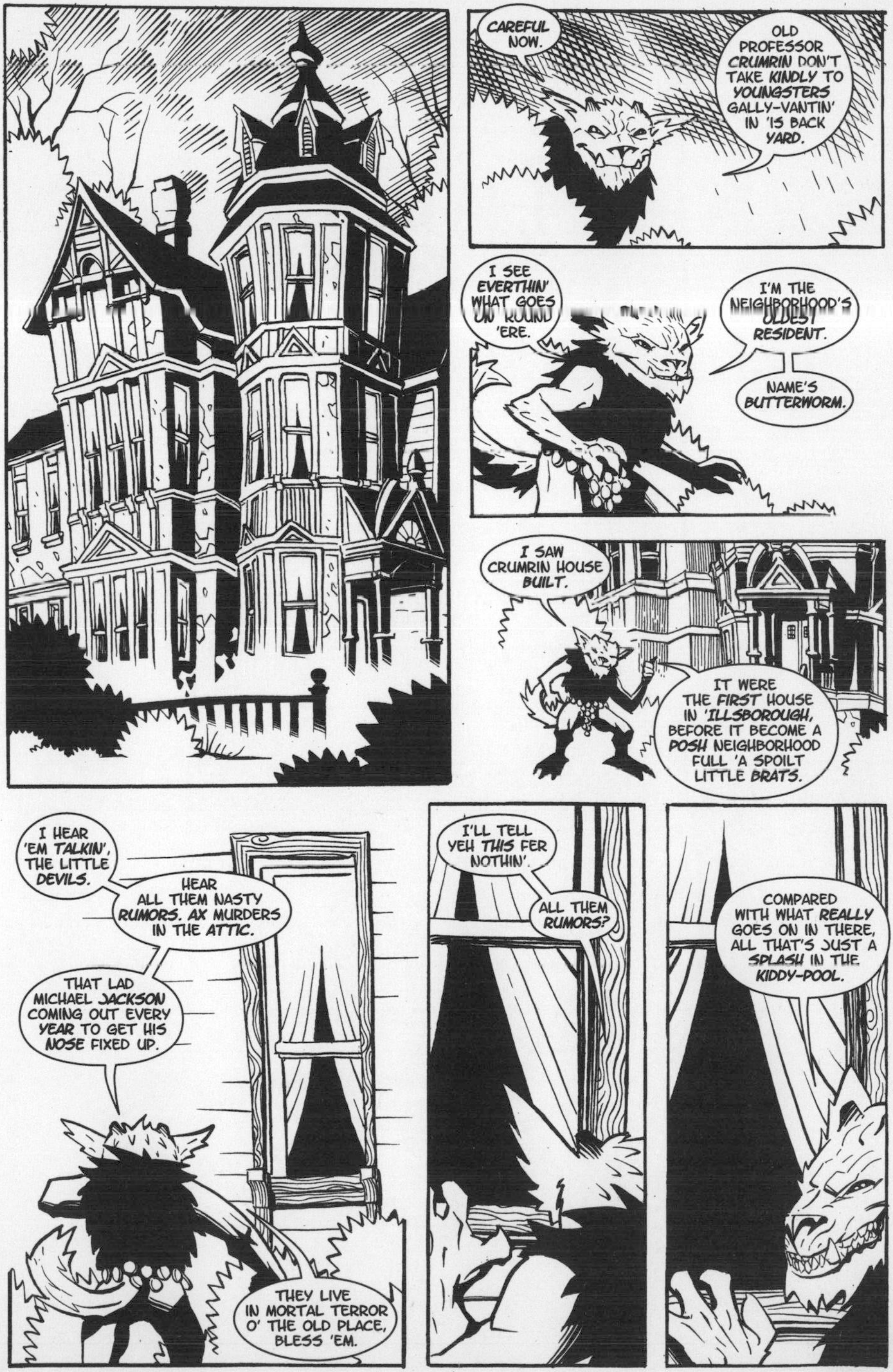
CAREFUL NOW.
OLD PROFESSOR CRUMRIN DON'T TAKE KINDLY TO YOUNGSTERS GALLY-VANTIN' IN 'IS BACK YARD.
I SEE EVERTHIN' WHAT GOES ON ROUND 'ERE.
I'M THE NEIGHBORHOOD'S OLDEST RESIDENT.
NAME'S BUTTERWORM.
I SAW CRUMRIN HOUSE BUILT.
IT WERE THE FIRST HOUSE IN 'ILLSBOROUGH, BEFORE IT BECOME A POSH NEIGHBORHOOD FULL 'A SPOILT LITTLE BRATS.
I HEAR 'EM TALKIN', THE LITTLE DEVILS.
HEAR ALL THEM NASTY RUMORS. AX MURDERS IN THE ATTIC.
THAT LAD MICHAEL JACKSON COMING OUT EVERY YEAR TO GET HIS NOSE FIXED UP.
THEY LIVE IN MORTAL TERROR O' THE OLD PLACE, BLESS 'EM.
I'LL TELL YEH THIS FER NOTHIN'.
ALL THEM RUMORS?
COMPARED WITH WHAT REALLY GOES ON IN THERE, ALL THAT'S JUST A SPLASH IN THE KIDDY-POOL.

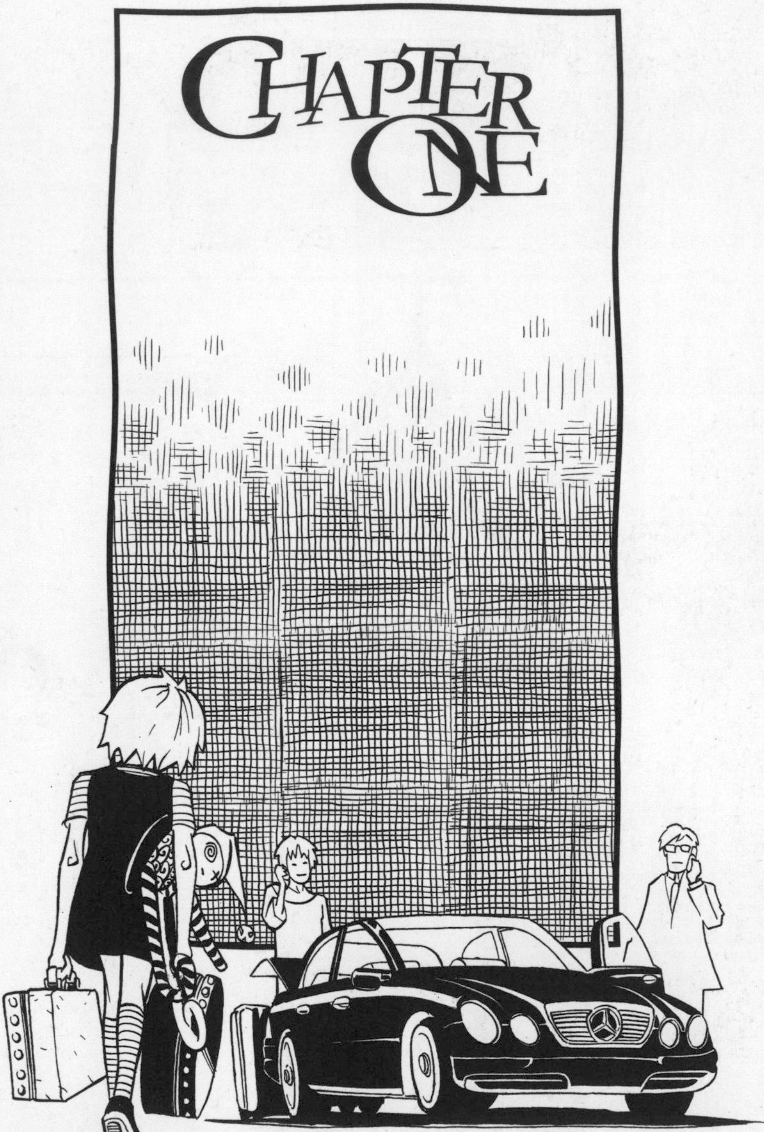
CHAPTER ONE

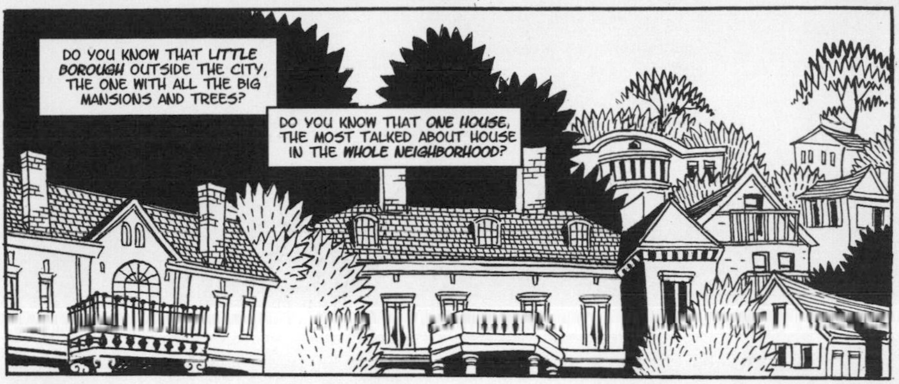
DO YOU KNOW THAT LITTLE BOROUGH OUTSIDE THE CITY, THE ONE WITH ALL THE BIG MANSIONS AND TREES?
DO YOU KNOW THAT ONE HOUSE, THE MOST TALKED ABOUT HOUSE IN THE WHOLE NEIGHBORHOOD?

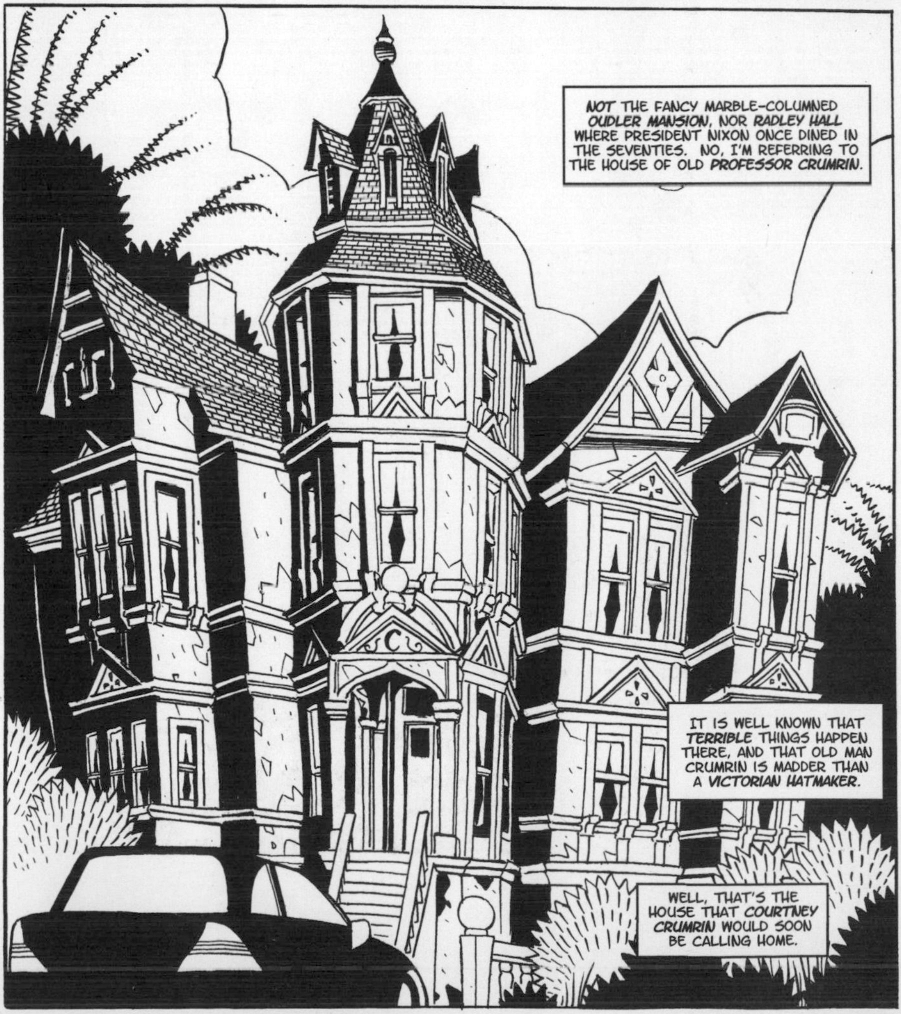
NOT THE FANCY MARBLE-COLUMNED OUDLER MANSION, NOR RADLEY HALL WHERE PRESIDENT NIXON ONCE DINED IN THE SEVENTIES. NO, I'M REFERRING TO THE HOUSE OF OLD PROFESSOR CRUMRIN.
C
IT IS WELL KNOWN THAT TERRIBLE THINGS HAPPEN THERE, AND THAT OLD MAN CRUMRIN IS MADDER THAN A VICTORIAN HATMAKER.
WELL, THAT'S THE HOUSE THAT COURTNEY CRUMRIN WOULD SOON BE CALLING HOME.

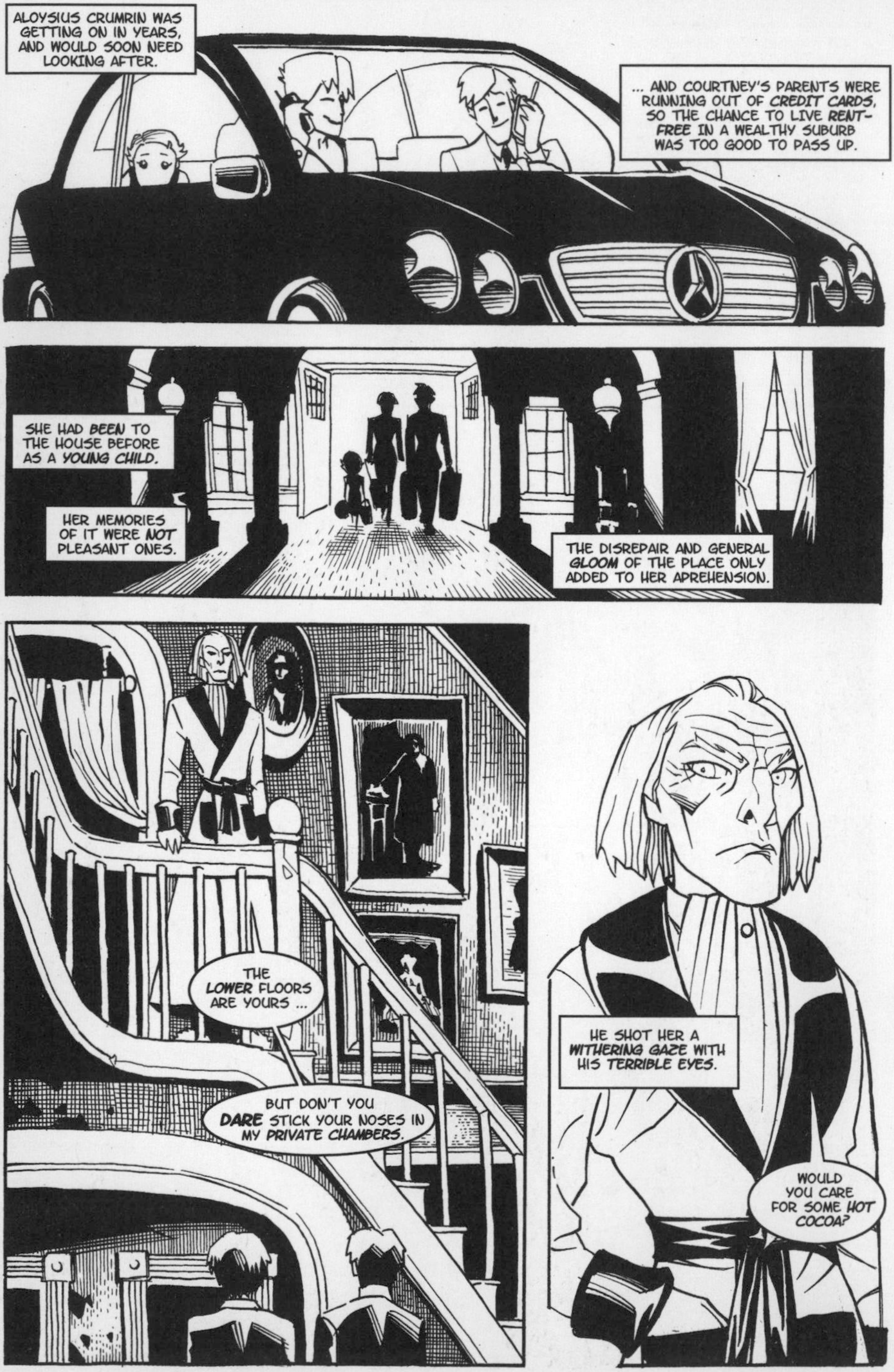
ALOYSIUS CRUMRIN WAS GETTING ON IN YEARS, AND WOULD SOON NEED LOOKING AFTER.
... AND COURTNEY'S PARENTS WERE RUNNING OUT OF CREDIT CARDS, SO THE CHANCE TO LIVE RENT-FREE IN A WEALTHY SUBURB WAS TOO GOOD TO PASS UP.
SHE HAD BEEN TO THE HOUSE BEFORE AS A YOUNG CHILD.
HER MEMORIES OF IT WERE NOT PLEASANT ONES.
THE DISREPAIR AND GENERAL GLOOM OF THE PLACE ONLY ADDED TO HER APREHENSION.
THE LOWER FLOORS ARE YOURS ...
BUT DON'T YOU DARE STICK YOUR NOSES IN MY PRIVATE CHAMBERS.
HE SHOT HER A WITHERING GAZE WITH HIS TERRIBLE EYES.
WOULD YOU CARE FOR SOME HOT COCOA?

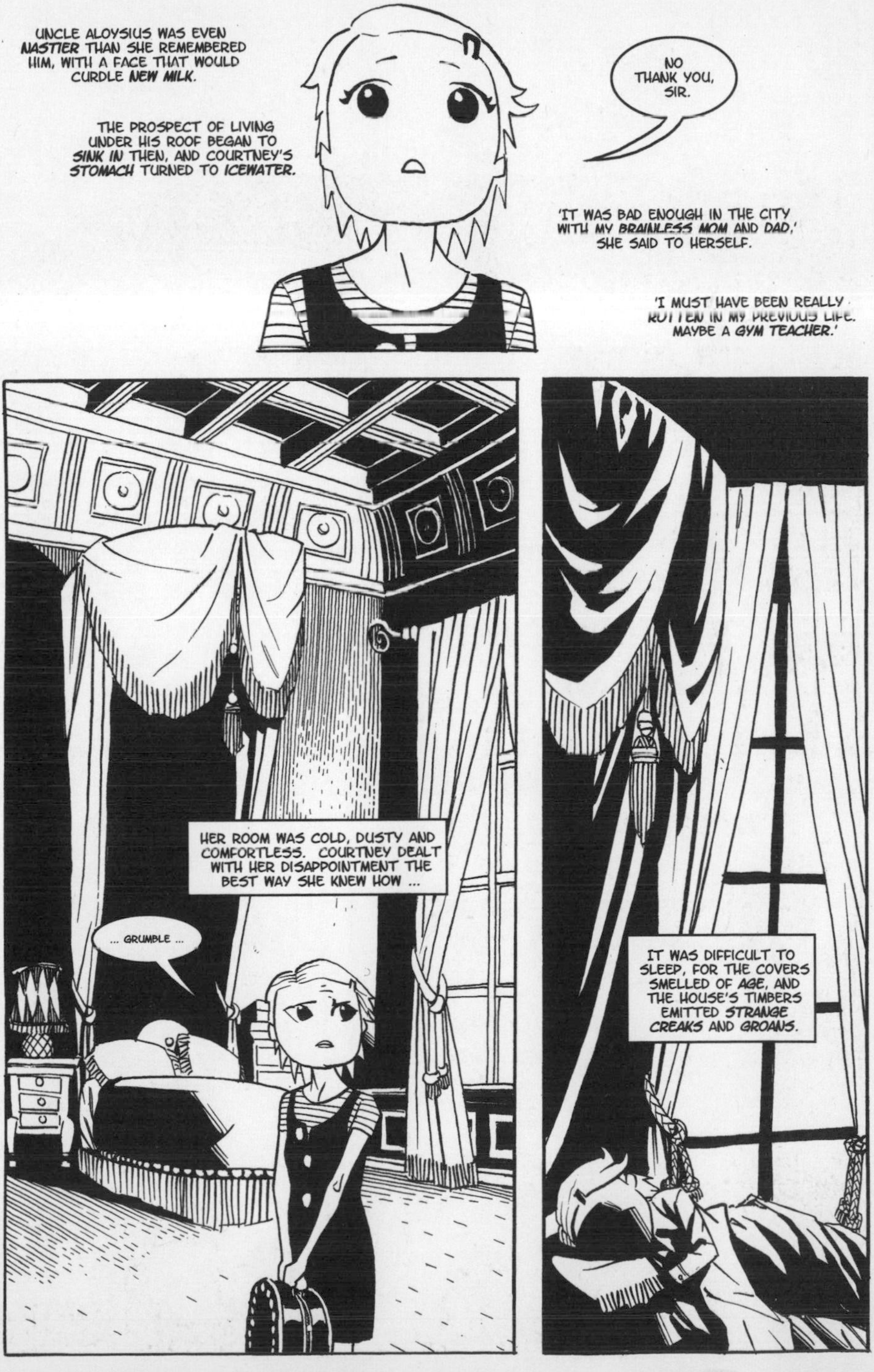
UNCLE ALOYSIUS WAS EVEN NASTIER THAN SHE REMEMBERED HIM, WITH A FACE THAT WOULD CURDLE NEW MILK.
THE PROSPECT OF LIVING UNDER HIS ROOF BEGAN TO SINK IN THEN, AND COURTNEY'S STOMACH TURNED TO ICEWATER.
NO THANK YOU, SIR.
'IT WAS BAD ENOUGH IN THE CITY WITH MY BRAINLESS MOM AND DAD,' SHE SAID TO HERSELF.
'I MUST HAVE BEEN REALLY ROTTEN IN MY PREVIOUS LIFE. MAYBE A GYM TEACHER.'
HER ROOM WAS COLD, DUSTY AND COMFORTLESS. COURTNEY DEALT WITH HER DISAPPOINTMENT THE BEST WAY SHE KNEW HOW ...
... GRUMBLE ...
IT WAS DIFFICULT TO SLEEP, FOR THE COVERS SMELLED OF AGE, AND THE HOUSE'S TIMBERS EMITTED STRANGE CREAKS AND GROANS.

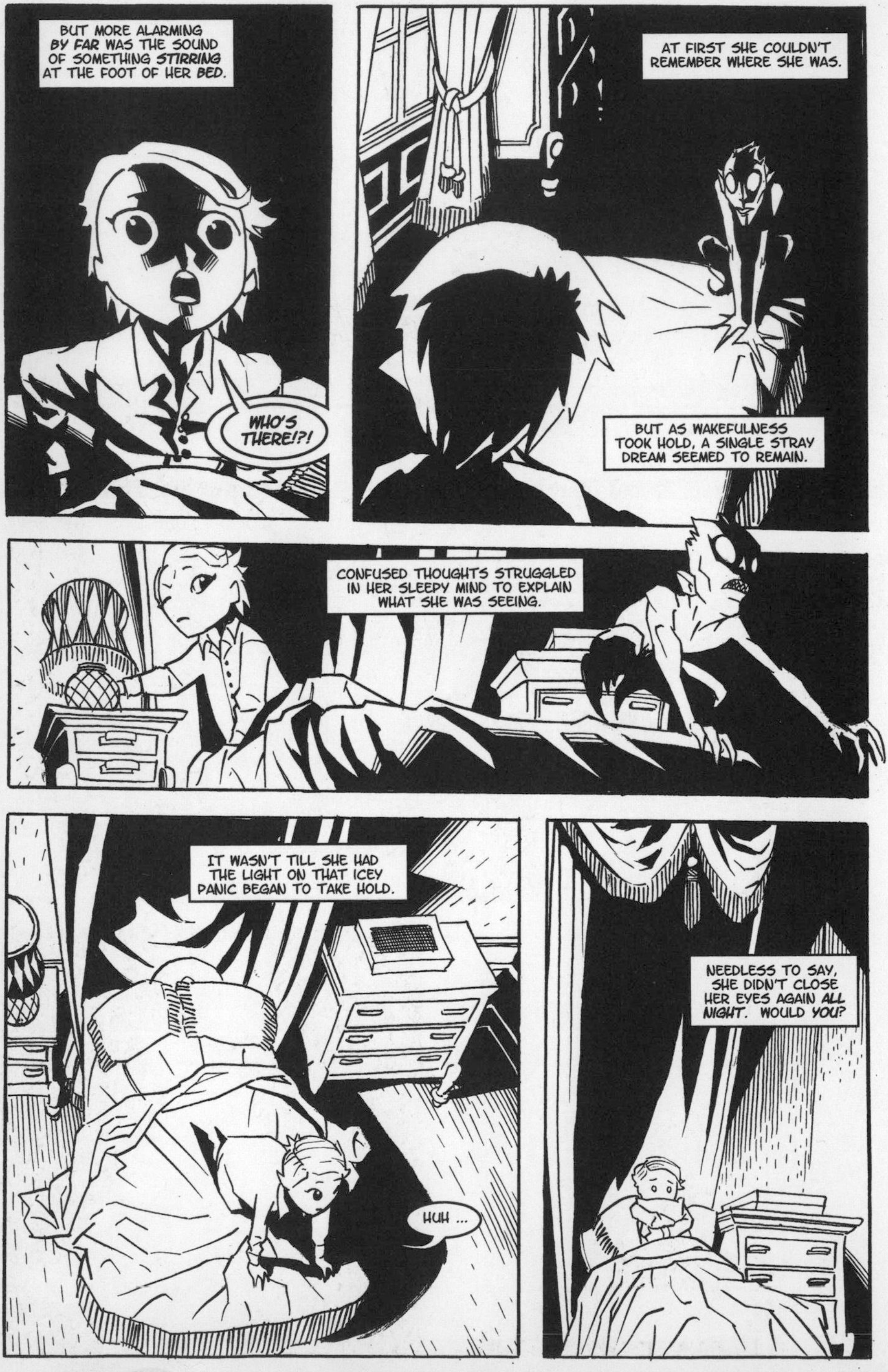
BUT MORE ALARMING BY FAR WAS THE SOUND OF SOMETHING STIRRING AT THE FOOT OF HER BED.
WHO'S THERE!?!
AT FIRST SHE COULDN'T REMEMBER WHERE SHE WAS.
BUT AS WAKEFULNESS TOOK HOLD, A SINGLE STRAY DREAM SEEMED TO REMAIN.
CONFUSED THOUGHTS STRUGGLED IN HER SLEEPY MIND TO EXPLAIN WHAT SHE WAS SEEING.
IT WASN'T TILL SHE HAD THE LIGHT ON THAT ICEY PANIC BEGAN TO TAKE HOLD.
HUH ...
NEEDLESS TO SAY, SHE DIDN'T CLOSE HER EYES AGAIN ALL NIGHT. WOULD YOU?

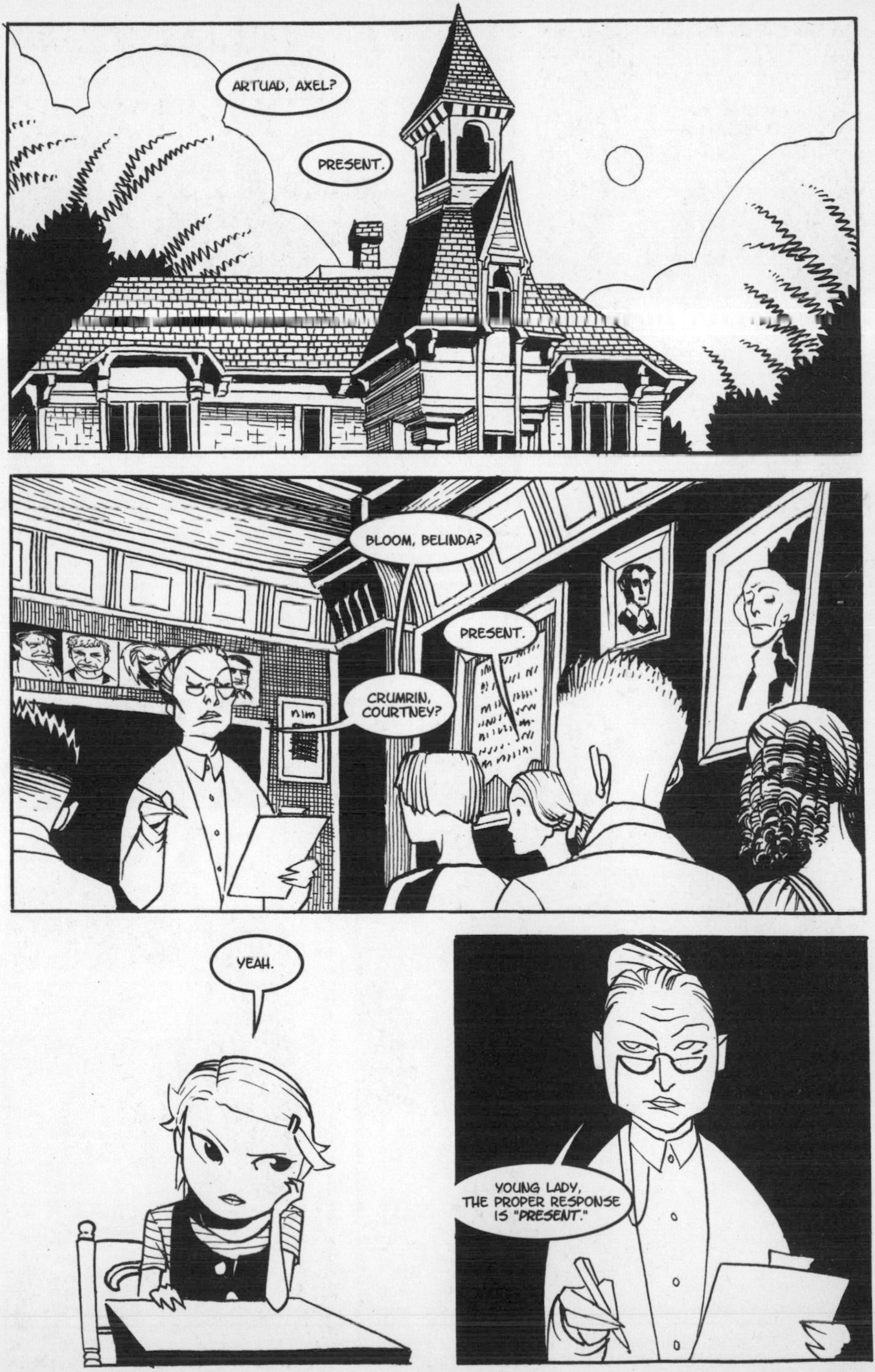
ARTUAD, AXEL?
PRESENT.
BLOOM, BELINDA?
PRESENT.
CRUMRIN, COURTNEY?
YEAH.
YOUNG LADY, THE PROPER RESPONSE IS "PRESENT."

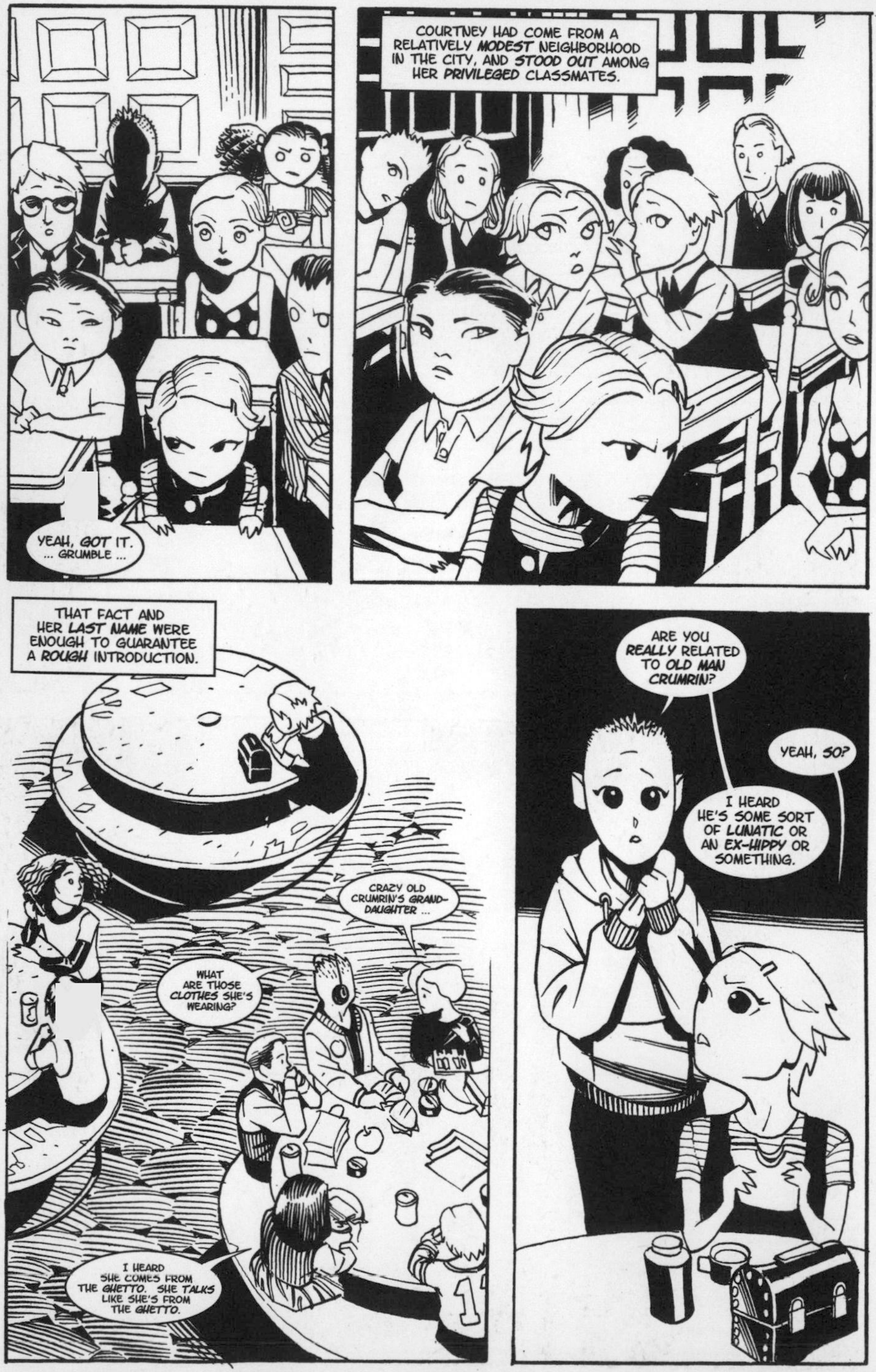
YEAH, GOT IT.
... GRUMBLE ...
COURTNEY HAD COME FROM A RELATIVELY MODEST NEIGHBORHOOD IN THE CITY, AND STOOD OUT AMONG HER PRIVILEGED CLASSMATES.
THAT FACT AND HER LAST NAME WERE ENOUGH TO GUARANTEE A ROUGH INTRODUCTION.
CRAZY OLD CRUMRIN'S GRAND-DAUGHTER ...
WHAT ARE THOSE CLOTHES SHE'S WEARING?
I HEARD SHE COMES FROM THE GHETTO. SHE TALKS LIKE SHE'S FROM THE GHETTO.
ARE YOU REALLY RELATED TO OLD MAN CRUMRIN?
YEAH, SO?
I HEARD HE'S SOME SORT OF LUNATIC OR AN EX-HIPPY OR SOMETHING.

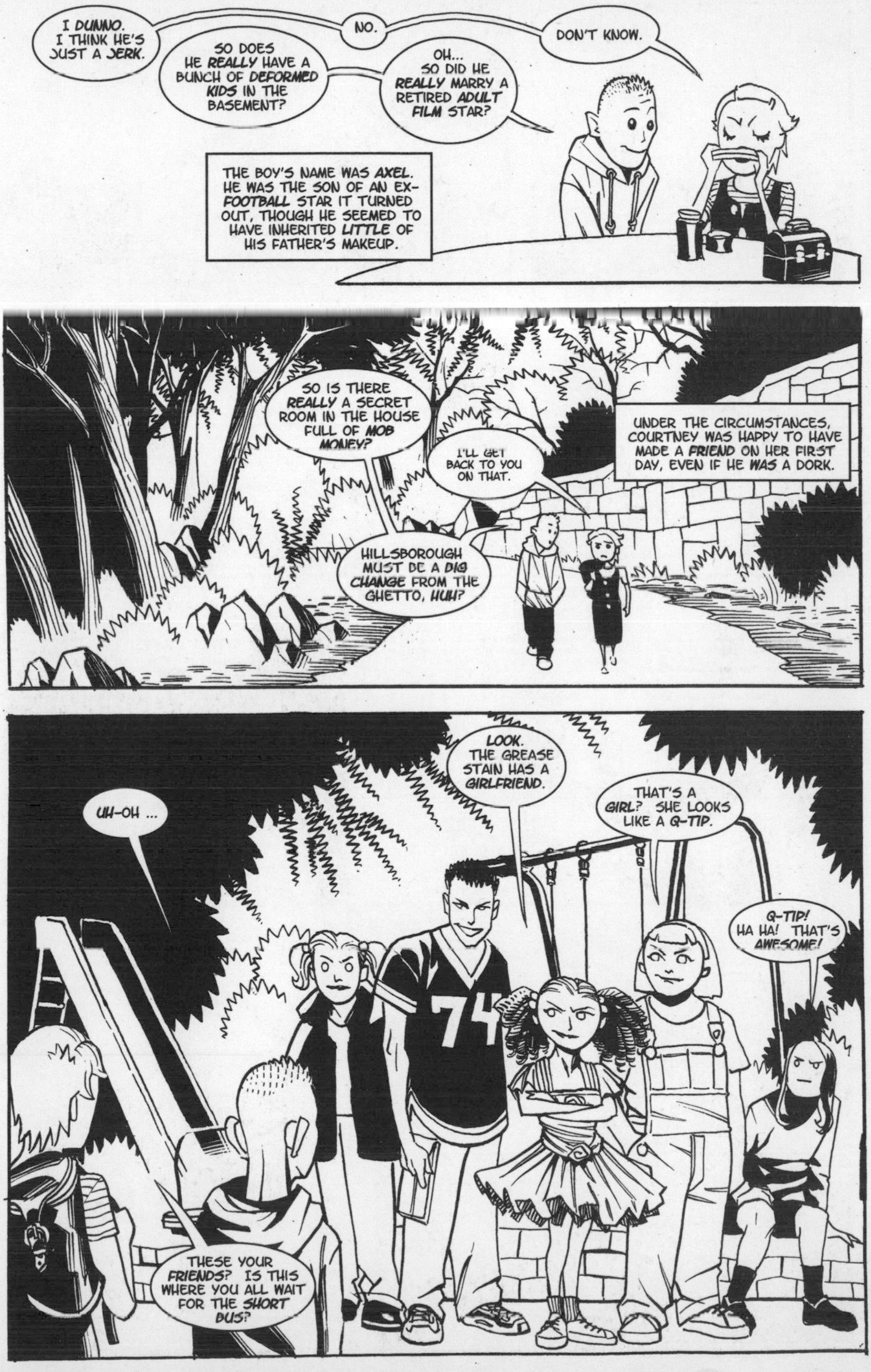
I DUNNO. I THINK HE'S JUST A JERK.
SO DOES HE REALLY HAVE A BUNCH OF DEFORMED KIDS IN THE BASEMENT?
NO.
OH... SO DID HE REALLY MARRY A RETIRED ADULT FILM STAR?
DON'T KNOW.
THE BOY'S NAME WAS AXEL. HE WAS THE SON OF AN EX-FOOTBALL STAR IT TURNED OUT, THOUGH HE SEEMED TO HAVE INHERITED LITTLE OF HIS FATHER'S MAKEUP.
SO IS THERE REALLY A SECRET ROOM IN THE HOUSE FULL OF MOB MONEY?
I'LL GET BACK TO YOU ON THAT.
UNDER THE CIRCUMSTANCES, COURTNEY WAS HAPPY TO HAVE MADE A FRIEND ON HER FIRST DAY, EVEN IF HE WAS A DORK.
HILLSBOROUGH MUST BE A BIG CHANGE FROM THE GHETTO, HUH?
UH-OH ...
LOOK. THE GREASE STAIN HAS A GIRLFRIEND.
THAT'S A GIRL? SHE LOOKS LIKE A Q-TIP.
Q-TIP! HA HA! THAT'S AWESOME!
74
THESE YOUR FRIENDS? IS THIS WHERE YOU ALL WAIT FOR THE SHORT BUS?

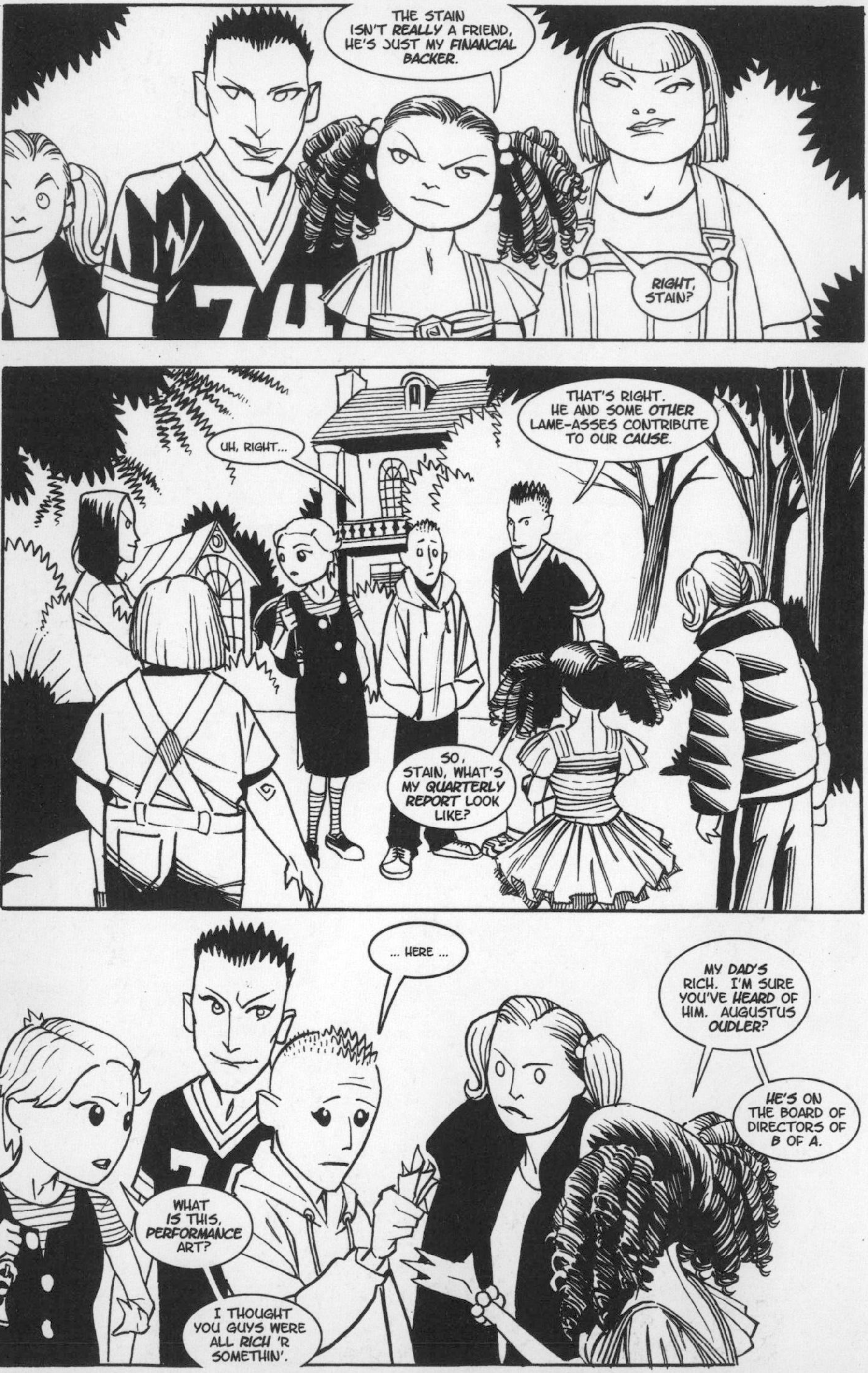
THE STAIN ISN'T REALLY A FRIEND, HE'S JUST MY FINANCIAL BACKER.
RIGHT, STAIN?
UH, RIGHT...
THAT'S RIGHT. HE AND SOME OTHER LAME-ASSES CONTRIBUTE TO OUR CAUSE.
SO, STAIN, WHAT'S MY QUARTERLY REPORT LOOK LIKE?
... HERE ...
MY DAD'S RICH. I'M SURE YOU'VE HEARD OF HIM. AUGUSTUS OUDLER?
HE'S ON THE BOARD OF DIRECTORS OF B OF A.
WHAT IS THIS, PERFORMANCE ART?
I THOUGHT YOU GUYS WERE ALL RICH 'R SOMETHIN'.

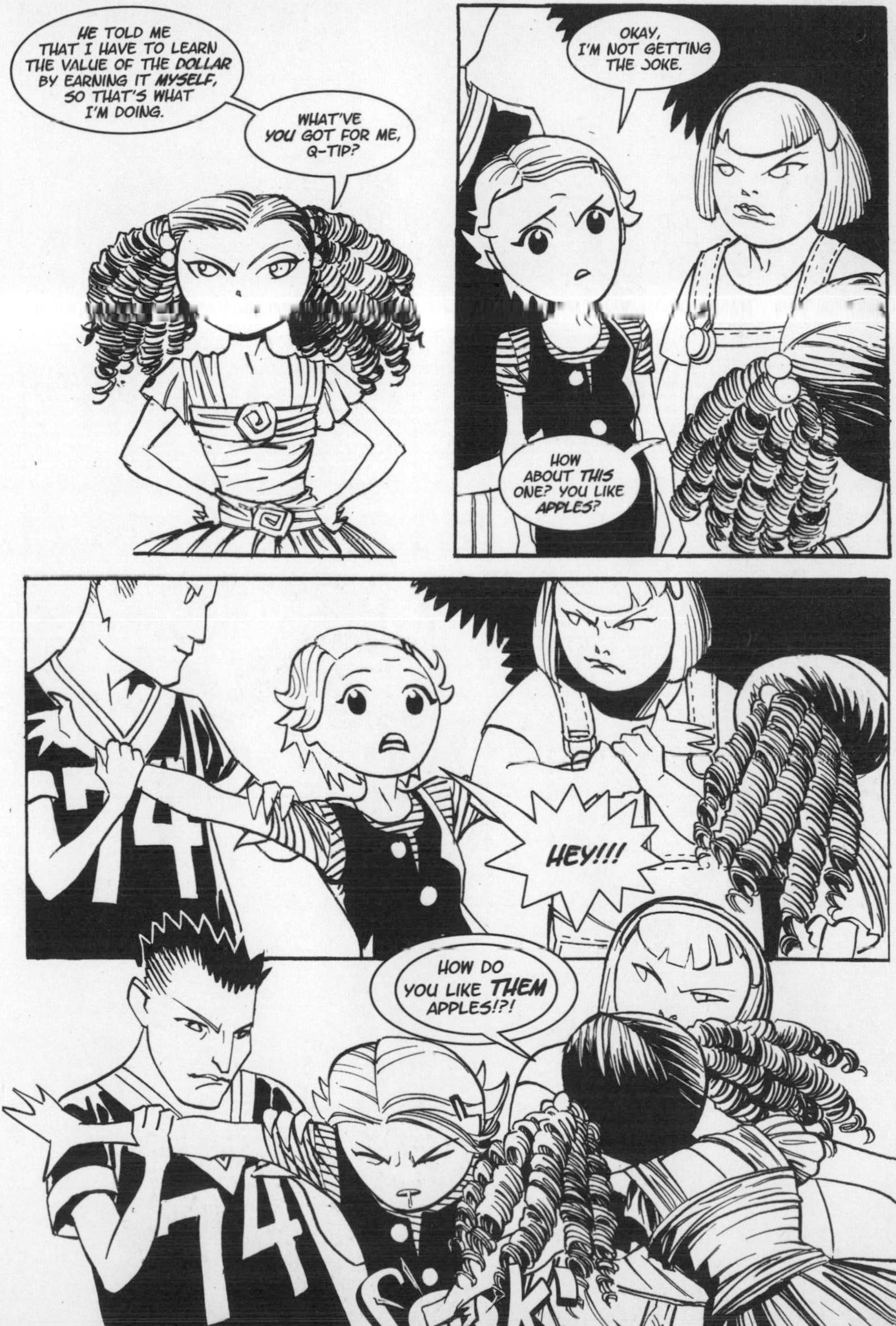
HE TOLD ME THAT I HAVE TO LEARN THE VALUE OF THE DOLLAR BY EARNING IT MYSELF, SO THAT'S WHAT I'M DOING.
WHAT'VE YOU GOT FOR ME, Q-TIP?
OKAY, I'M NOT GETTING THE JOKE.
HOW ABOUT THIS ONE? YOU LIKE APPLES?
HEY!!!
HOW DO YOU LIKE THEM APPLES!?!
SOCK!

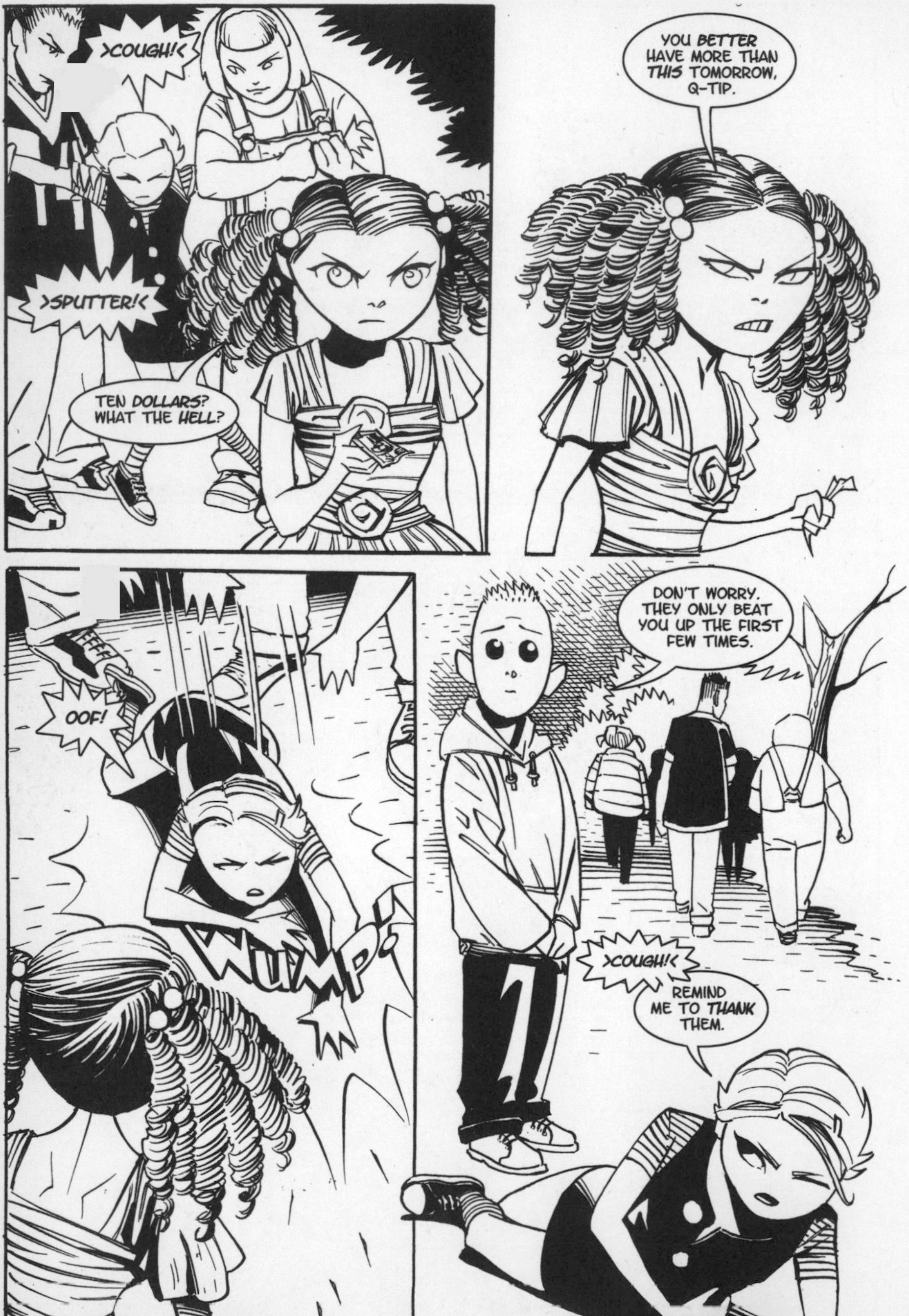
>COUGH!<
>SPUTTER!<
TEN DOLLARS? WHAT THE HELL?
YOU BETTER HAVE MORE THAN THIS TOMORROW, Q-TIP.
OOF!
WUMP!
DON'T WORRY. THEY ONLY BEAT YOU UP THE FIRST FEW TIMES.
>COUGH!<
REMIND ME TO THANK THEM.

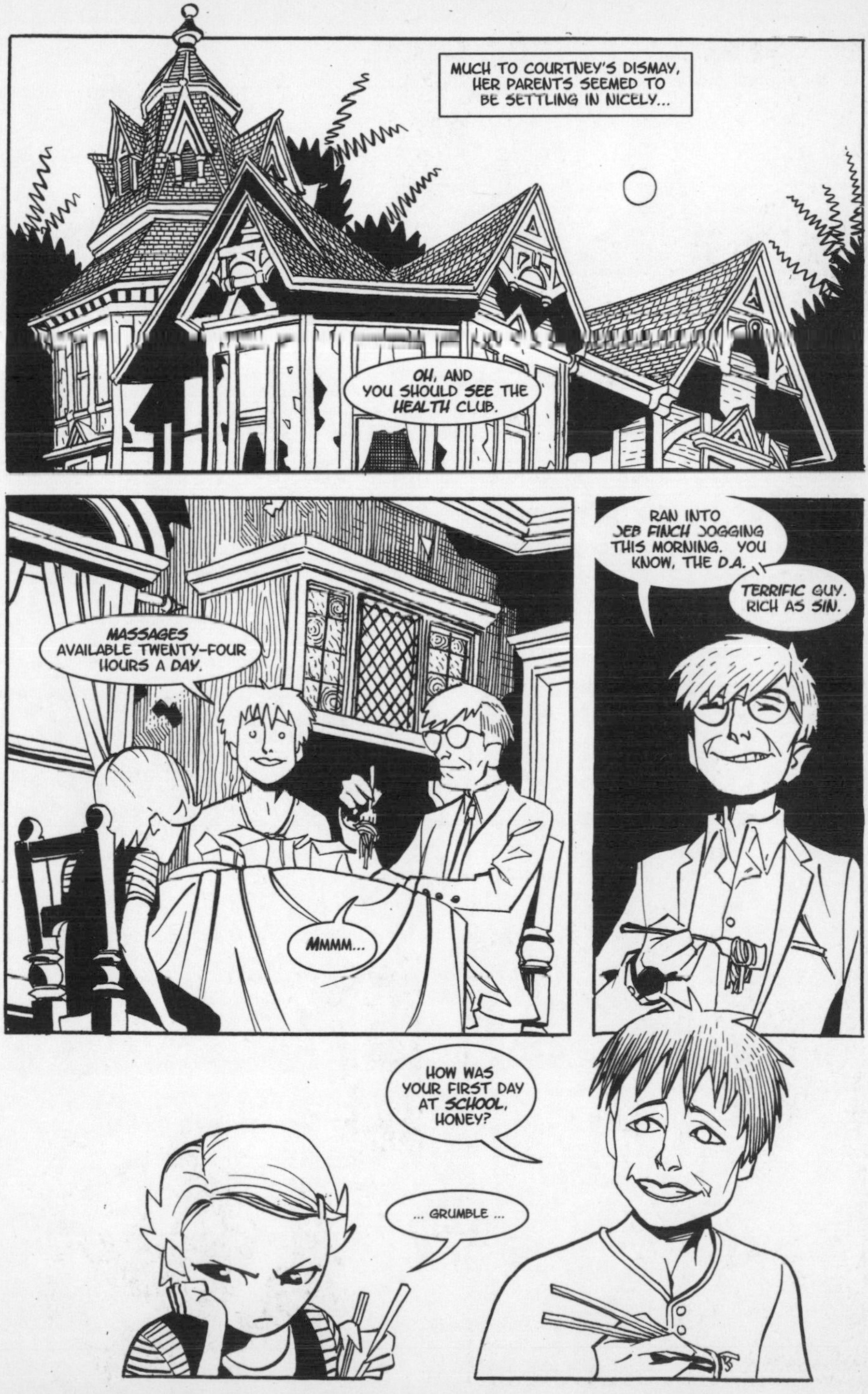

MUCH TO COURTNEY'S DISMAY, HER PARENTS SEEMED TO BE SETTLING IN NICELY...
OH, AND YOU SHOULD SEE THE HEALTH CLUB.
MASSAGES AVAILABLE TWENTY-FOUR HOURS A DAY.
MMMM...
RAN INTO JEB FINCH JOGGING THIS MORNING. YOU KNOW, THE D.A.
TERRIFIC GUY. RICH AS SIN.
HOW WAS YOUR FIRST DAY AT SCHOOL, HONEY?
... GRUMBLE ...

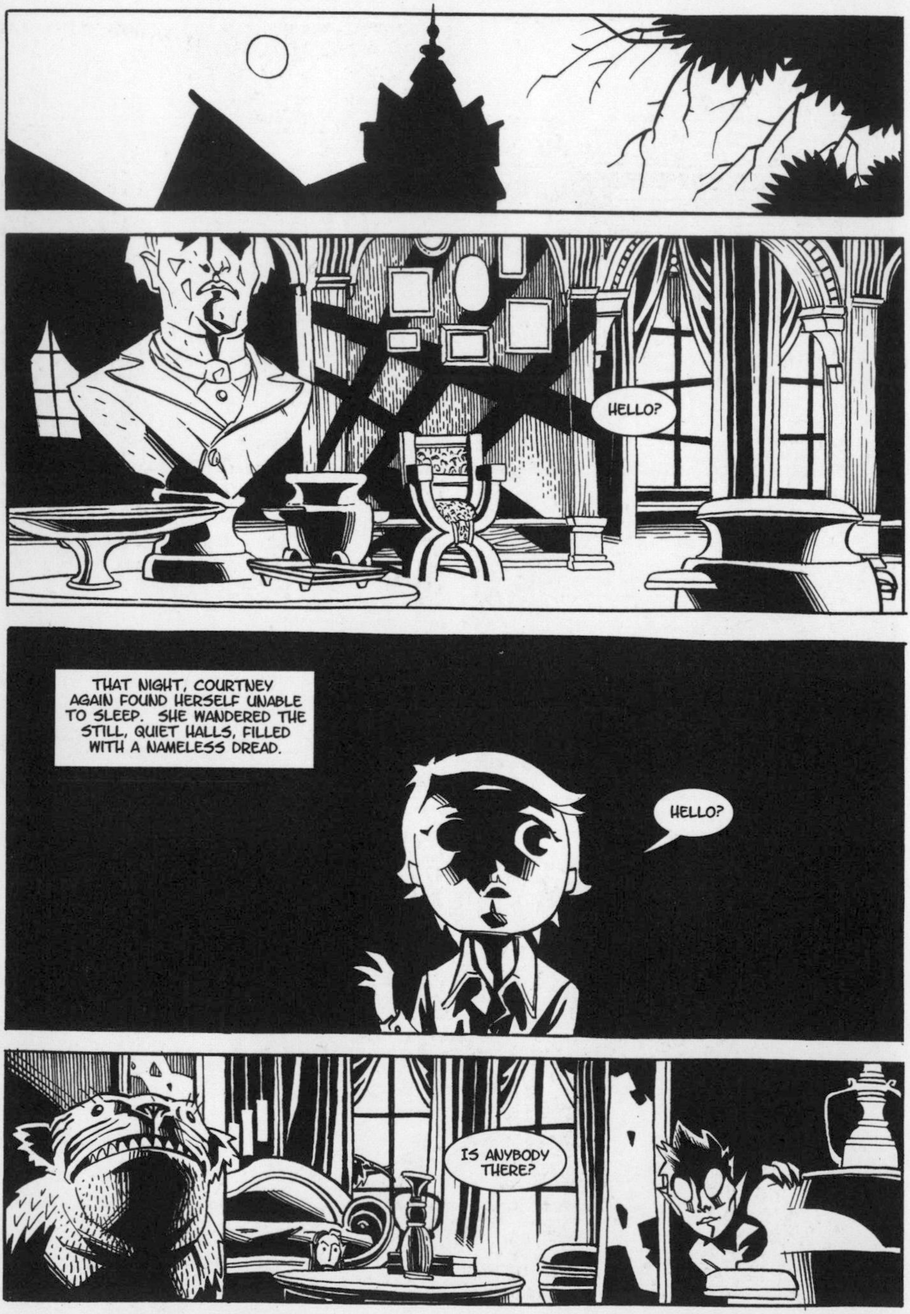
HELLO?
THAT NIGHT, COURTNEY AGAIN FOUND HERSELF UNABLE TO SLEEP. SHE WANDERED THE STILL, QUIET HALLS, FILLED WITH A NAMELESS DREAD.
HELLO?
IS ANYBODY THERE?

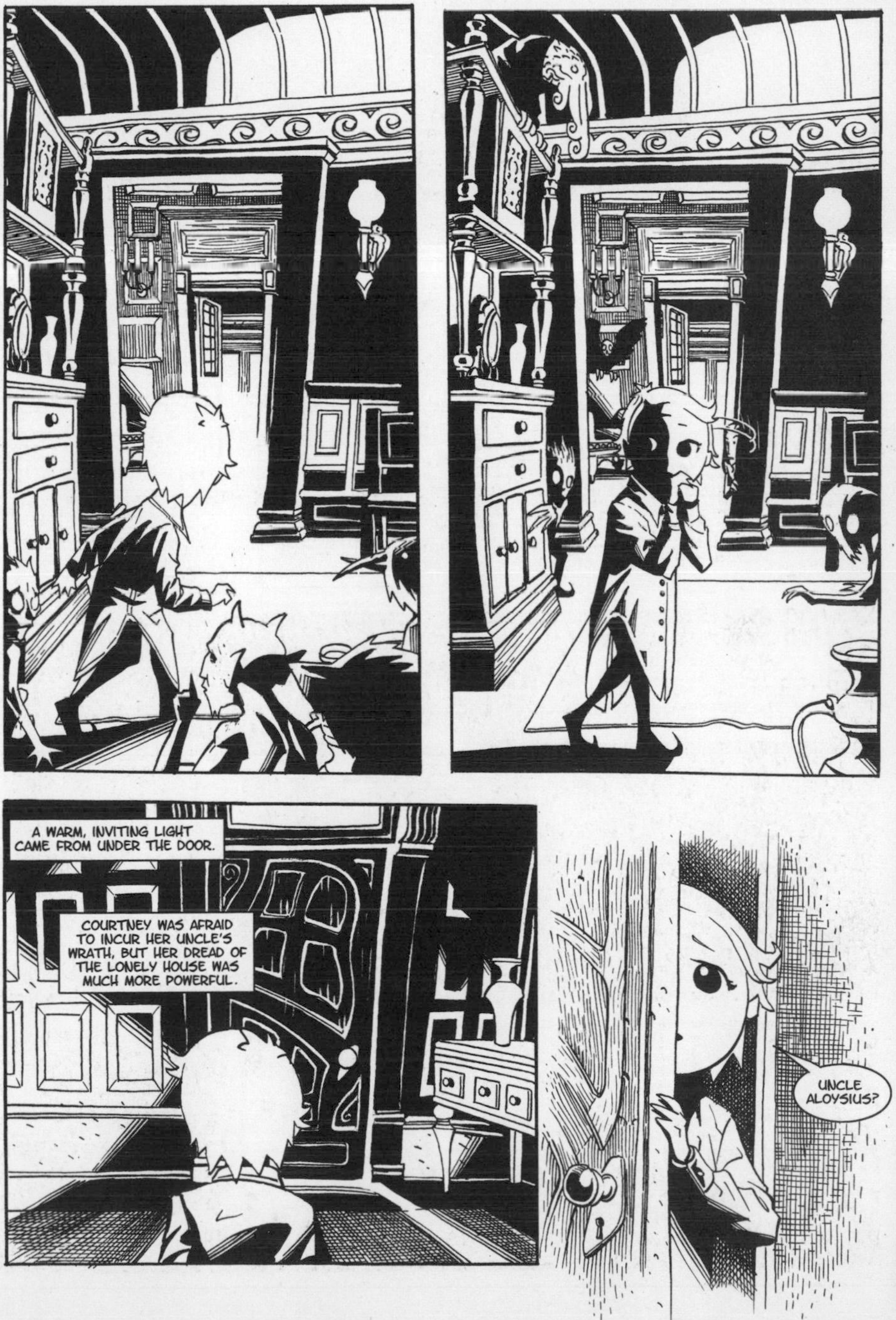
A WARM, INVITING LIGHT CAME FROM UNDER THE DOOR.
COURTNEY WAS AFRAID TO INCUR HER UNCLE'S WRATH, BUT HER DREAD OF THE LONELY HOUSE WAS MUCH MORE POWERFUL.
UNCLE ALOYSIUS?

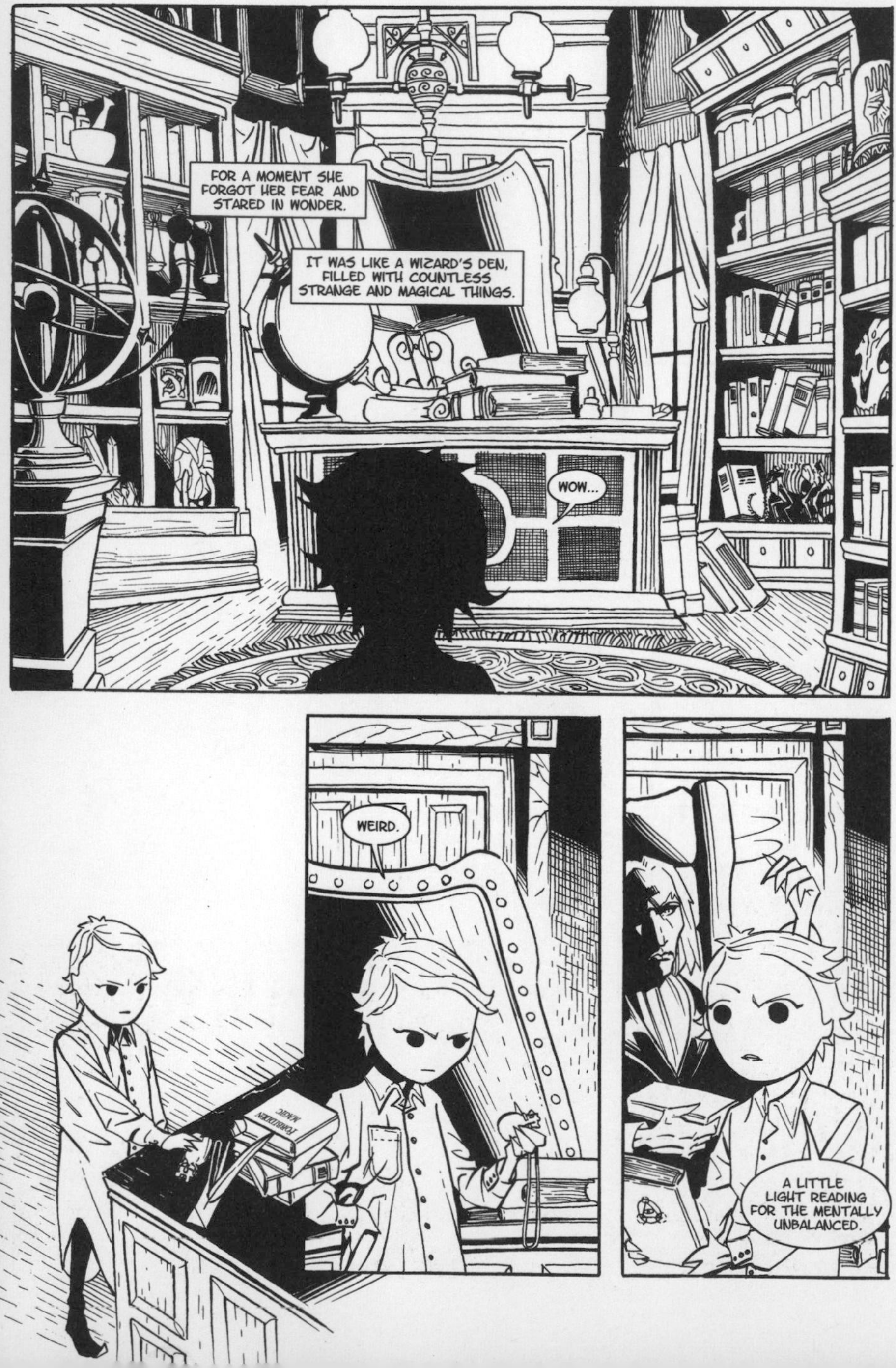
FOR A MOMENT SHE FORGOT HER FEAR AND STARED IN WONDER.
IT WAS LIKE A WIZARD'S DEN, FILLED WITH COUNTLESS STRANGE AND MAGICAL THINGS.
WOW...
FORBIDDEN MAGIC
WEIRD.
A LITTLE LIGHT READING FOR THE MENTALLY UNBALANCED.

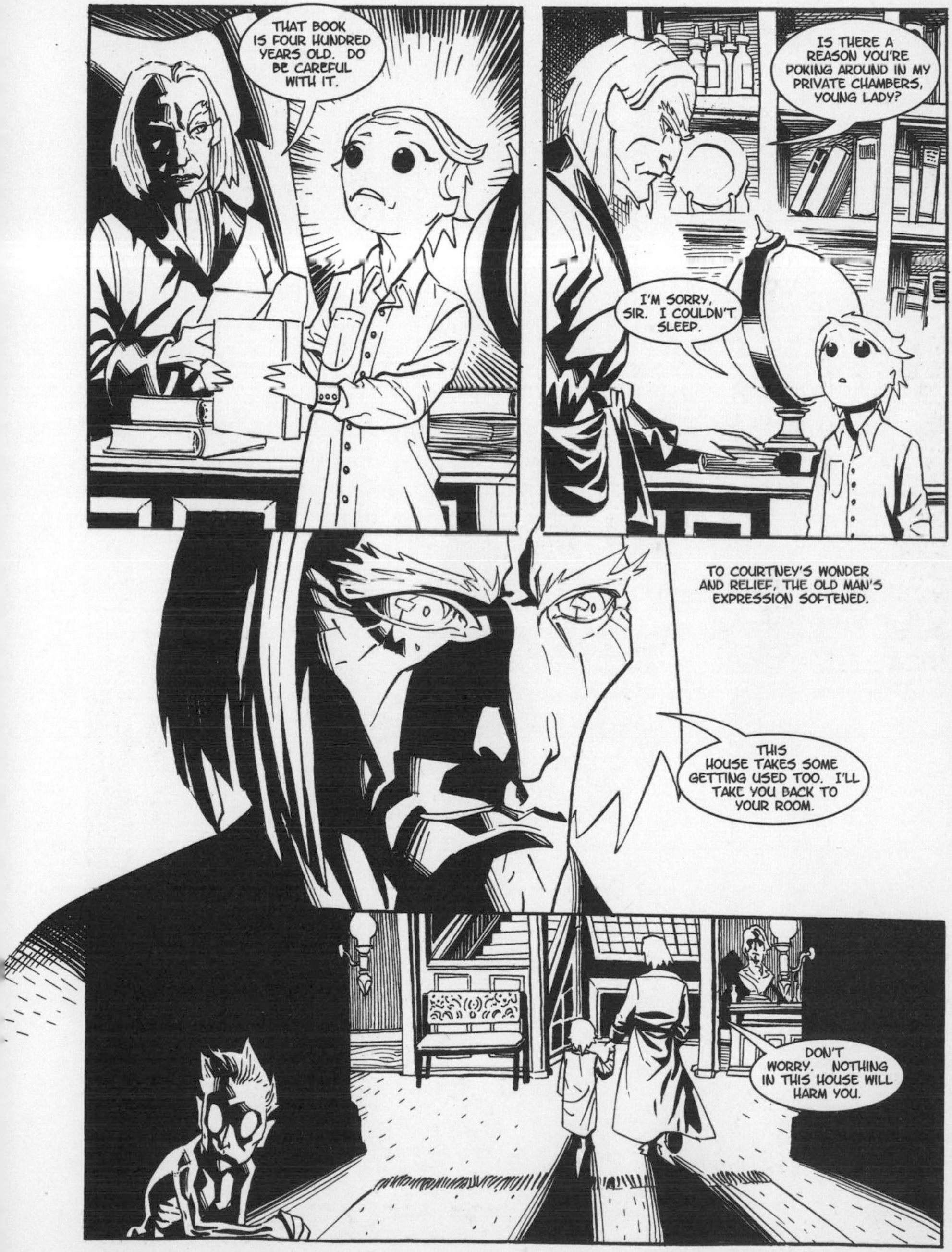
THAT BOOK IS FOUR HUNDRED YEARS OLD. DO BE CAREFUL WITH IT.
IS THERE A REASON YOU'RE POKING AROUND IN MY PRIVATE CHAMBERS, YOUNG LADY?
I'M SORRY, SIR. I COULDN'T SLEEP.
TO COURTNEY'S WONDER AND RELIEF, THE OLD MAN'S EXPRESSION SOFTENED.
THIS HOUSE TAKES SOME GETTING USED TOO. I'LL TAKE YOU BACK TO YOUR ROOM.
DON'T WORRY. NOTHING IN THIS HOUSE WILL HARM YOU.

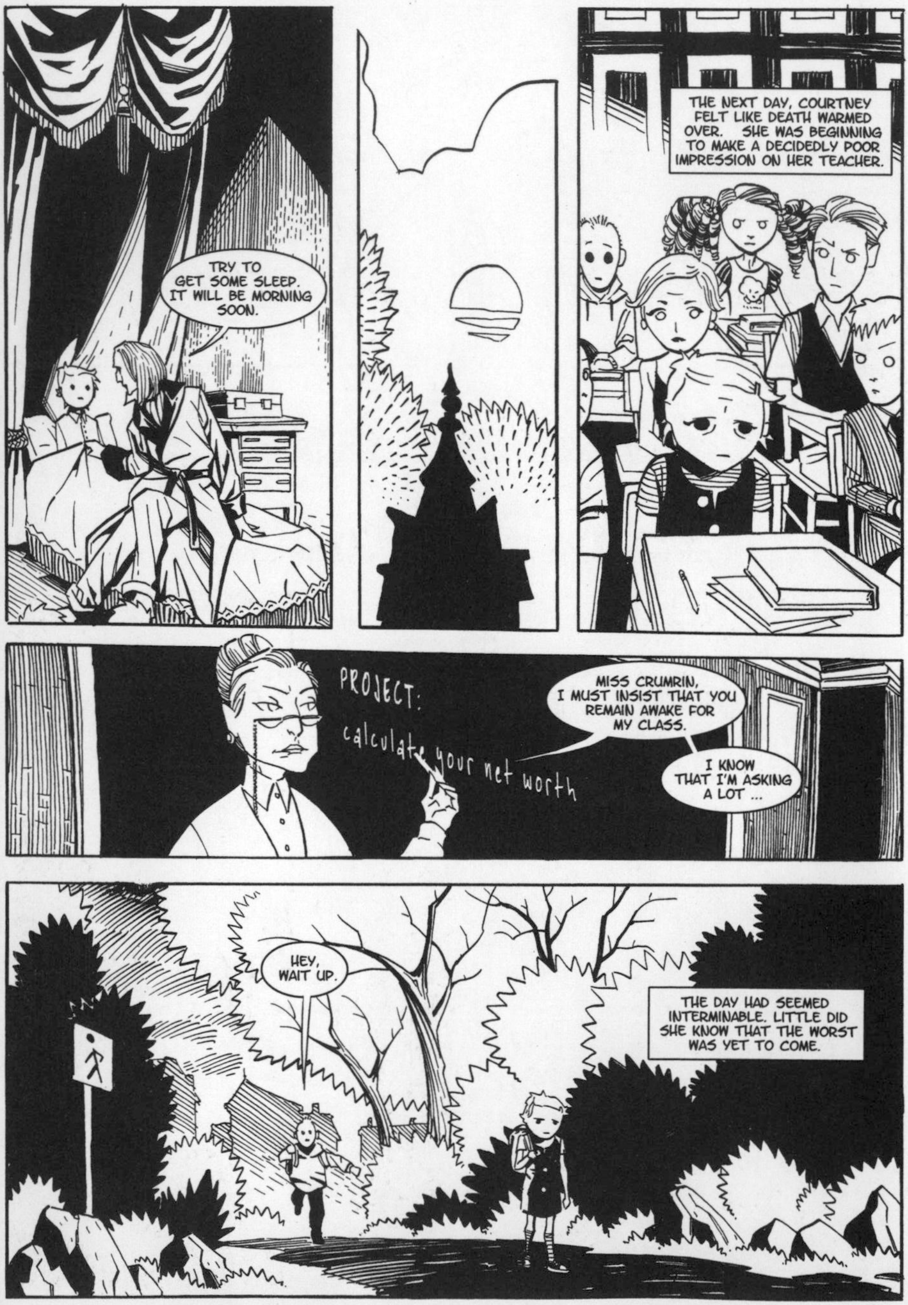

TRY TO GET SOME SLEEP. IT WILL BE MORNING SOON.
THE NEXT DAY, COURTNEY FELT LIKE DEATH WARMED OVER. SHE WAS BEGINNING TO MAKE A DECIDEDLY POOR IMPRESSION ON HER TEACHER.
PROJECT:
calculate your net worth
MISS CRUMRIN, I MUST INSIST THAT YOU REMAIN AWAKE FOR MY CLASS.
I KNOW THAT I'M ASKING A LOT ...
HEY, WAIT UP.
THE DAY HAD SEEMED INTERMINABLE. LITTLE DID SHE KNOW THAT THE WORST WAS YET TO COME.

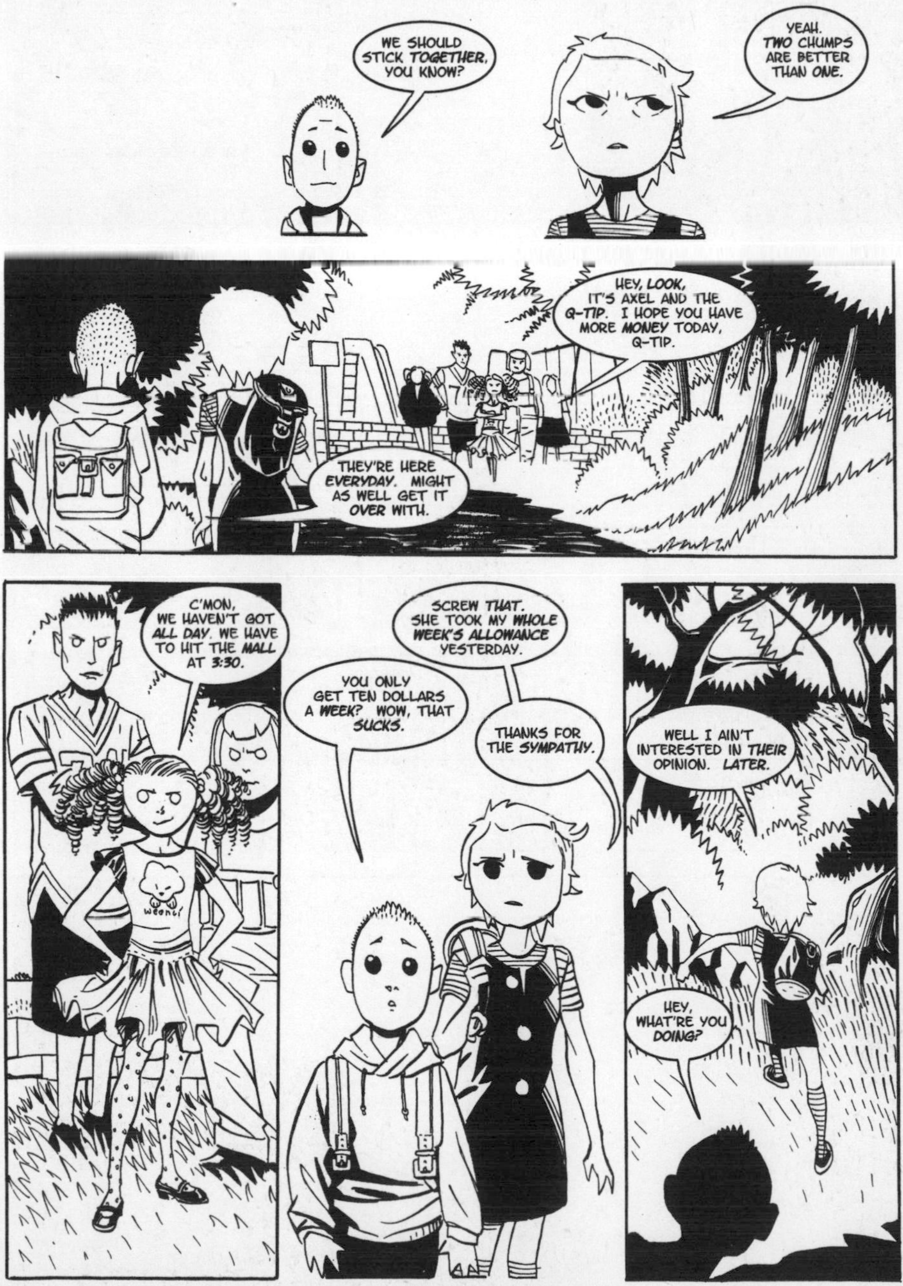
WE SHOULD STICK TOGETHER, YOU KNOW?
YEAH. TWO CHUMPS ARE BETTER THAN ONE.
HEY, LOOK, IT'S AXEL AND THE Q-TIP. I HOPE YOU HAVE MORE MONEY TODAY, Q-TIP.
THEY'RE HERE EVERYDAY. MIGHT AS WELL GET IT OVER WITH.
C'MON, WE HAVEN'T GOT ALL DAY. WE HAVE TO HIT THE MALL AT 3:30.
weenie
SCREW THAT. SHE TOOK MY WHOLE WEEK'S ALLOWANCE YESTERDAY.
YOU ONLY GET TEN DOLLARS A WEEK? WOW, THAT SUCKS.
THANKS FOR THE SYMPATHY.
WELL I AIN'T INTERESTED IN THEIR OPINION. LATER.
HEY, WHAT'RE YOU DOING?

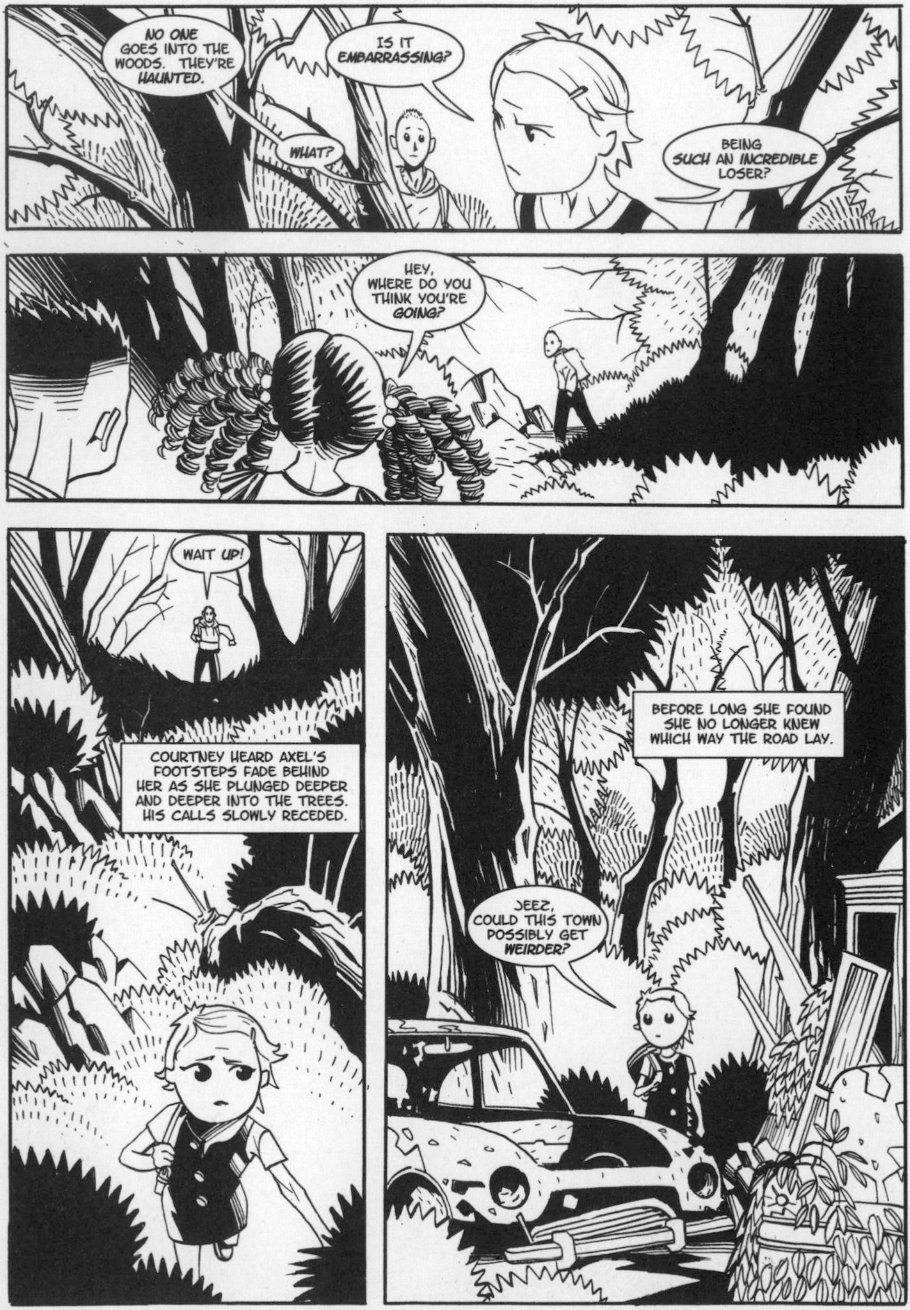
NO ONE GOES INTO THE WOODS. THEY'RE HAUNTED.
WHAT?
IS IT EMBARRASSING?
BEING SUCH AN INCREDIBLE LOSER?
HEY, WHERE DO YOU THINK YOU'RE GOING?
WAIT UP!
COURTNEY HEARD AXEL'S FOOTSTEPS FADE BEHIND HER AS SHE PLUNGED DEEPER AND DEEPER INTO THE TREES. HIS CALLS SLOWLY RECEDED.
BEFORE LONG SHE FOUND SHE NO LONGER KNEW WHICH WAY THE ROAD LAY.
JEEZ, COULD THIS TOWN POSSIBLY GET WEIRDER?

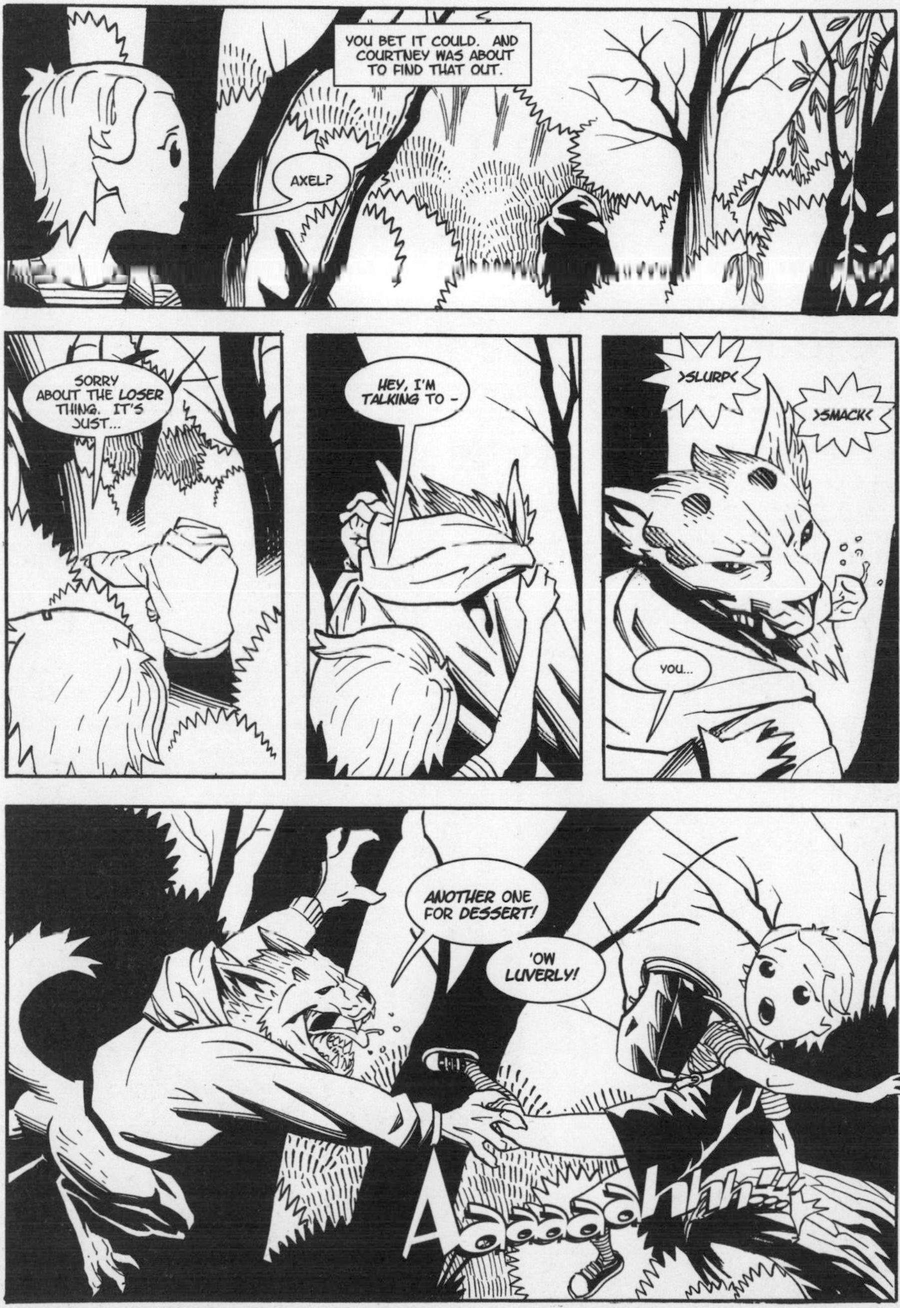
YOU BET IT COULD. AND COURTNEY WAS ABOUT TO FIND THAT OUT.
AXEL?
SORRY ABOUT THE LOSER THING. IT'S JUST...
HEY, I'M TALKING TO -
>SLURP<
>SMACK<
YOU...
ANOTHER ONE FOR DESSERT!
'OW LUVERLY!
Aaaaaahhh!!

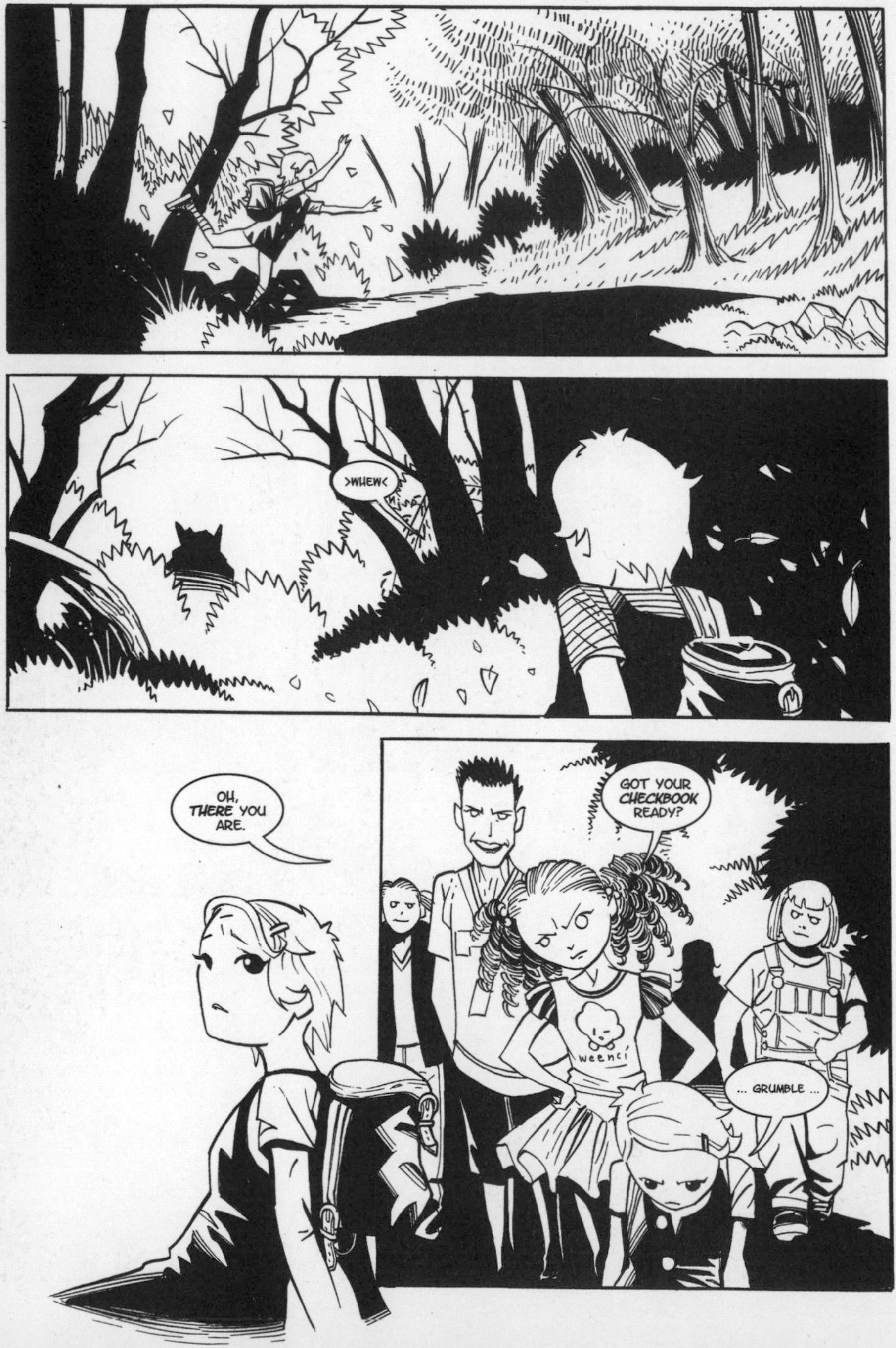
>WHEW<
OH, THERE YOU ARE.
GOT YOUR CHECKBOOK READY?
... GRUMBLE ...

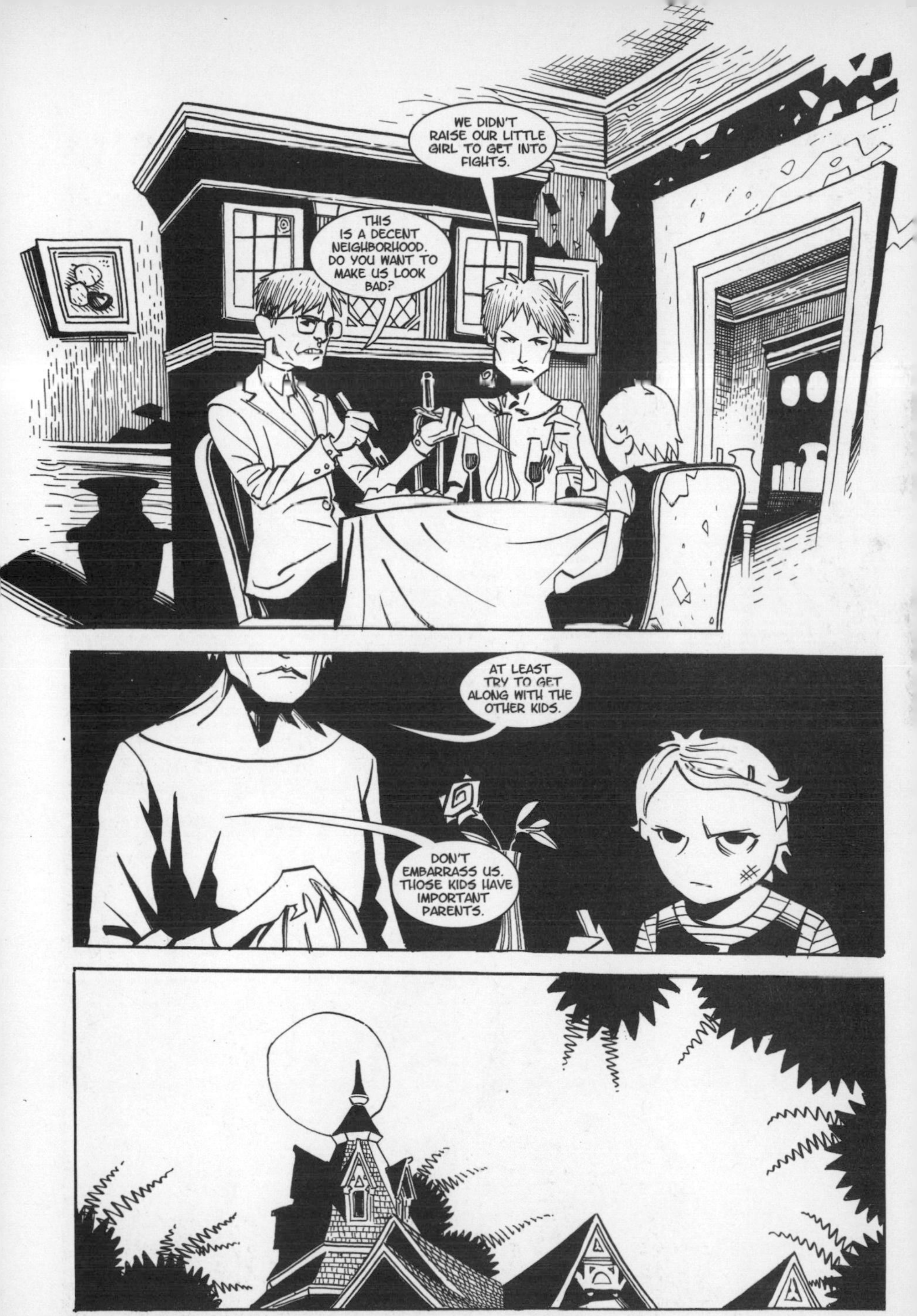
THIS IS A DECENT NEIGHBORHOOD. DO YOU WANT TO MAKE US LOOK BAD?
WE DIDN'T RAISE OUR LITTLE GIRL TO GET INTO FIGHTS.
AT LEAST TRY TO GET ALONG WITH THE OTHER KIDS.
DON'T EMBARRASS US. THOSE KIDS HAVE IMPORTANT PARENTS.

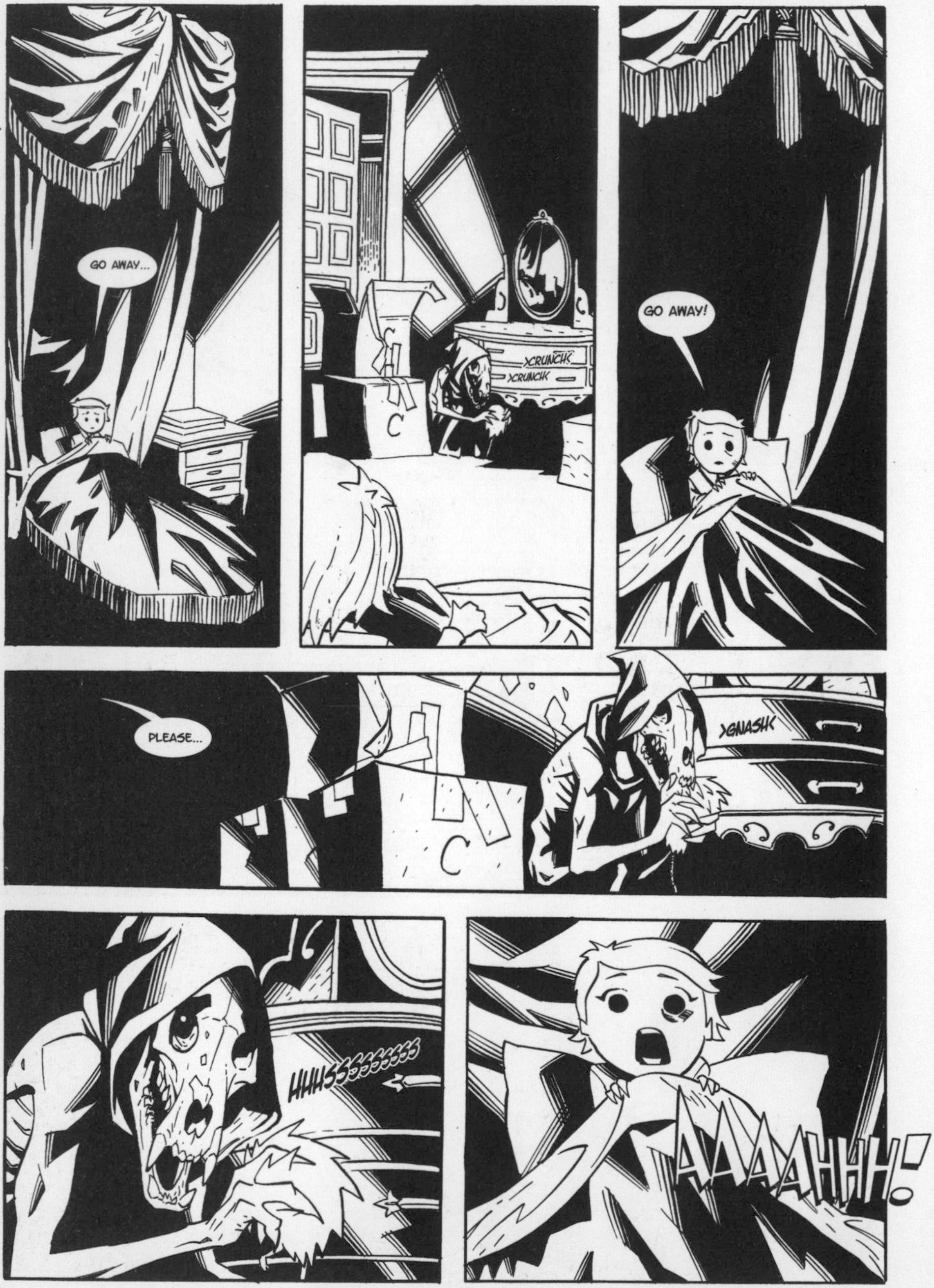
GO AWAY...
>CRUNCH<
>CRUNCH<
GO AWAY!
PLEASE...
>GNASH<
HHHSSSSSSSSS
AAAAHHH!

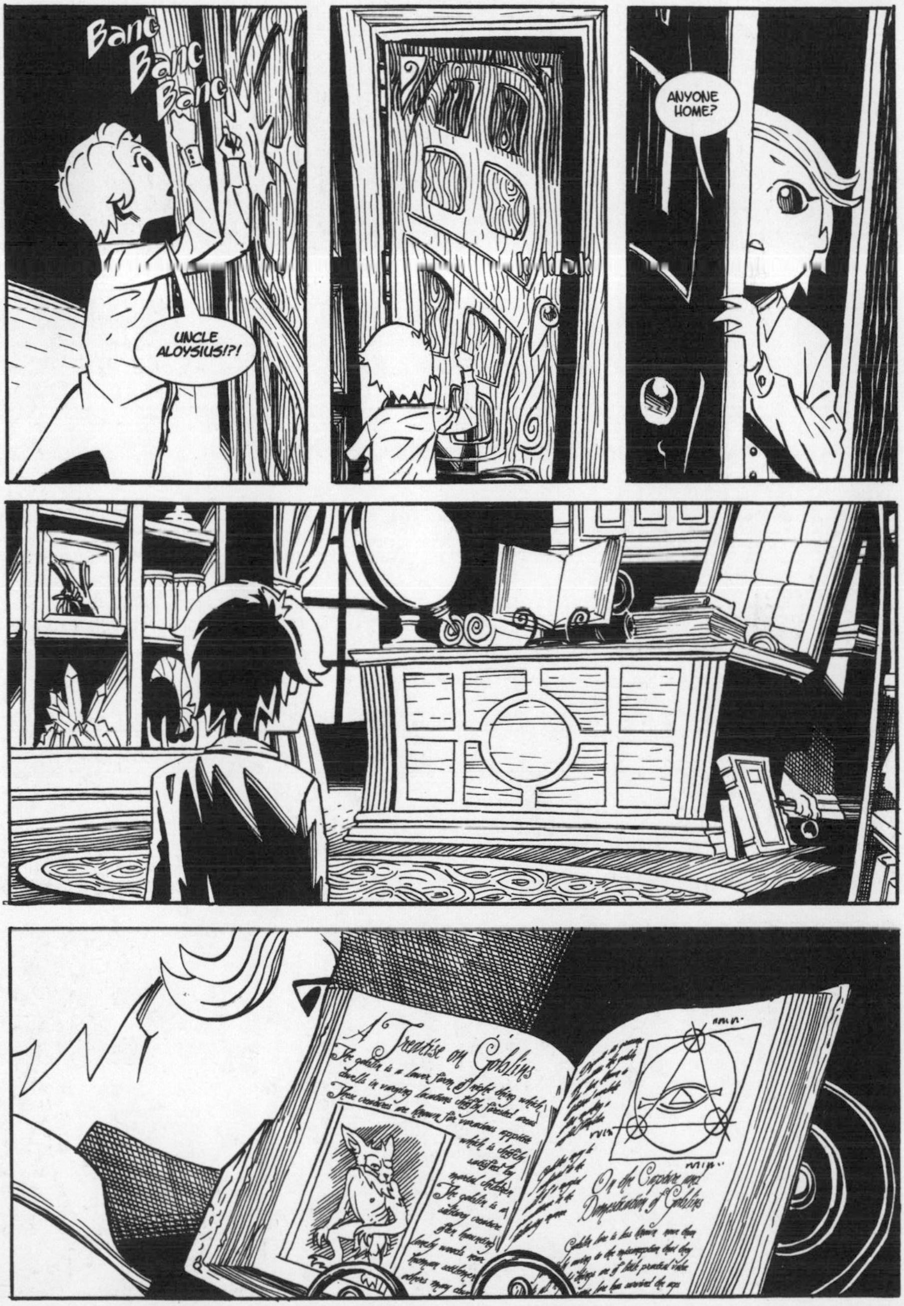

Bang
Bang
Bang
UNCLE ALOYSIUS!?!
ANYONE HOME?
A Treatise on Goblins
On the Capture and Domestication of Goblins

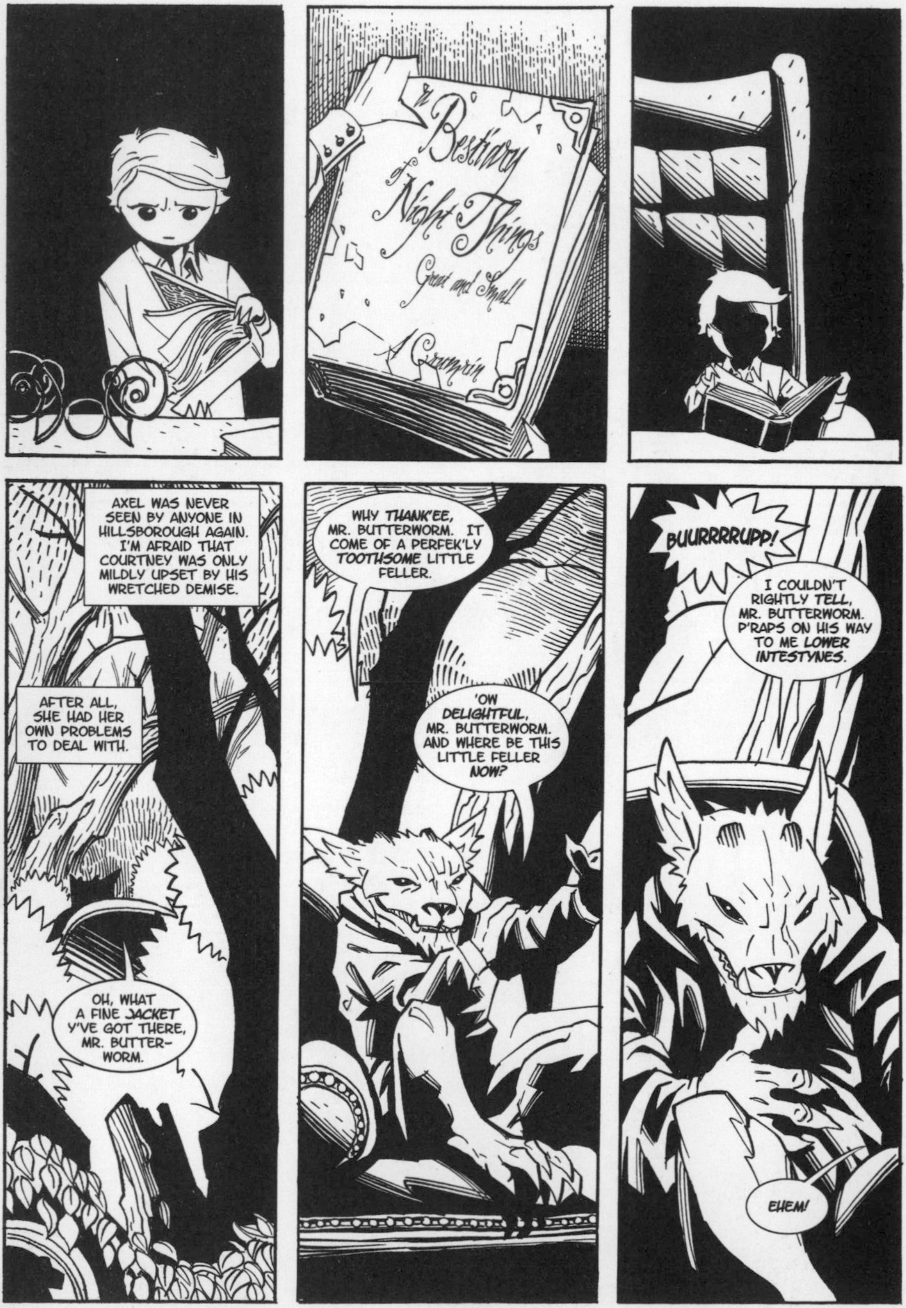
Bestiary
of
Night Things
Great and Small
AXEL WAS NEVER SEEN BY ANYONE IN HILLSBOROUGH AGAIN. I'M AFRAID THAT COURTNEY WAS ONLY MILDLY UPSET BY HIS WRETCHED DEMISE.
AFTER ALL, SHE HAD HER OWN PROBLEMS TO DEAL WITH.
OH, WHAT A FINE *JACKET* Y'VE GOT THERE, MR. BUTTER-WORM.
WHY *THANK'EE*, MR. BUTTERWORM. IT COME OF A PERFEK'LY *TOOTHSOME* LITTLE FELLER.
'OW *DELIGHTFUL*, MR. BUTTERWORM. AND WHERE BE THIS LITTLE FELLER *NOW?*
BUURRRRUPP!
I COULDN'T RIGHTLY *TELL*, MR. BUTTERWORM. P'RAPS ON HIS WAY TO ME *LOWER INTESTYNES*.
EHEM!

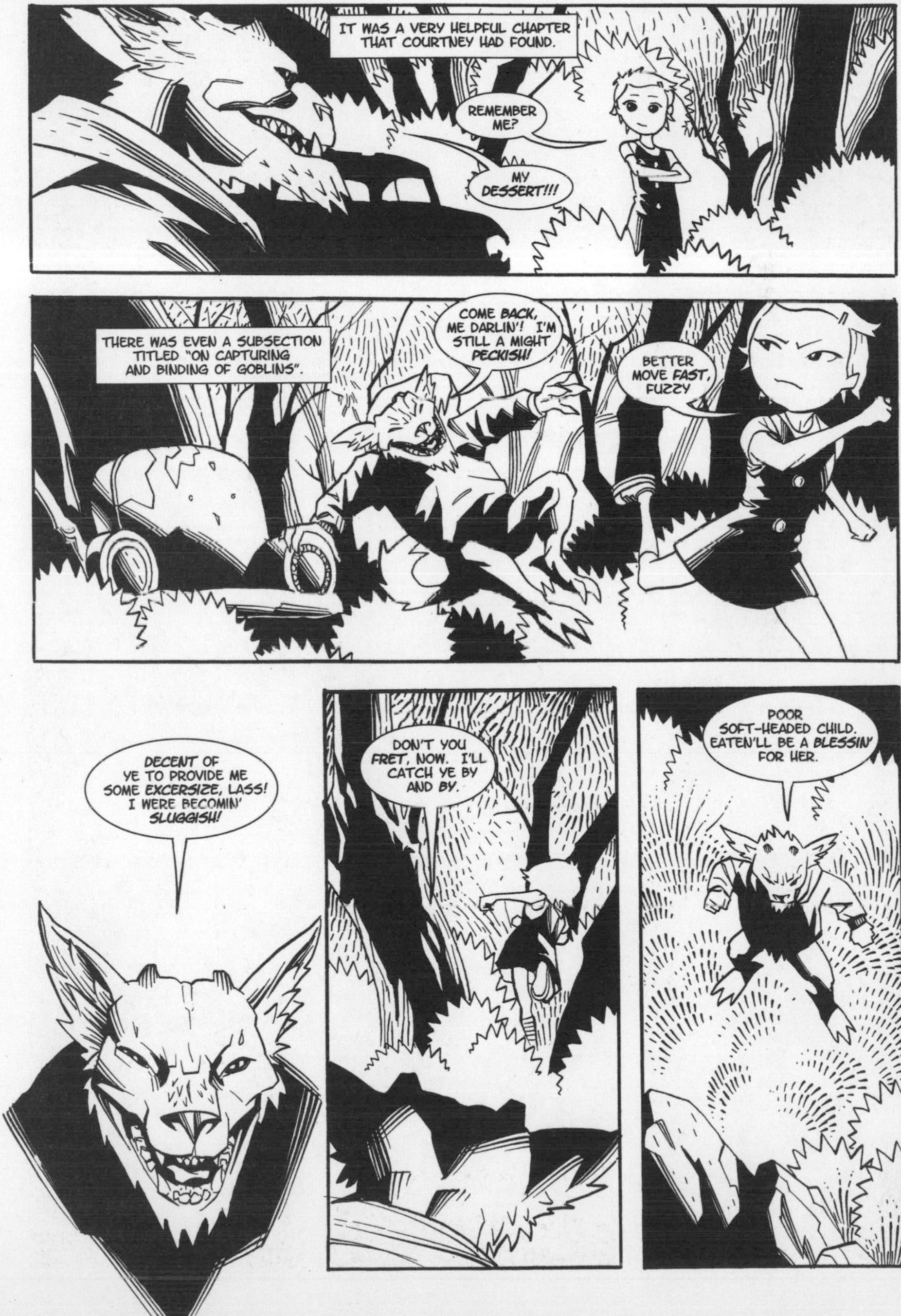

IT WAS A VERY HELPFUL CHAPTER THAT COURTNEY HAD FOUND.
REMEMBER ME?
MY DESSERT!!!
THERE WAS EVEN A SUBSECTION TITLED "ON CAPTURING AND BINDING OF GOBLINS".
COME BACK, ME DARLIN'! I'M STILL A MIGHT PECKISH!
BETTER MOVE FAST, FUZZY
DECENT OF YE TO PROVIDE ME SOME EXCERSIZE, LASS! I WERE BECOMIN' SLUGGISH!
DON'T YOU FRET, NOW. I'LL CATCH YE BY AND BY.
POOR SOFT-HEADED CHILD. EATEN'LL BE A BLESSIN' FOR HER.

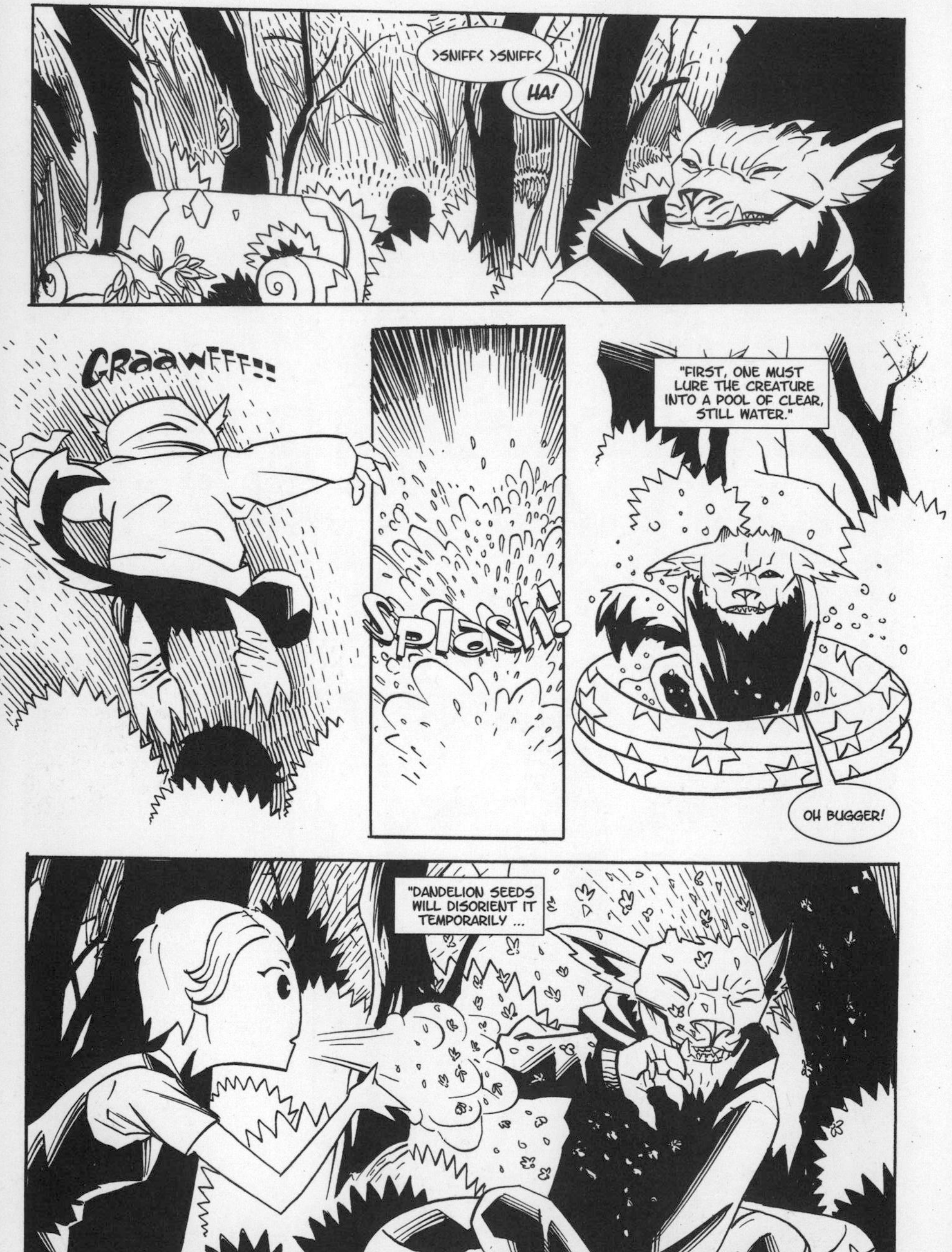
>SNIFF< >SNIFF<
HA!
GRAAWFFF!!
Splash!
"FIRST, ONE MUST LURE THE CREATURE INTO A POOL OF CLEAR, STILL WATER."
OH BUGGER!
"DANDELION SEEDS WILL DISORIENT IT TEMPORARILY ...

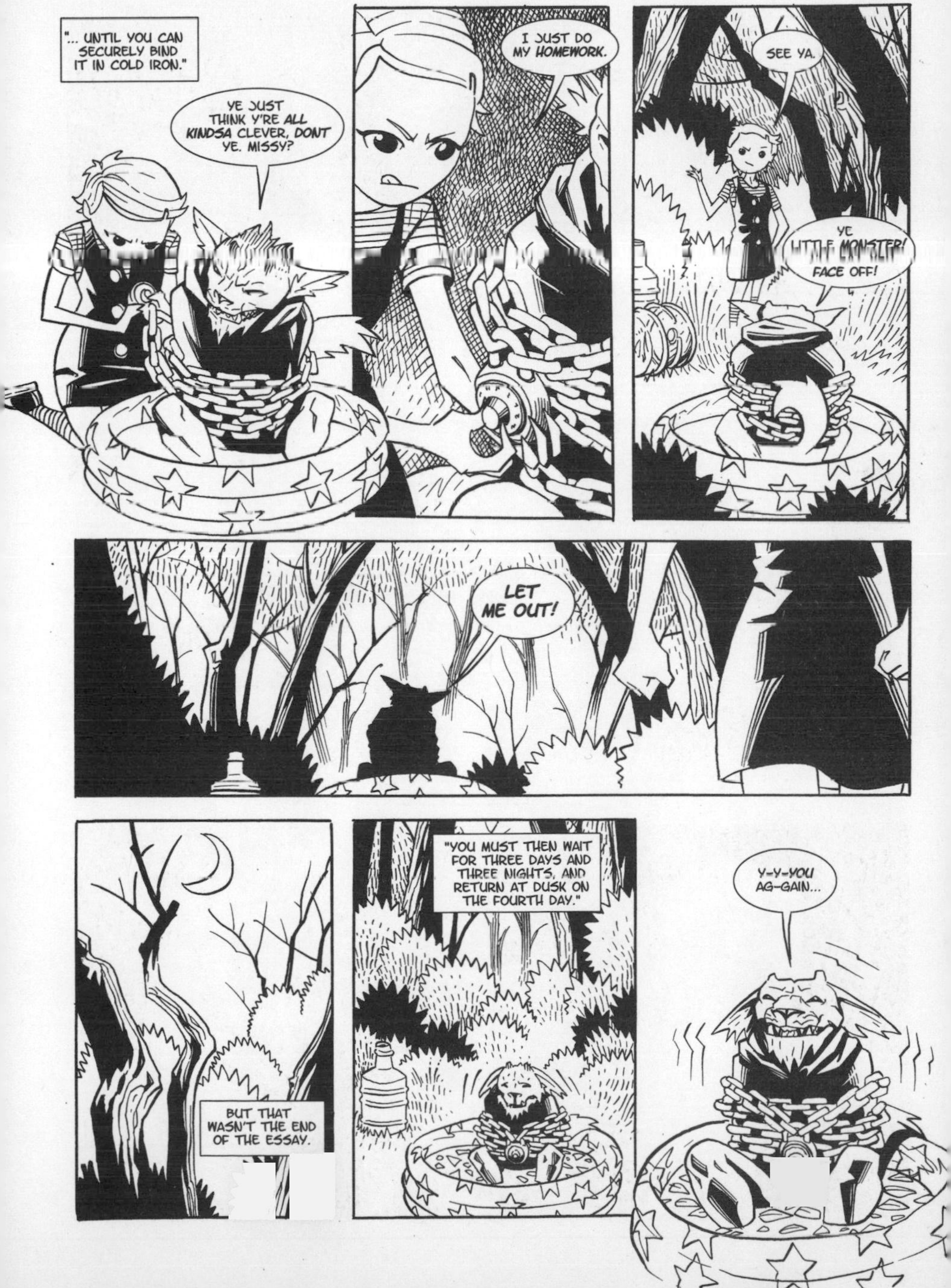
"... UNTIL YOU CAN SECURELY BIND IT IN COLD IRON."
YE JUST THINK Y'RE ALL KINDSA CLEVER, DONT YE. MISSY?
I JUST DO MY HOMEWORK.
SEE YA.
YE LITTLE MONSTER! FACE OFF!
LET ME OUT!
BUT THAT WASN'T THE END OF THE ESSAY.
"YOU MUST THEN WAIT FOR THREE DAYS AND THREE NIGHTS, AND RETURN AT DUSK ON THE FOURTH DAY."
Y-Y-YOU AG-GAIN...

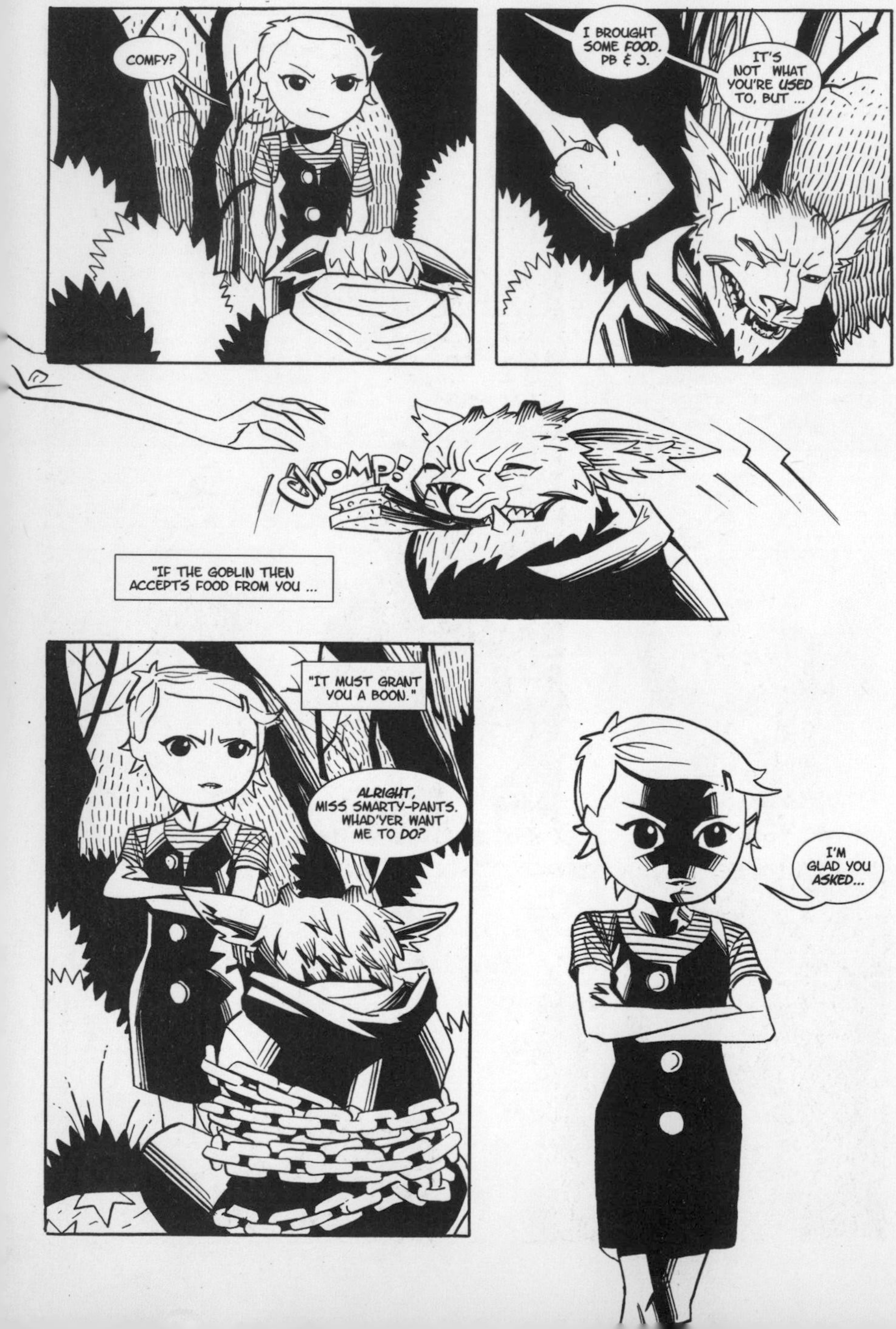
COMFY?
I BROUGHT SOME FOOD. PB & J.
IT'S NOT WHAT YOU'RE USED TO, BUT ...
CHOMP!
"IF THE GOBLIN THEN ACCEPTS FOOD FROM YOU ...
"IT MUST GRANT YOU A BOON."
ALRIGHT, MISS SMARTY-PANTS. WHAD'YER WANT ME TO DO?
I'M GLAD YOU ASKED...

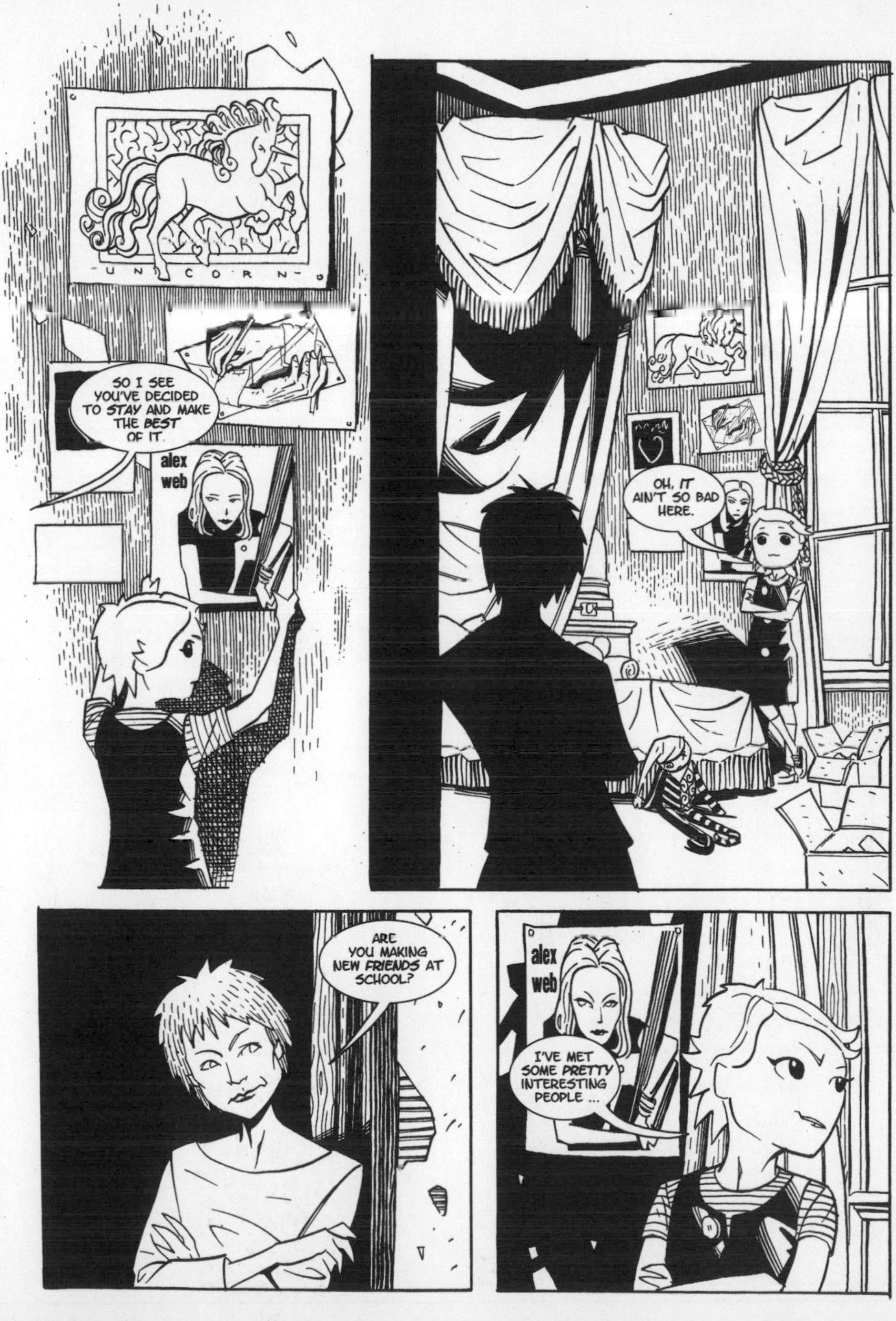
UNICORN
SO I SEE YOU'VE DECIDED TO STAY AND MAKE THE BEST OF IT.
alex web
OH, IT AIN'T SO BAD HERE.
ARE YOU MAKING NEW FRIENDS AT SCHOOL?
alex web
I'VE MET SOME PRETTY INTERESTING PEOPLE ...

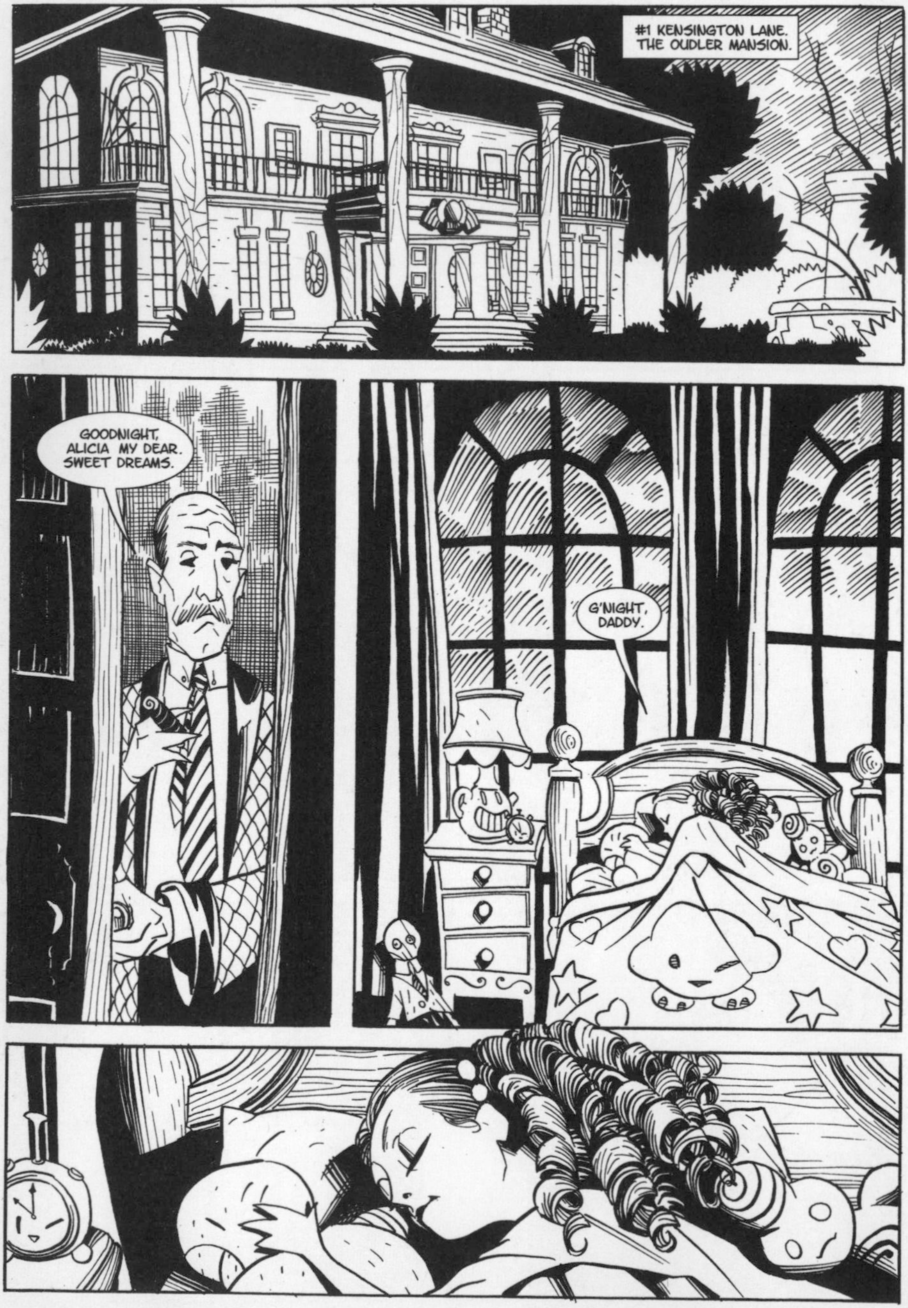
#1 KENSINGTON LANE. THE OUDLER MANSION.
GOODNIGHT, ALICIA MY DEAR. SWEET DREAMS.
G'NIGHT, DADDY.

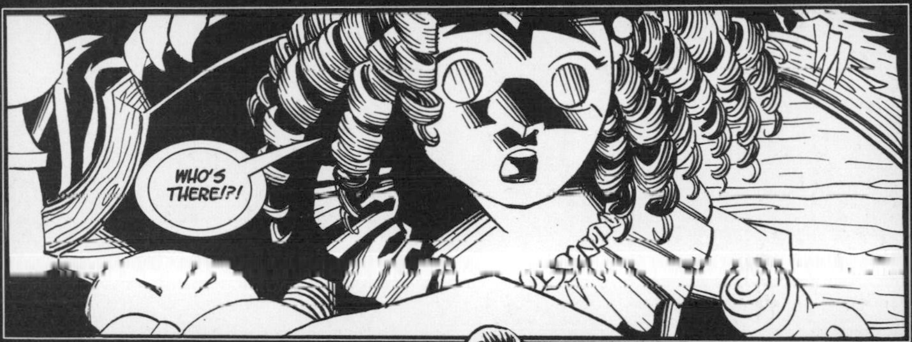
WHO'S THERE!?!

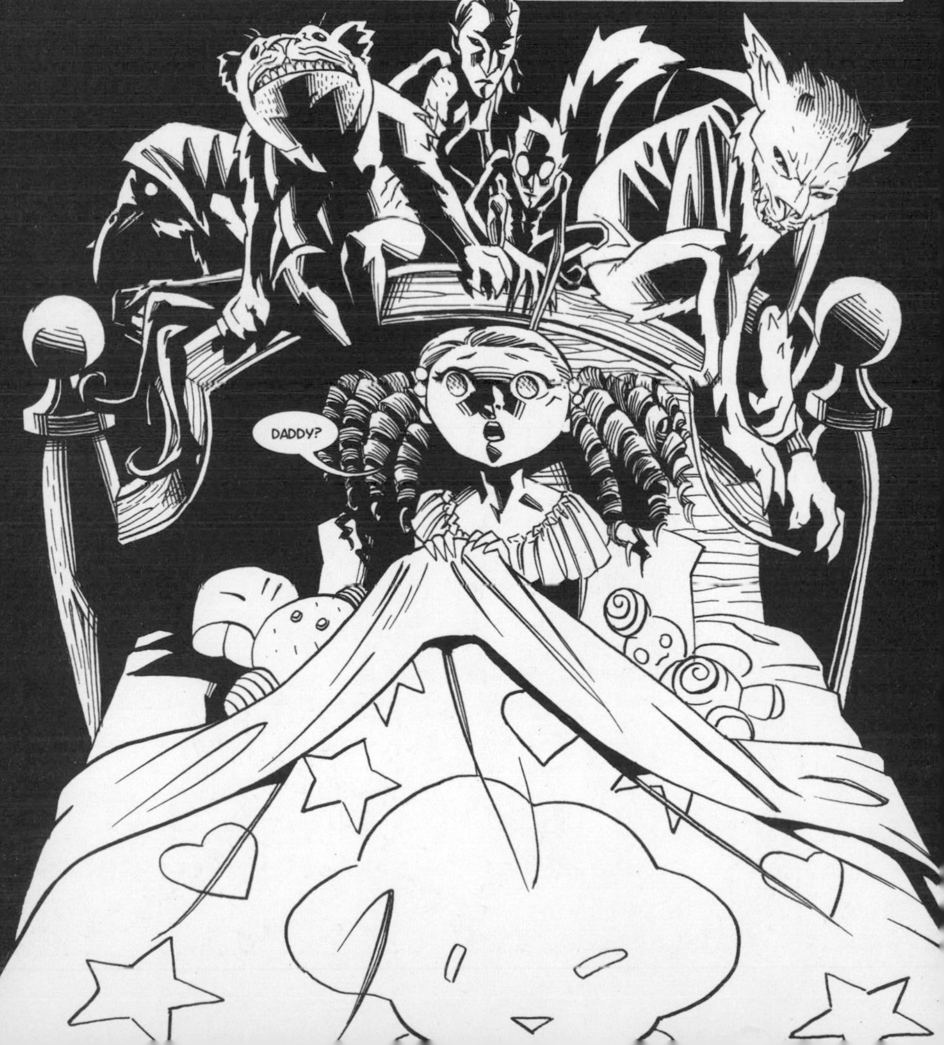
DADDY?

Chapter Two

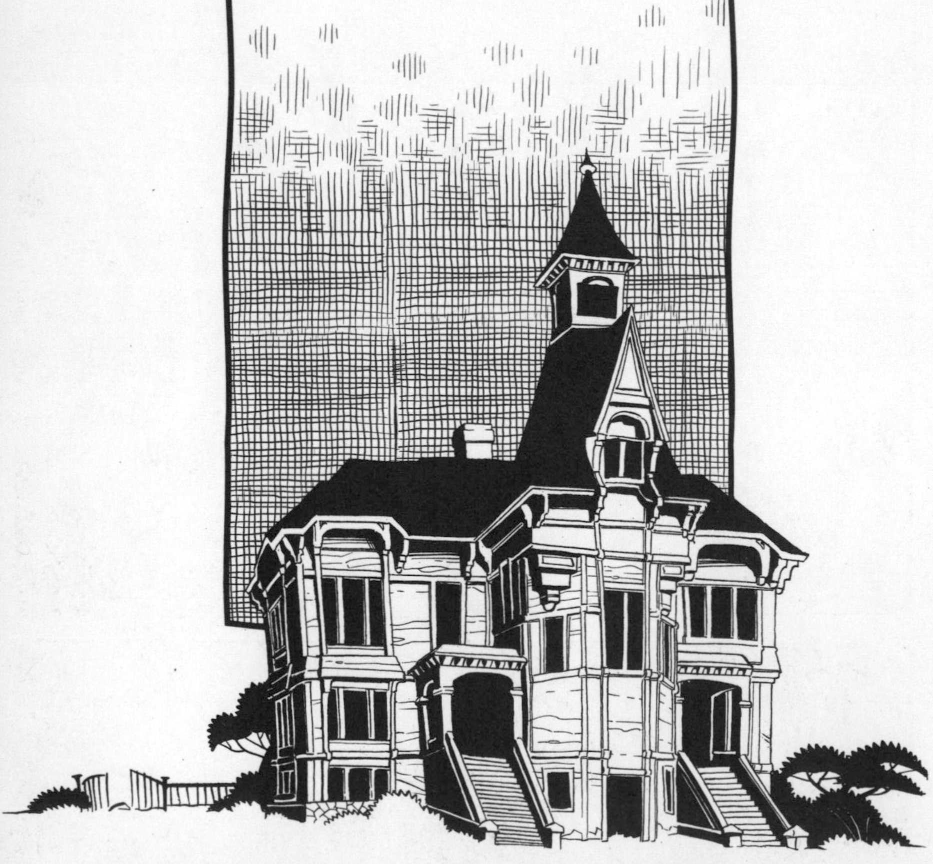

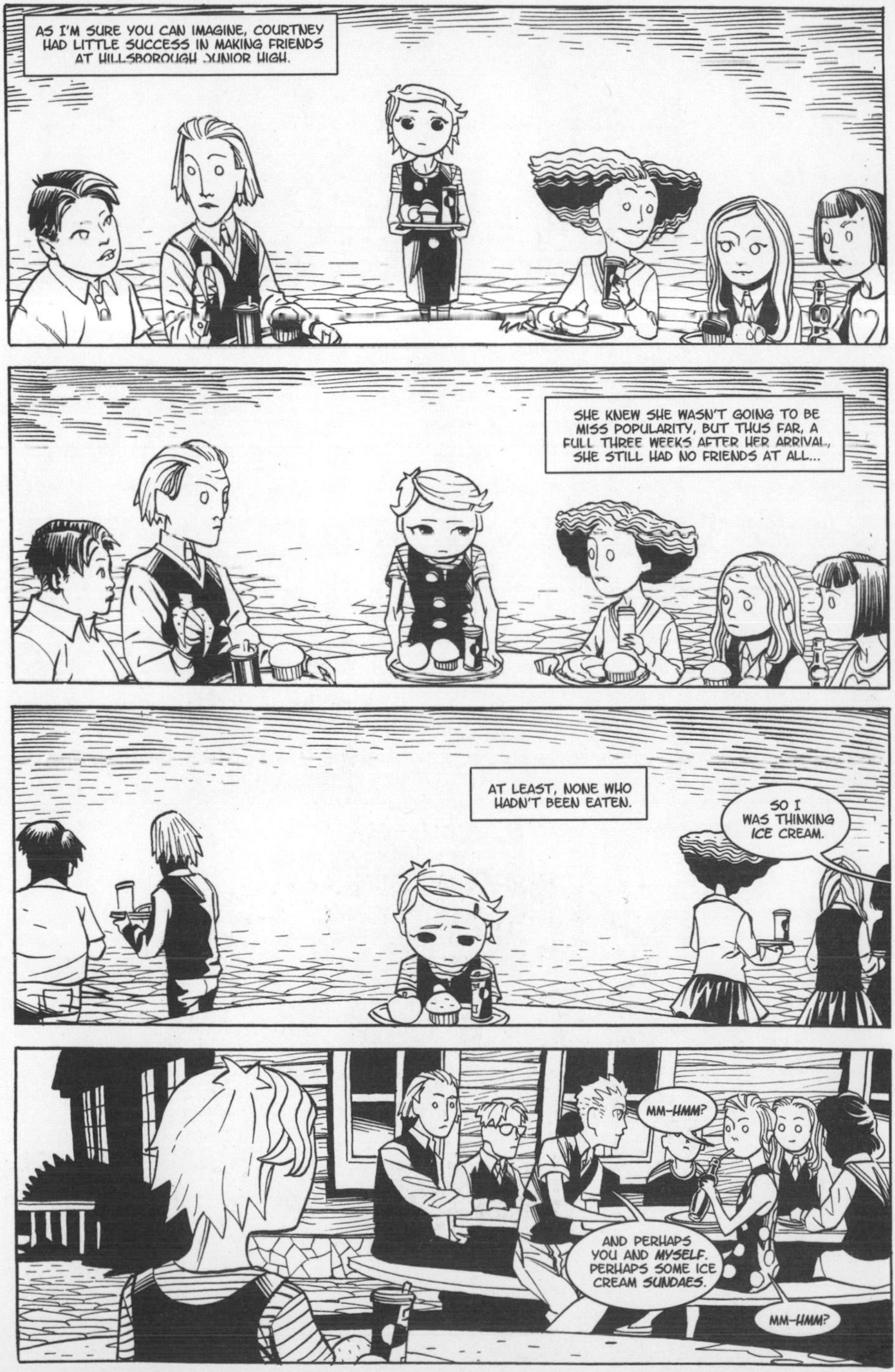
AS I'M SURE YOU CAN IMAGINE, COURTNEY HAD LITTLE SUCCESS IN MAKING FRIENDS AT HILLSBOROUGH JUNIOR HIGH.
SHE KNEW SHE WASN'T GOING TO BE MISS POPULARITY, BUT THUS FAR, A FULL THREE WEEKS AFTER HER ARRIVAL, SHE STILL HAD NO FRIENDS AT ALL...
AT LEAST, NONE WHO HADN'T BEEN EATEN.
SO I WAS THINKING ICE CREAM.
MM-HMM?
AND PERHAPS YOU AND MYSELF. PERHAPS SOME ICE CREAM SUNDAES.
MM-HMM?

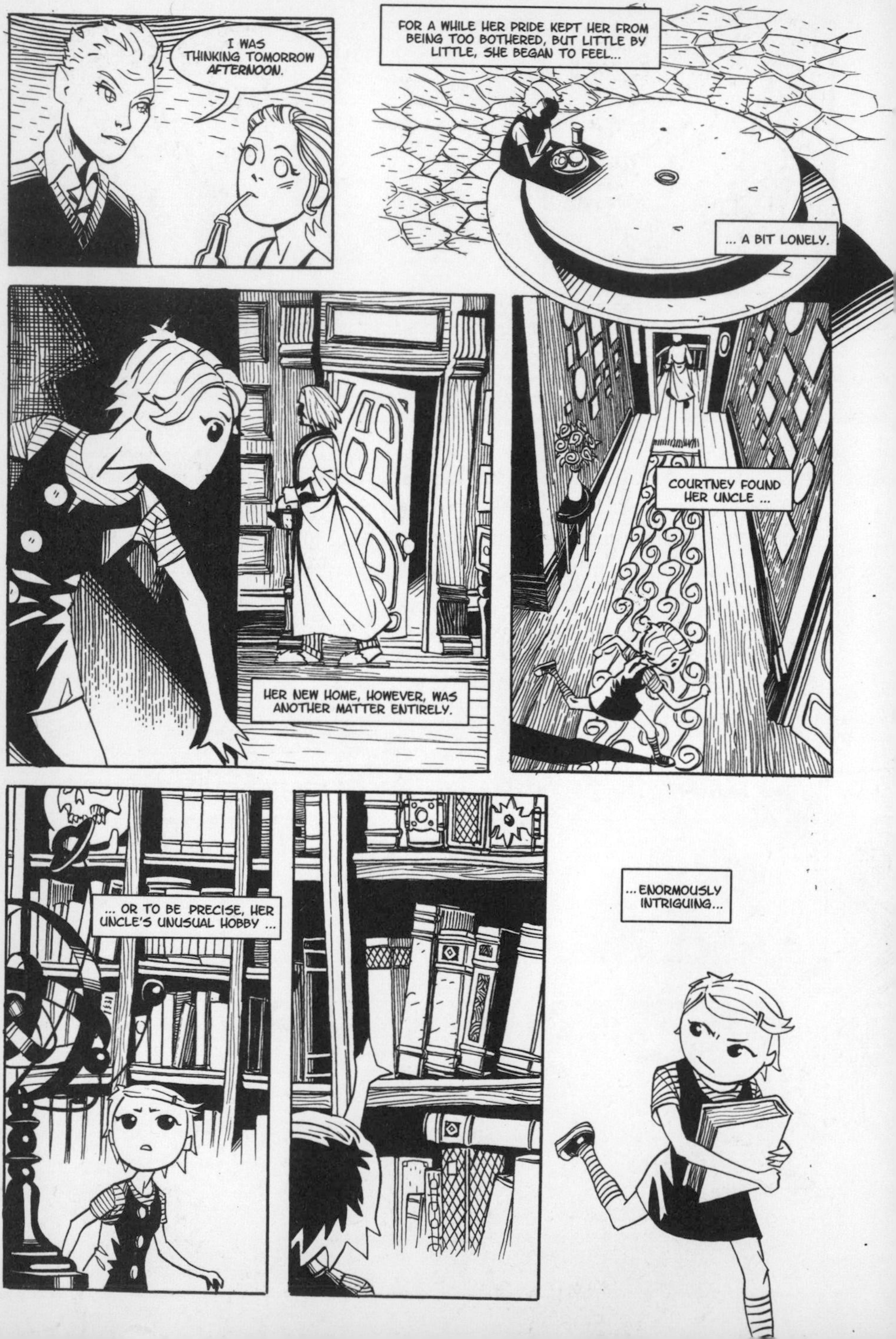
I WAS THINKING TOMORROW AFTERNOON.
FOR A WHILE HER PRIDE KEPT HER FROM BEING TOO BOTHERED, BUT LITTLE BY LITTLE, SHE BEGAN TO FEEL...
... A BIT LONELY.
HER NEW HOME, HOWEVER, WAS ANOTHER MATTER ENTIRELY.
COURTNEY FOUND HER UNCLE ...
... OR TO BE PRECISE, HER UNCLE'S UNUSUAL HOBBY ...
...ENORMOUSLY INTRIGUING...

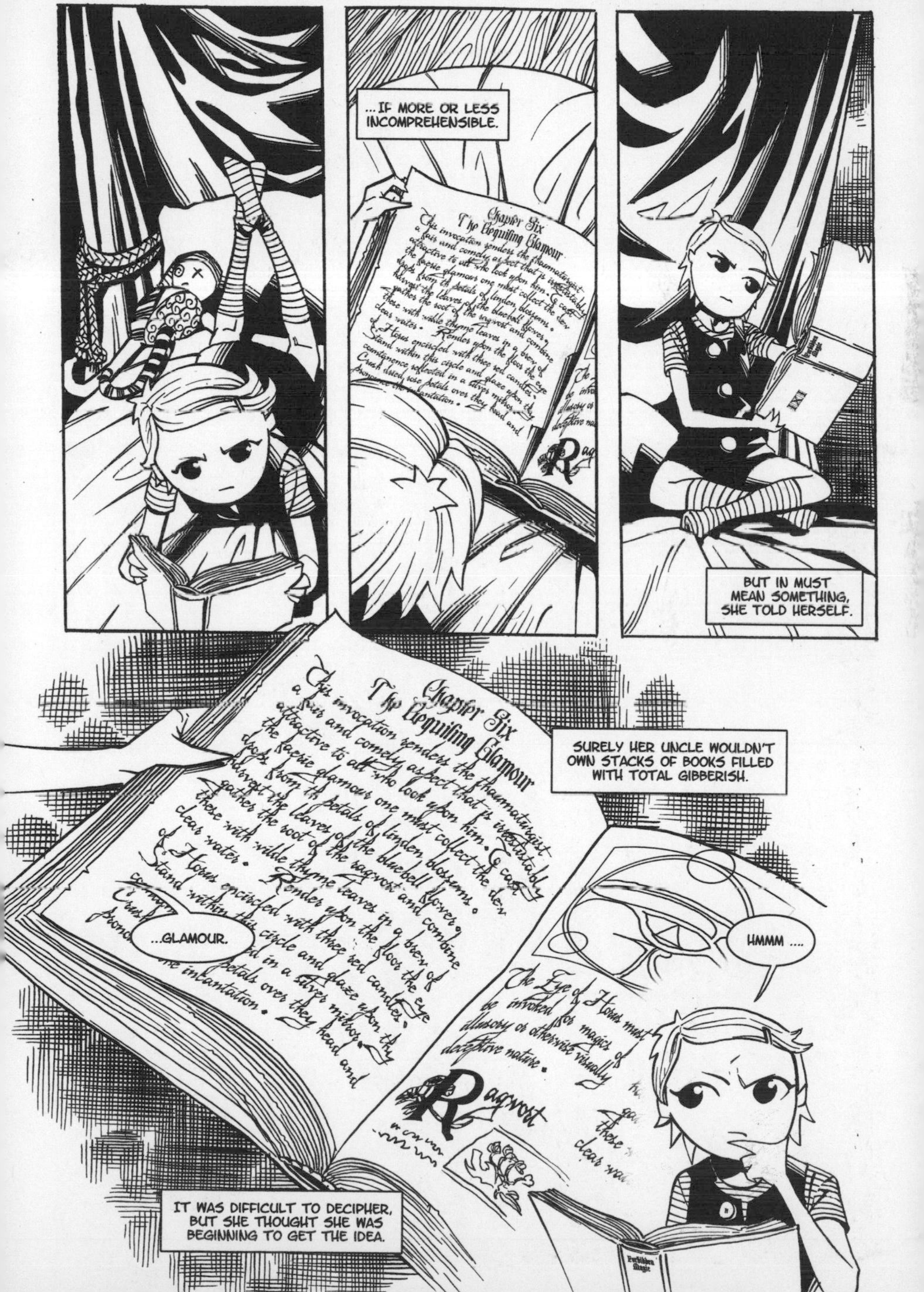
...IF MORE OR LESS INCOMPREHENSIBLE.
BUT IN MUST MEAN SOMETHING, SHE TOLD HERSELF.
SURELY HER UNCLE WOULDN'T OWN STACKS OF BOOKS FILLED WITH TOTAL GIBBERISH.
...GLAMOUR.
HMMM ....
IT WAS DIFFICULT TO DECIPHER, BUT SHE THOUGHT SHE WAS BEGINNING TO GET THE IDEA.

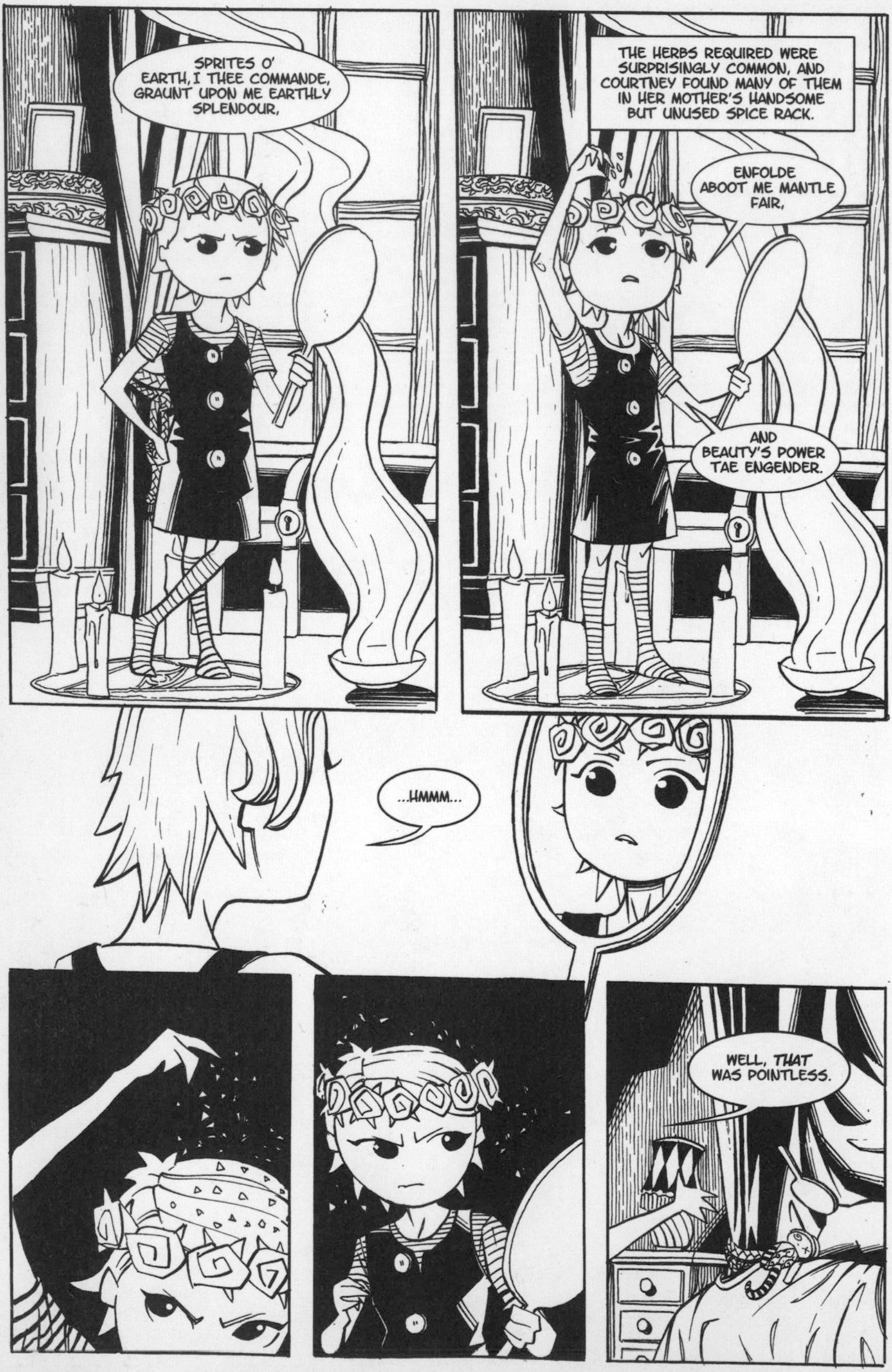
SPRITES O' EARTH, I THEE COMMANDE, GRAUNT UPON ME EARTHLY SPLENDOUR,
THE HERBS REQUIRED WERE SURPRISINGLY COMMON, AND COURTNEY FOUND MANY OF THEM IN HER MOTHER'S HANDSOME BUT UNUSED SPICE RACK.
ENFOLDE ABOOT ME MANTLE FAIR,
AND BEAUTY'S POWER TAE ENGENDER.
...HMMM...
WELL, THAT WAS POINTLESS.

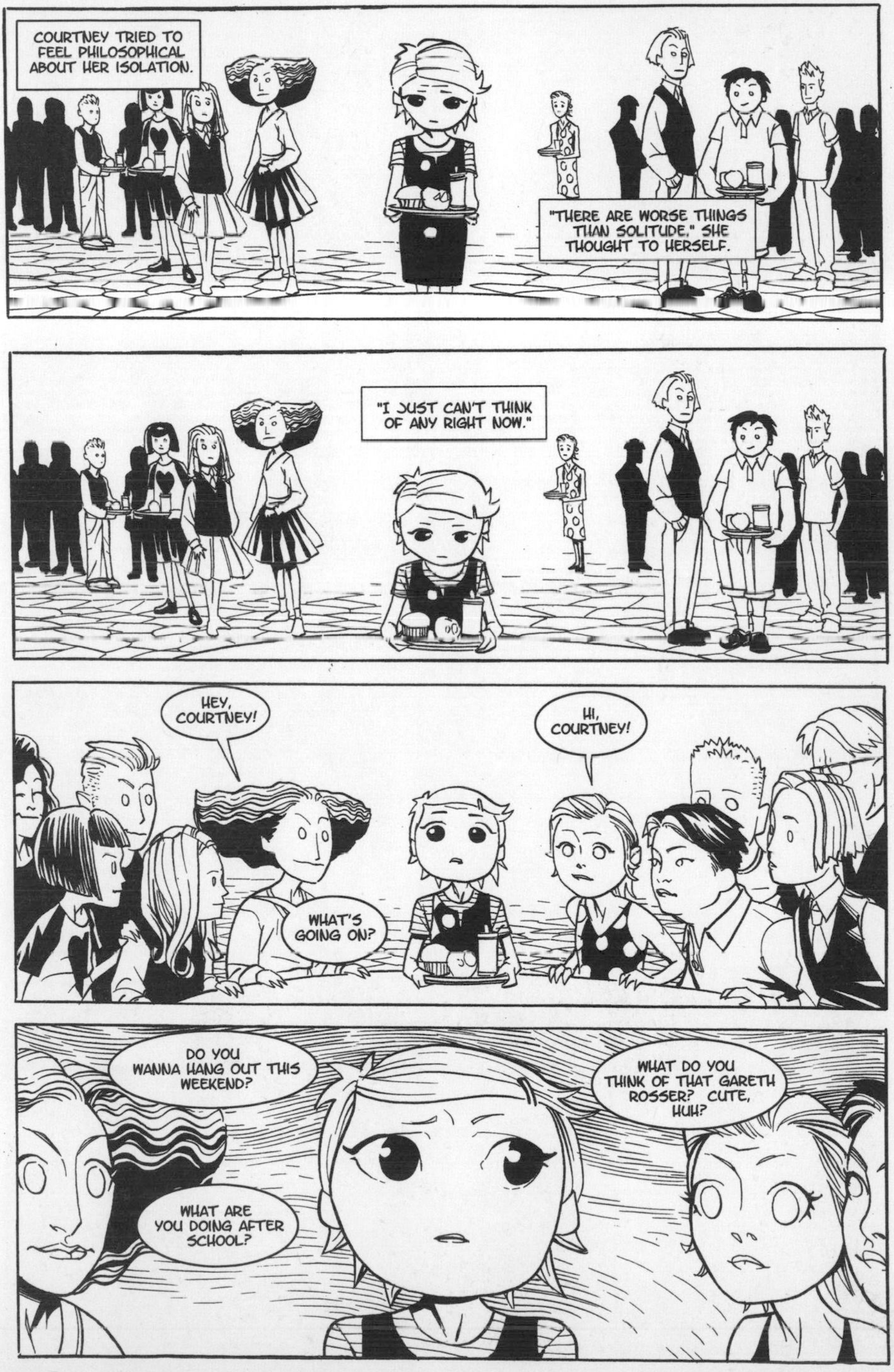
COURTNEY TRIED TO FEEL PHILOSOPHICAL ABOUT HER ISOLATION.
"THERE ARE WORSE THINGS THAN SOLITUDE," SHE THOUGHT TO HERSELF.
"I JUST CAN'T THINK OF ANY RIGHT NOW."
HEY, COURTNEY!
HI, COURTNEY!
WHAT'S GOING ON?
DO YOU WANNA HANG OUT THIS WEEKEND?
WHAT DO YOU THINK OF THAT GARETH ROSSER? CUTE, HUH?
WHAT ARE YOU DOING AFTER SCHOOL?

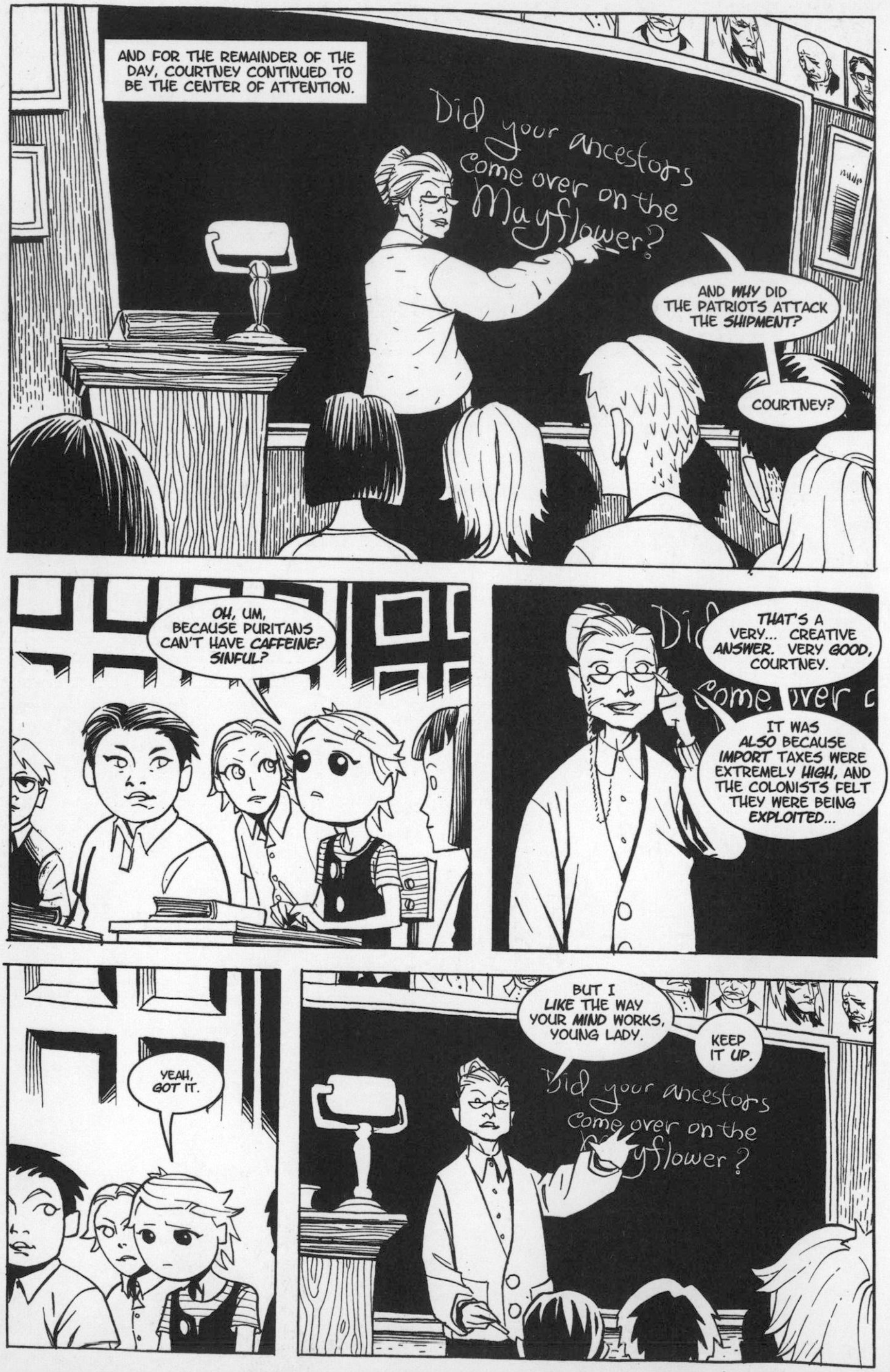
AND FOR THE REMAINDER OF THE DAY, COURTNEY CONTINUED TO BE THE CENTER OF ATTENTION.
Did your ancestors come over on the Mayflower?
AND WHY DID THE PATRIOTS ATTACK THE SHIPMENT?
COURTNEY?
OH, UM, BECAUSE PURITANS CAN'T HAVE CAFFEINE? SINFUL?
THAT'S A VERY... CREATIVE ANSWER. VERY GOOD, COURTNEY.
IT WAS ALSO BECAUSE IMPORT TAXES WERE EXTREMELY HIGH, AND THE COLONISTS FELT THEY WERE BEING EXPLOITED...
YEAH, GOT IT.
BUT I LIKE THE WAY YOUR MIND WORKS, YOUNG LADY.
KEEP IT UP.
Did your ancestors come over on the Mayflower?

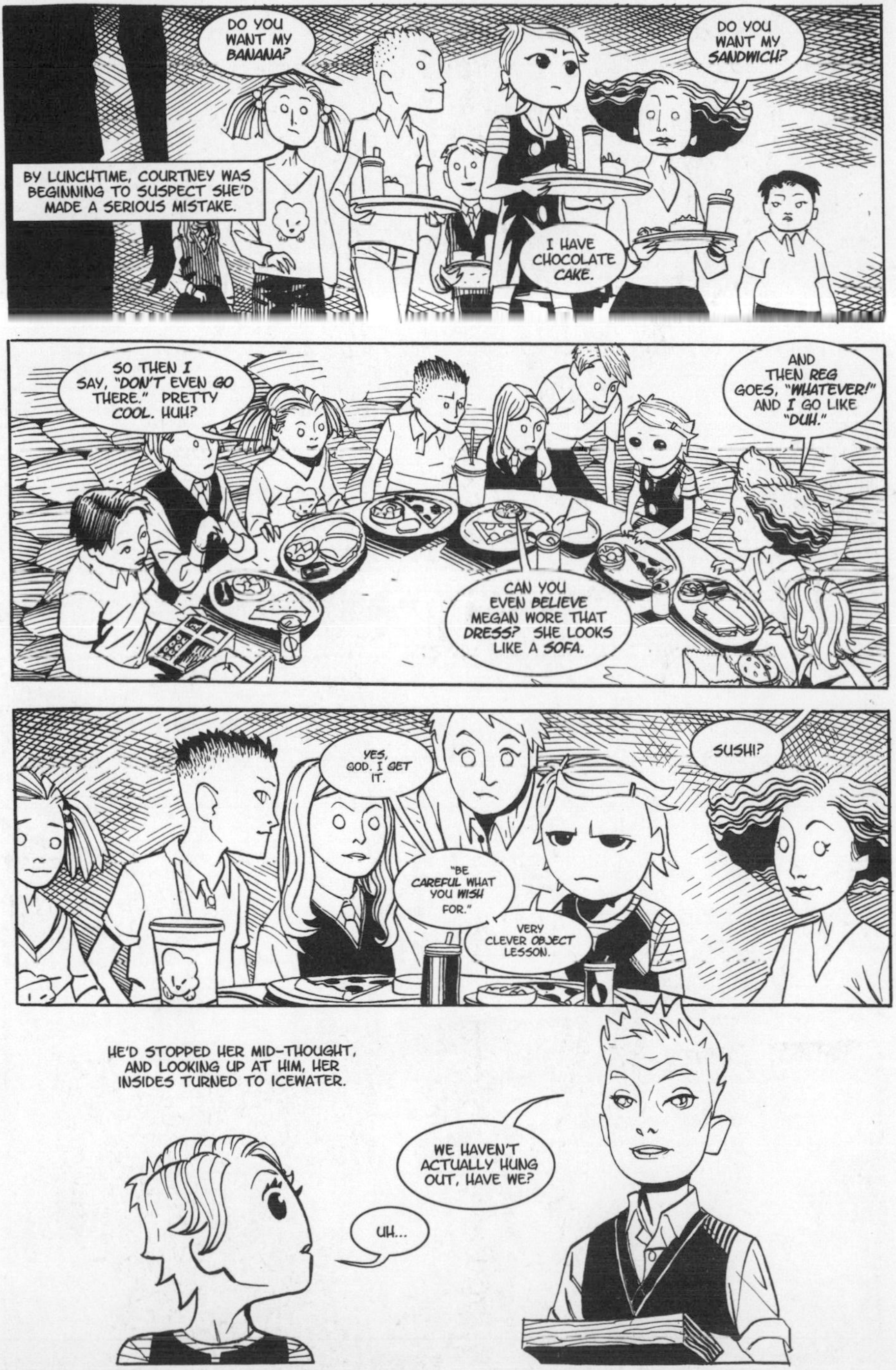

BY LUNCHTIME, COURTNEY WAS BEGINNING TO SUSPECT SHE'D MADE A SERIOUS MISTAKE.
DO YOU WANT MY BANANA?
I HAVE CHOCOLATE CAKE.
DO YOU WANT MY SANDWICH?
SO THEN I SAY, "DON'T EVEN GO THERE." PRETTY COOL. HUH?
AND THEN REG GOES, "WHATEVER!" AND I GO LIKE "DUH."
CAN YOU EVEN BELIEVE MEGAN WORE THAT DRESS? SHE LOOKS LIKE A SOFA.
YES, GOD. I GET IT.
"BE CAREFUL WHAT YOU WISH FOR."
VERY CLEVER OBJECT LESSON.
SUSHI?
HE'D STOPPED HER MID-THOUGHT, AND LOOKING UP AT HIM, HER INSIDES TURNED TO ICEWATER.
WE HAVEN'T ACTUALLY HUNG OUT, HAVE WE?
UH...

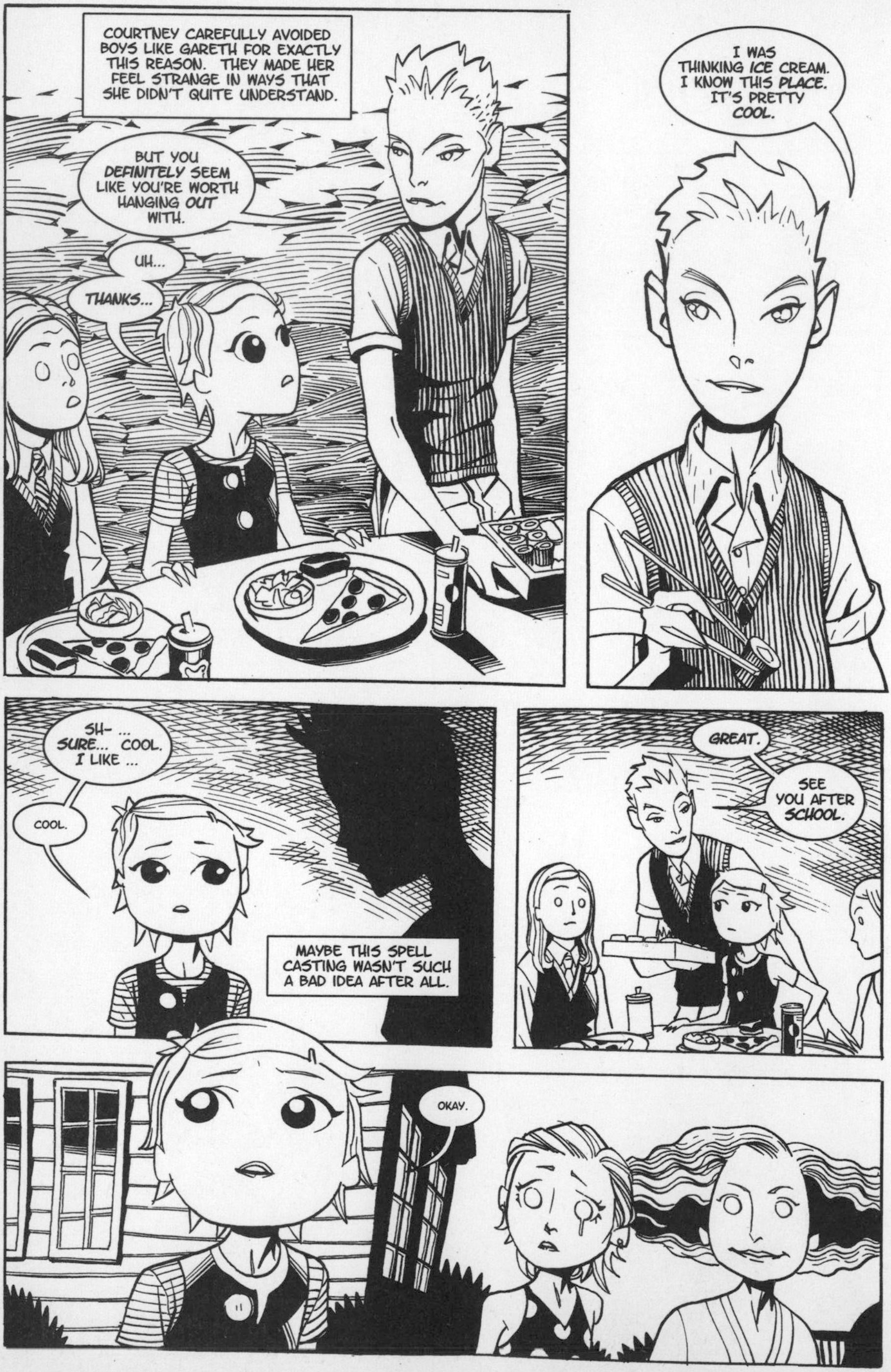
COURTNEY CAREFULLY AVOIDED BOYS LIKE GARETH FOR EXACTLY THIS REASON. THEY MADE HER FEEL STRANGE IN WAYS THAT SHE DIDN'T QUITE UNDERSTAND.
BUT YOU DEFINITELY SEEM LIKE YOU'RE WORTH HANGING OUT WITH.
UH...
THANKS...
I WAS THINKING ICE CREAM. I KNOW THIS PLACE. IT'S PRETTY COOL.
SH- ... SURE... COOL. I LIKE ...
COOL.
MAYBE THIS SPELL CASTING WASN'T SUCH A BAD IDEA AFTER ALL.
GREAT.
SEE YOU AFTER SCHOOL.
OKAY.

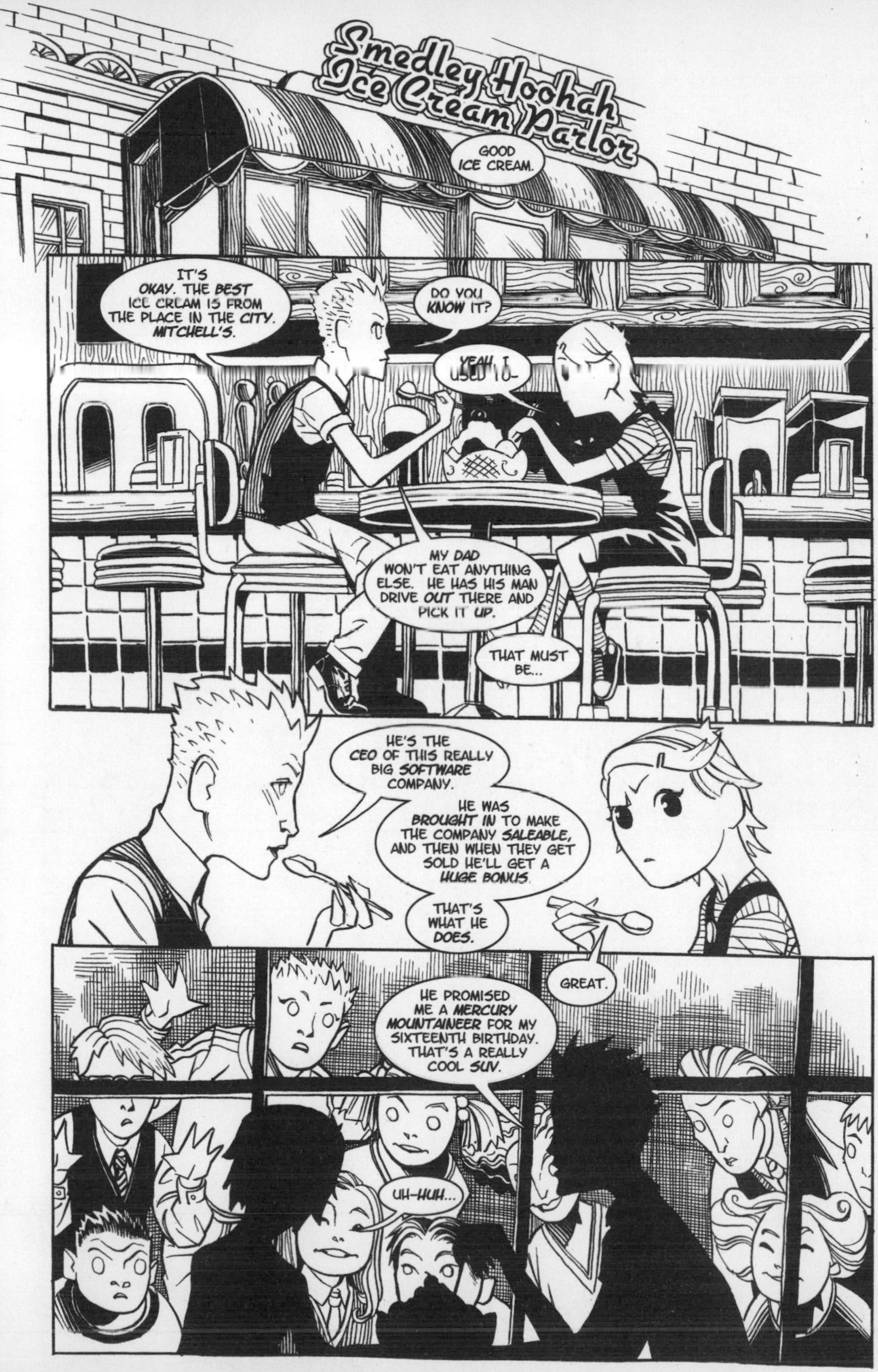
Smedley Hoohah Ice Cream Parlor
GOOD ICE CREAM.
IT'S OKAY. THE BEST ICE CREAM IS FROM THE PLACE IN THE CITY. MITCHELL'S.
DO YOU KNOW IT?
YEAH, I USED TO–
MY DAD WON'T EAT ANYTHING ELSE. HE HAS HIS MAN DRIVE OUT THERE AND PICK IT UP.
THAT MUST BE...
HE'S THE CEO OF THIS REALLY BIG SOFTWARE COMPANY.
HE WAS BROUGHT IN TO MAKE THE COMPANY SALEABLE, AND THEN WHEN THEY GET SOLD HE'LL GET A HUGE BONUS.
THAT'S WHAT HE DOES.
GREAT.
HE PROMISED ME A MERCURY MOUNTAINEER FOR MY SIXTEENTH BIRTHDAY. THAT'S A REALLY COOL SUV.
UH-HUH...

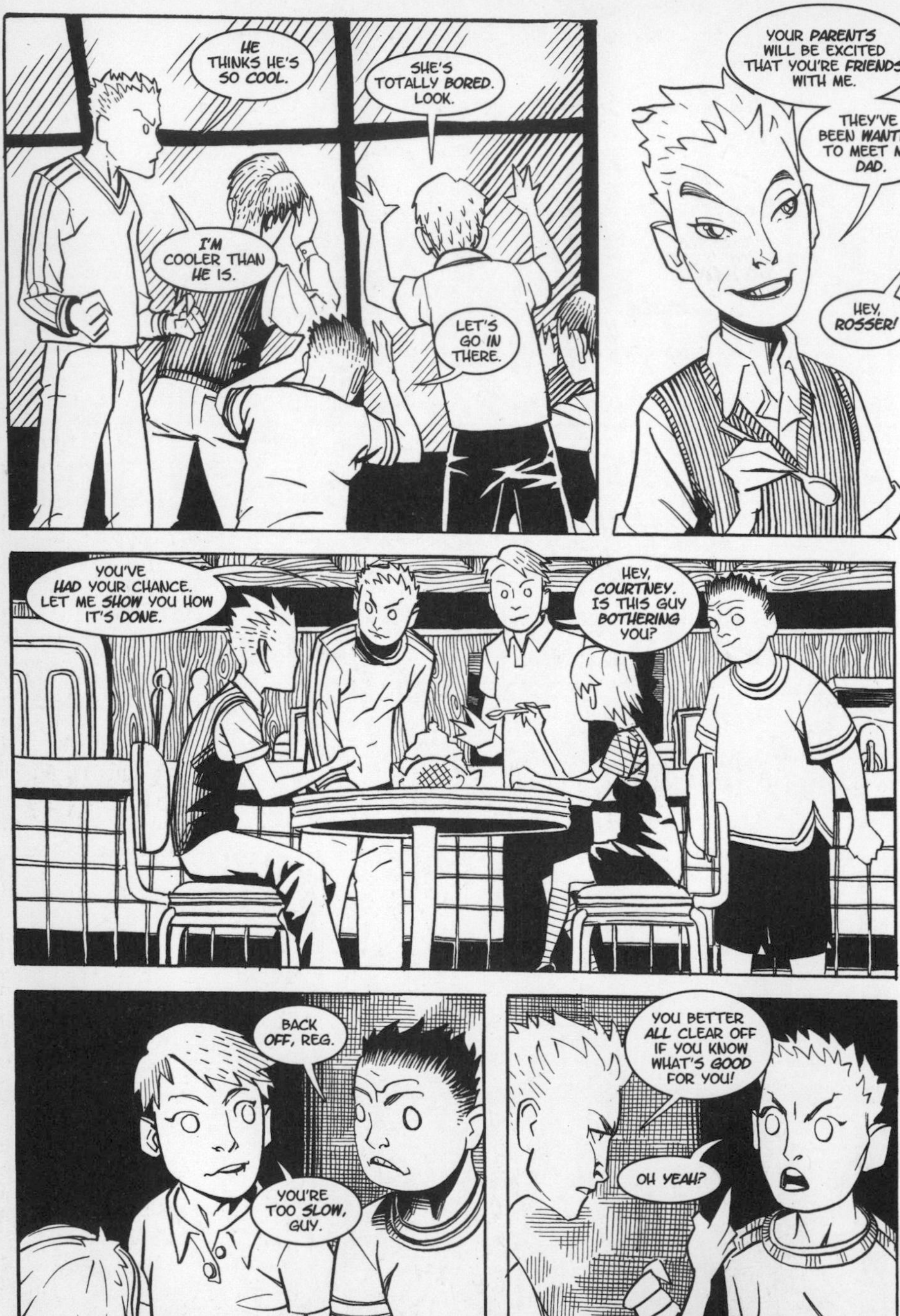
HE THINKS HE'S SO COOL.
SHE'S TOTALLY BORED. LOOK.
I'M COOLER THAN HE IS.
LET'S GO IN THERE.
YOUR PARENTS WILL BE EXCITED THAT YOU'RE FRIENDS WITH ME.
THEY'VE BEEN WANTING TO MEET MY DAD.
HEY, ROSSER!
YOU'VE HAD YOUR CHANCE. LET ME SHOW YOU HOW IT'S DONE.
HEY, COURTNEY. IS THIS GUY BOTHERING YOU?
BACK OFF, REG.
YOU'RE TOO SLOW, GUY.
YOU BETTER ALL CLEAR OFF IF YOU KNOW WHAT'S GOOD FOR YOU!
OH YEAH?

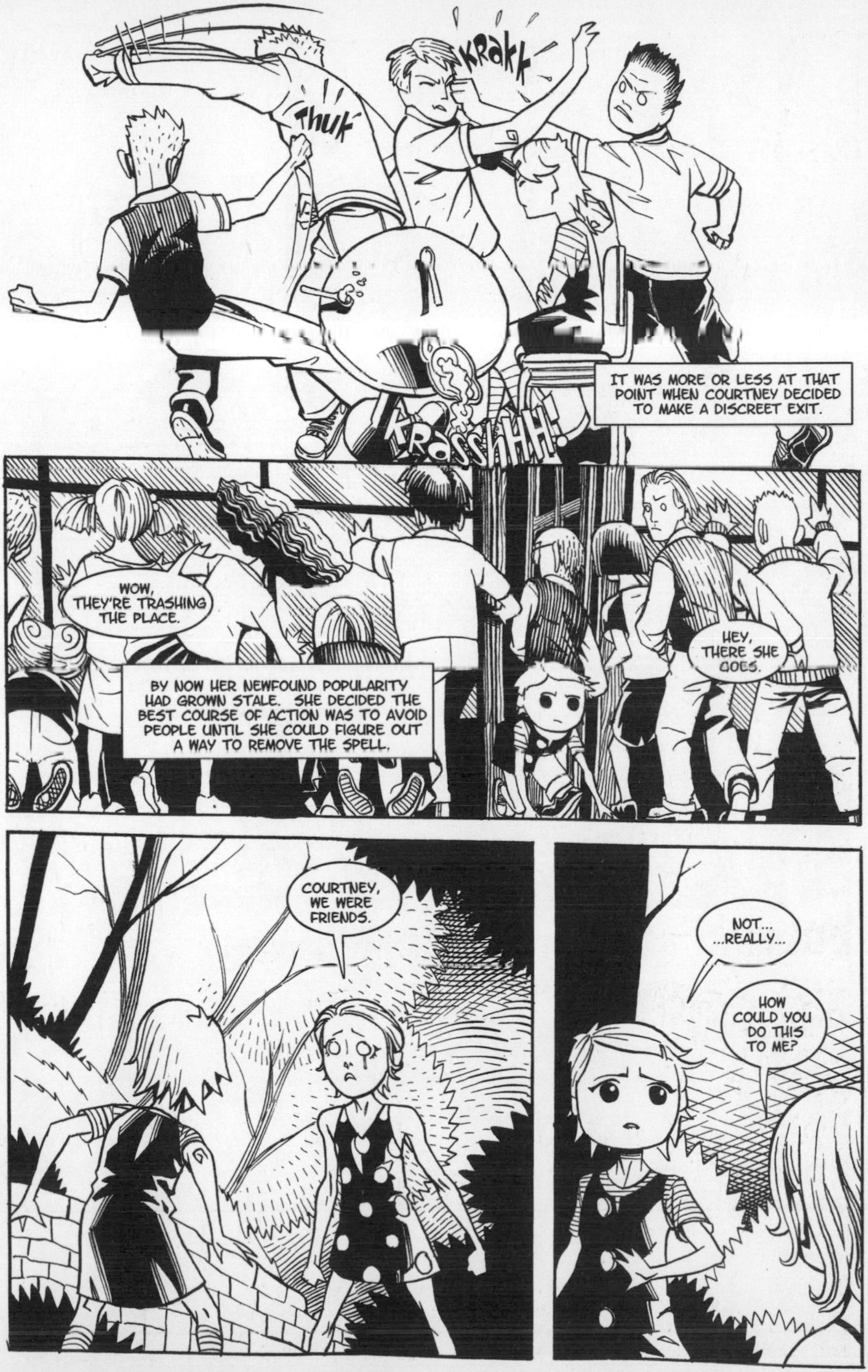
KRAKK
THUK
KRASSHHH!
IT WAS MORE OR LESS AT THAT POINT WHEN COURTNEY DECIDED TO MAKE A DISCREET EXIT.
WOW, THEY'RE TRASHING THE PLACE.
BY NOW HER NEWFOUND POPULARITY HAD GROWN STALE. SHE DECIDED THE BEST COURSE OF ACTION WAS TO AVOID PEOPLE UNTIL SHE COULD FIGURE OUT A WAY TO REMOVE THE SPELL.
HEY, THERE SHE GOES.
COURTNEY, WE WERE FRIENDS.
NOT... ...REALLY...
HOW COULD YOU DO THIS TO ME?

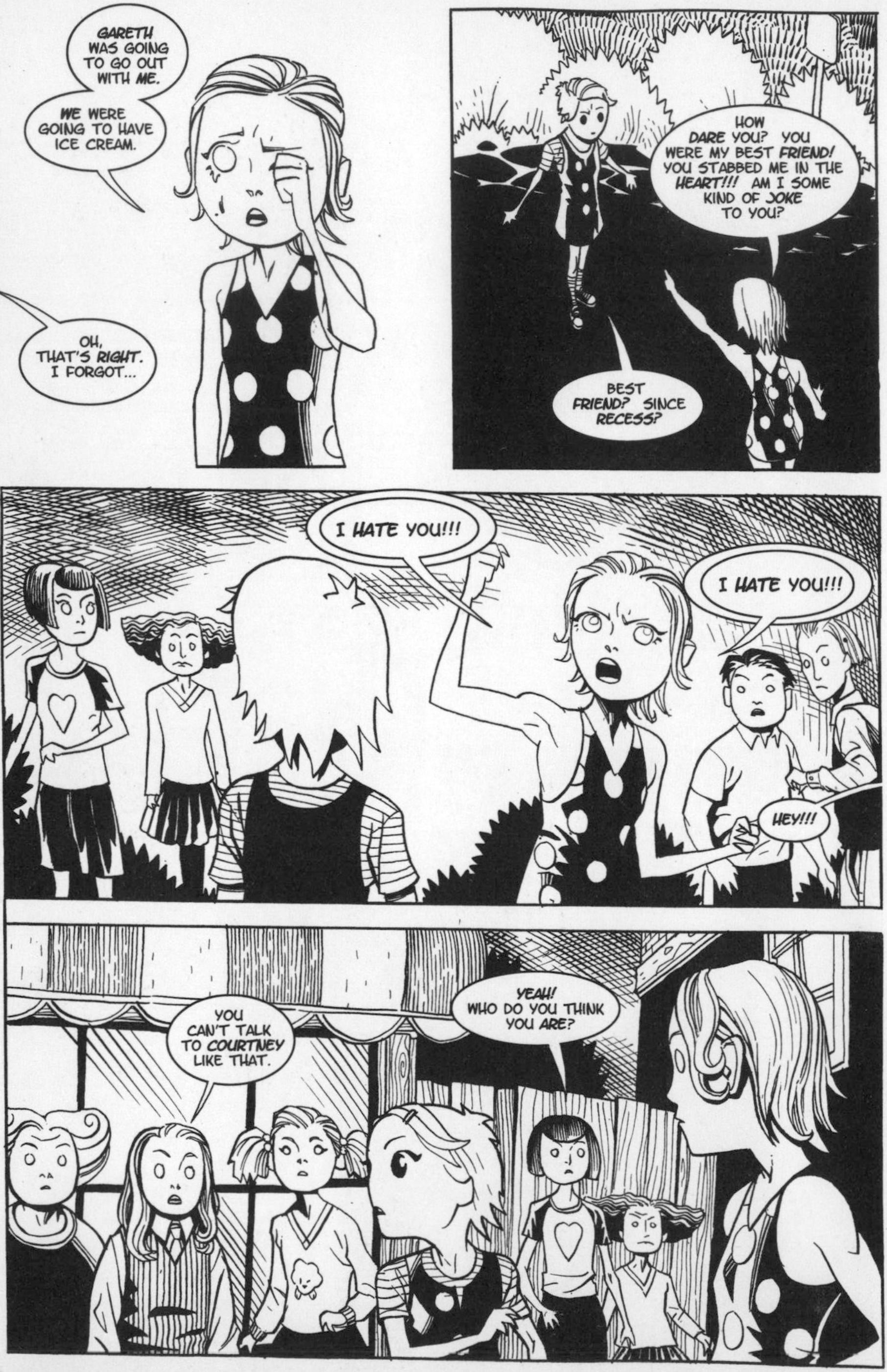
GARETH WAS GOING TO GO OUT WITH ME.
WE WERE GOING TO HAVE ICE CREAM.
OH, THAT'S RIGHT. I FORGOT...
HOW DARE YOU? YOU WERE MY BEST FRIEND! YOU STABBED ME IN THE HEART!!! AM I SOME KIND OF JOKE TO YOU?
BEST FRIEND? SINCE RECESS?
I HATE YOU!!!
I HATE YOU!!!
HEY!!!
YOU CAN'T TALK TO COURTNEY LIKE THAT.
YEAH! WHO DO YOU THINK YOU ARE?

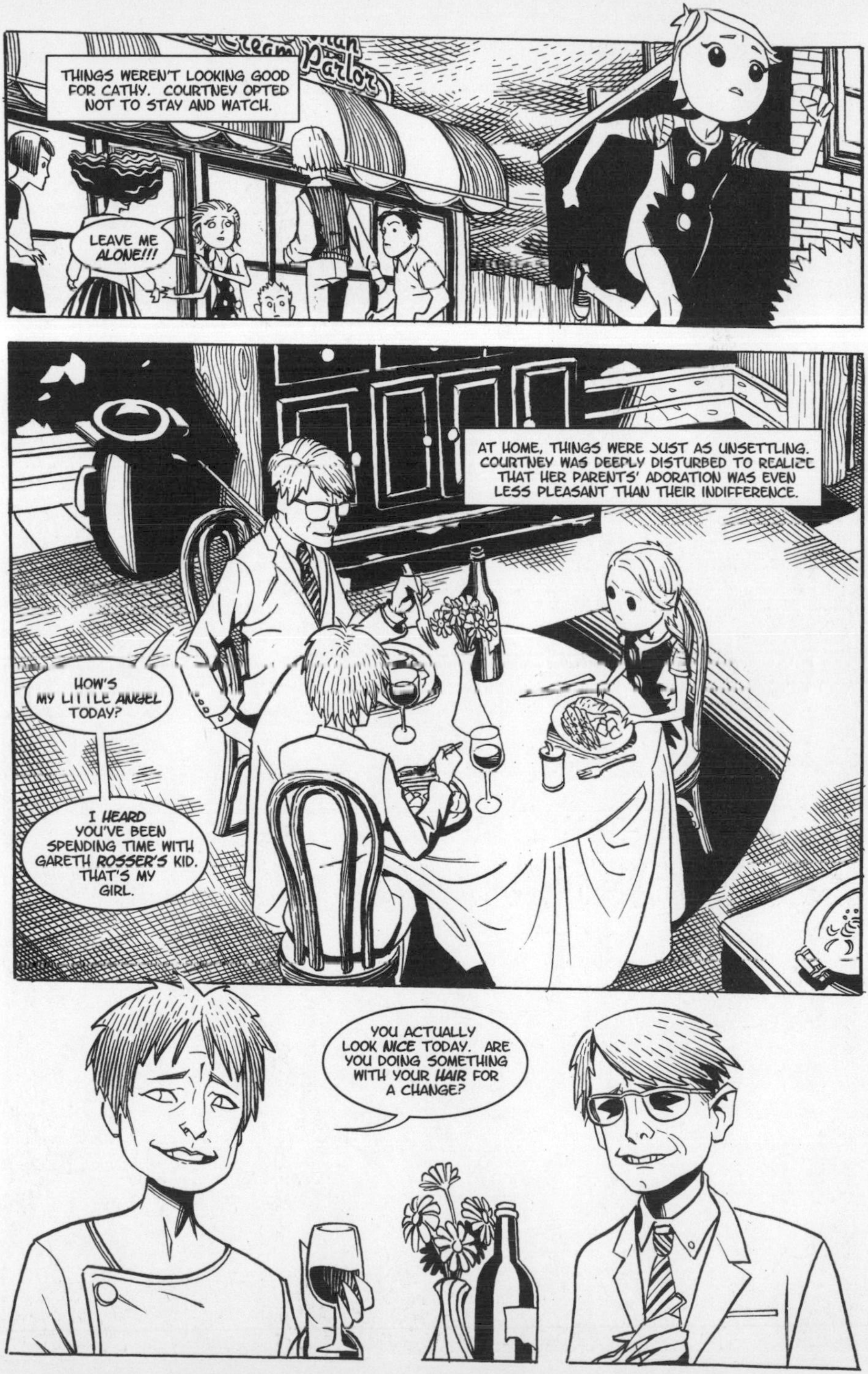

THINGS WEREN'T LOOKING GOOD FOR CATHY. COURTNEY OPTED NOT TO STAY AND WATCH.
LEAVE ME ALONE!!!
AT HOME, THINGS WERE JUST AS UNSETTLING. COURTNEY WAS DEEPLY DISTURBED TO REALIZE THAT HER PARENTS' ADORATION WAS EVEN LESS PLEASANT THAN THEIR INDIFFERENCE.
HOW'S MY LITTLE ANGEL TODAY?
I HEARD YOU'VE BEEN SPENDING TIME WITH GARETH ROSSER'S KID. THAT'S MY GIRL.
YOU ACTUALLY LOOK NICE TODAY. ARE YOU DOING SOMETHING WITH YOUR HAIR FOR A CHANGE?

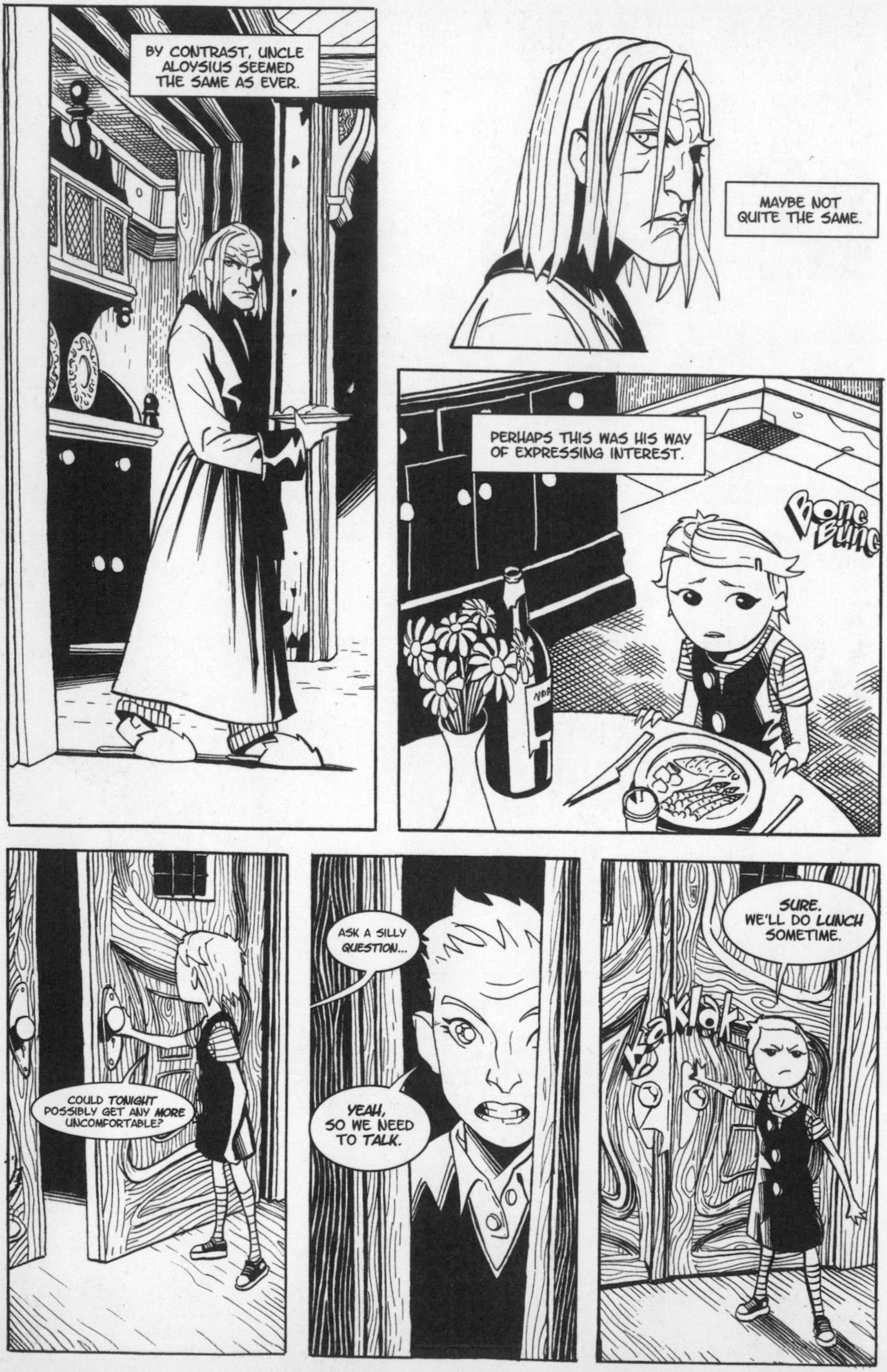
BY CONTRAST, UNCLE ALOYSIUS SEEMED THE SAME AS EVER.
MAYBE NOT QUITE THE SAME.
PERHAPS THIS WAS HIS WAY OF EXPRESSING INTEREST.
Bonc Bunc
COULD TONIGHT POSSIBLY GET ANY MORE UNCOMFORTABLE?
ASK A SILLY QUESTION...
YEAH, SO WE NEED TO TALK.
SURE. WE'LL DO LUNCH SOMETIME.
KaKlok

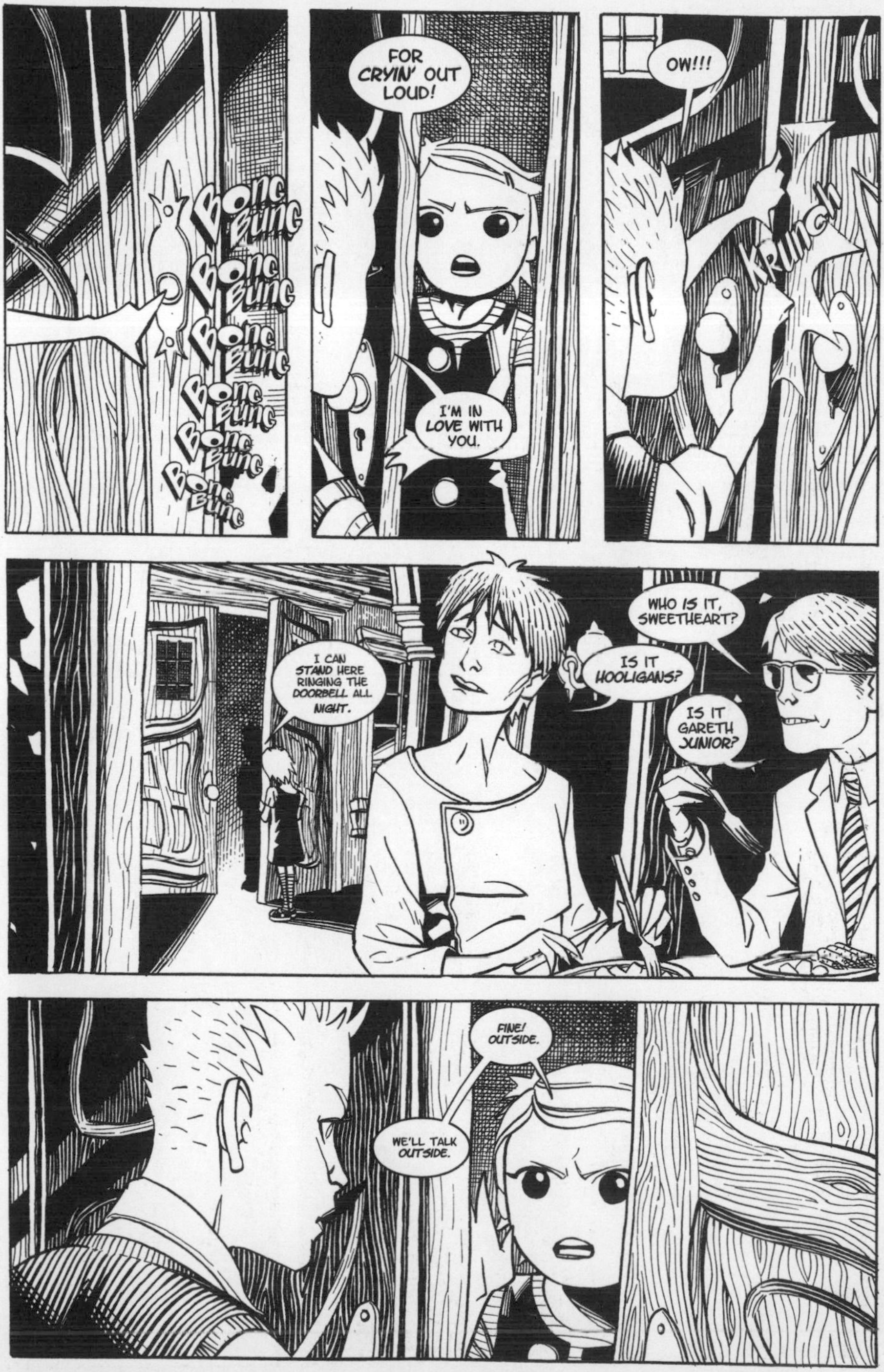
BONG BUNG
BONG BUNG
BONG BUNG
BONG BUNG
BONG BUNG
BONG BUNG
FOR CRYIN' OUT LOUD!
I'M IN LOVE WITH YOU.
OW!!!
KRUNCH
I CAN STAND HERE RINGING THE DOORBELL ALL NIGHT.
WHO IS IT, SWEETHEART?
IS IT HOOLIGANS?
IS IT GARETH JUNIOR?
FINE! OUTSIDE.
WE'LL TALK OUTSIDE.

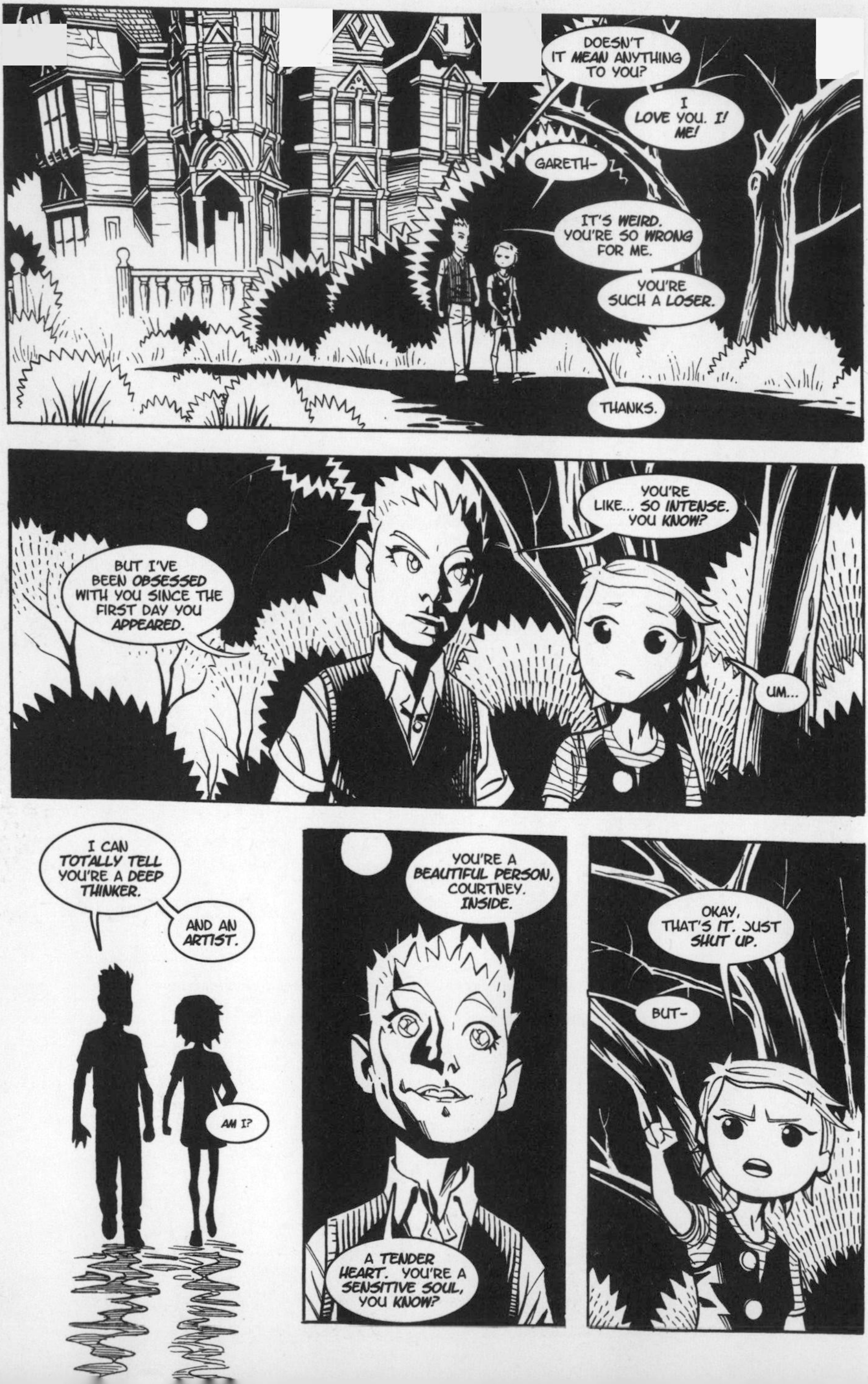
DOESN'T IT MEAN ANYTHING TO YOU?
I LOVE YOU. I! ME!
GARETH-
IT'S WEIRD. YOU'RE SO WRONG FOR ME.
YOU'RE SUCH A LOSER.
THANKS.
YOU'RE LIKE... SO INTENSE. YOU KNOW?
BUT I'VE BEEN OBSESSED WITH YOU SINCE THE FIRST DAY YOU APPEARED.
UM...
I CAN TOTALLY TELL YOU'RE A DEEP THINKER.
AND AN ARTIST.
AM I?
YOU'RE A BEAUTIFUL PERSON, COURTNEY. INSIDE.
A TENDER HEART. YOU'RE A SENSITIVE SOUL, YOU KNOW?
OKAY, THAT'S IT. JUST SHUT UP.
BUT-

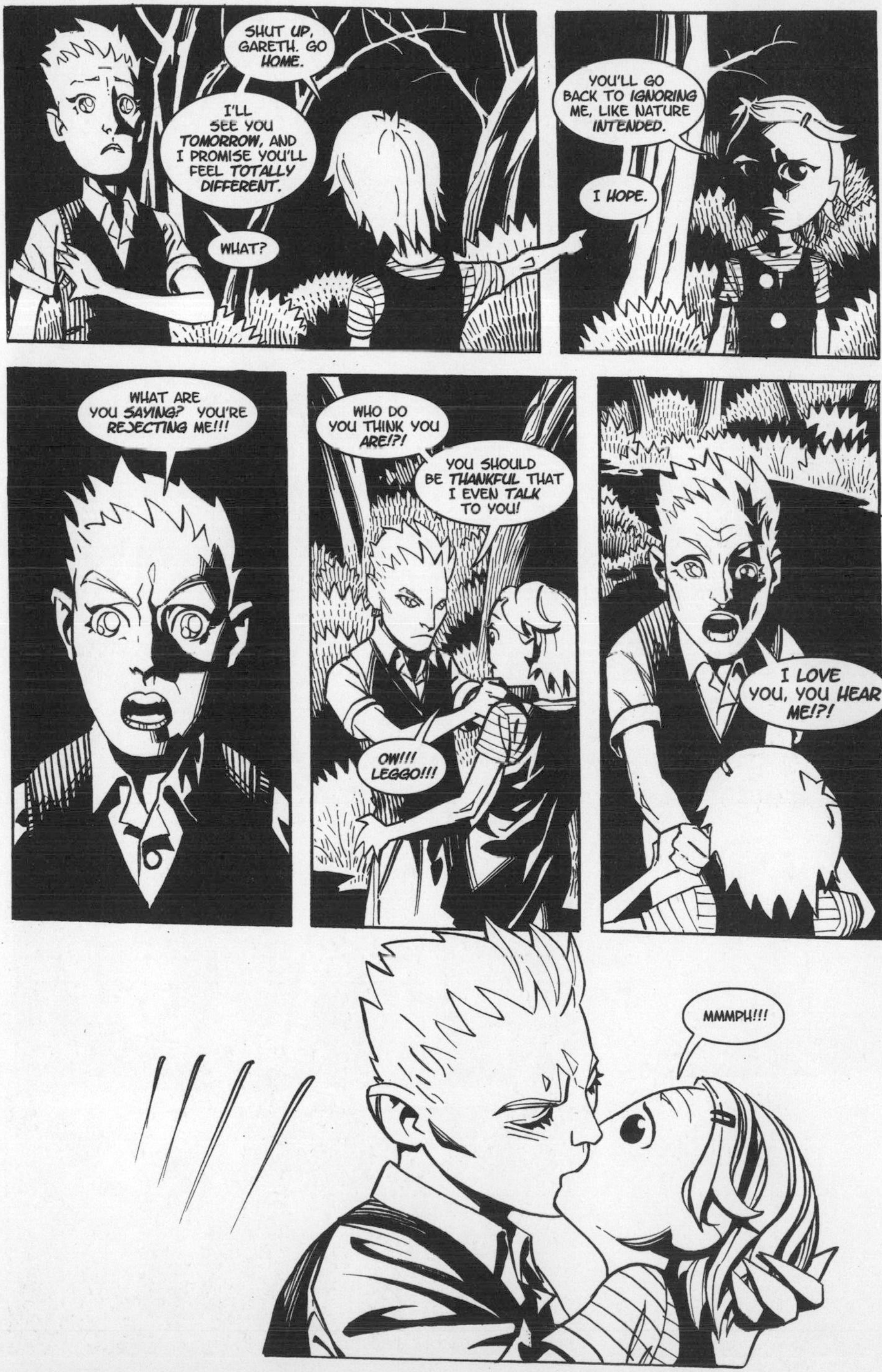
SHUT UP, GARETH. GO HOME.
I'LL SEE YOU TOMORROW, AND I PROMISE YOU'LL FEEL TOTALLY DIFFERENT.
WHAT?
YOU'LL GO BACK TO IGNORING ME, LIKE NATURE INTENDED.
I HOPE.
WHAT ARE YOU SAYING? YOU'RE REJECTING ME!!!
WHO DO YOU THINK YOU ARE!?!
YOU SHOULD BE THANKFUL THAT I EVEN TALK TO YOU!
OW!!! LEGGO!!!
I LOVE YOU, YOU HEAR ME!?!
MMMPH!!!

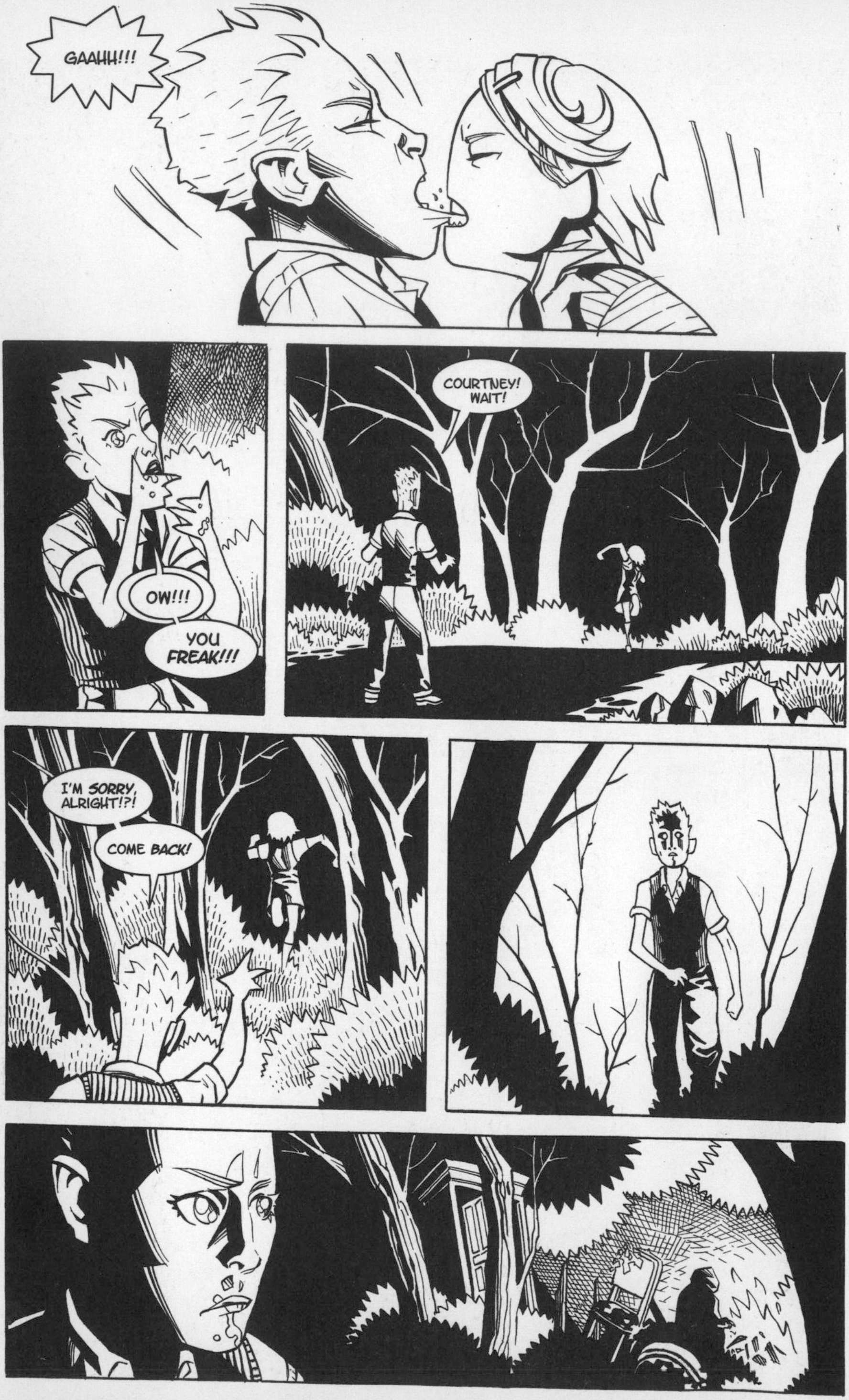
GAAHH!!!
OW!!!
YOU FREAK!!!
COURTNEY! WAIT!
I'M SORRY, ALRIGHT!?!
COME BACK!

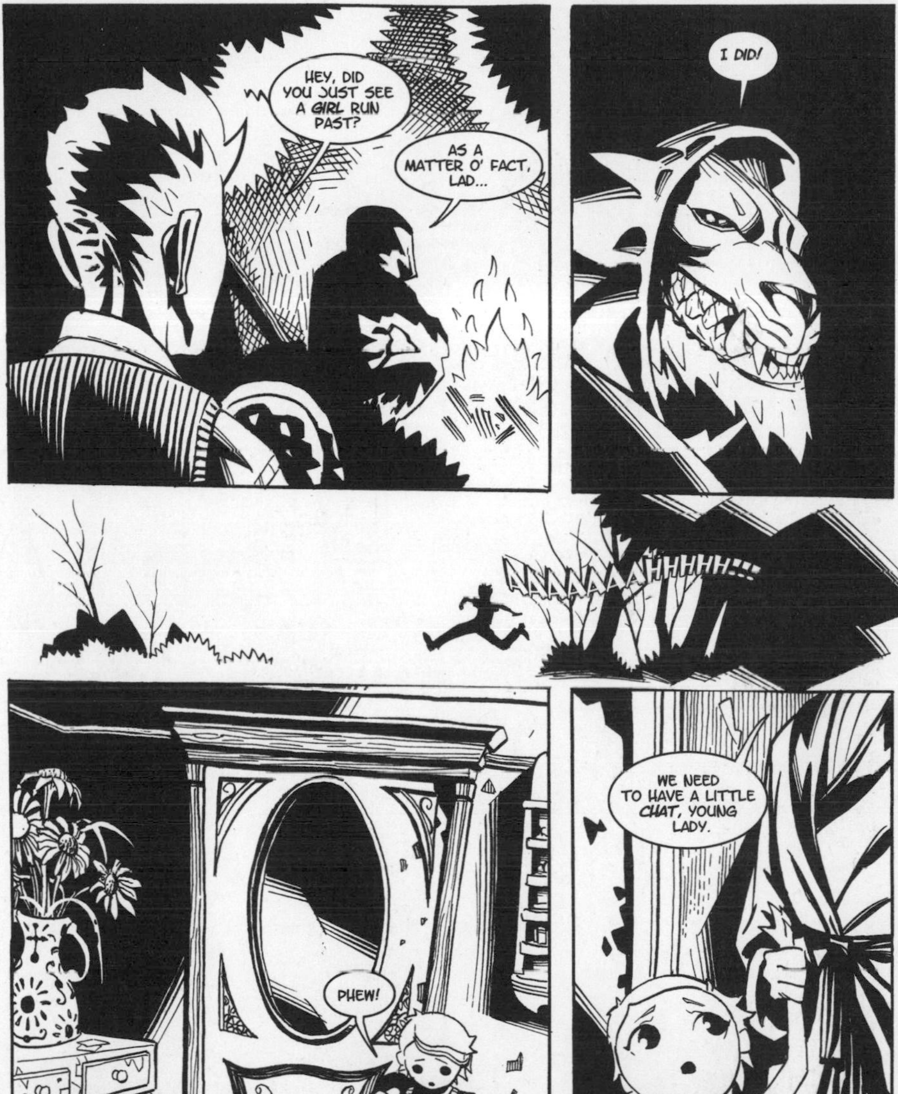
HEY, DID YOU JUST SEE A GIRL RUN PAST?
AS A MATTER O' FACT, LAD...
I DID!
AAAAAAAAHHHHHH!!!
PHEW!
WE NEED TO HAVE A LITTLE CHAT, YOUNG LADY.

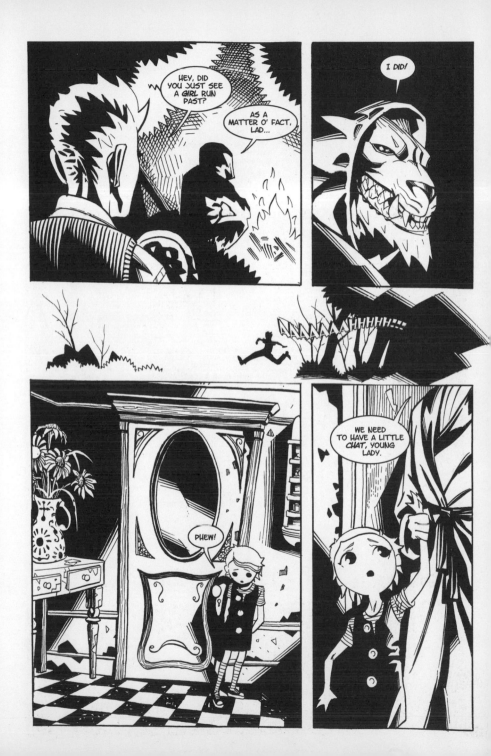

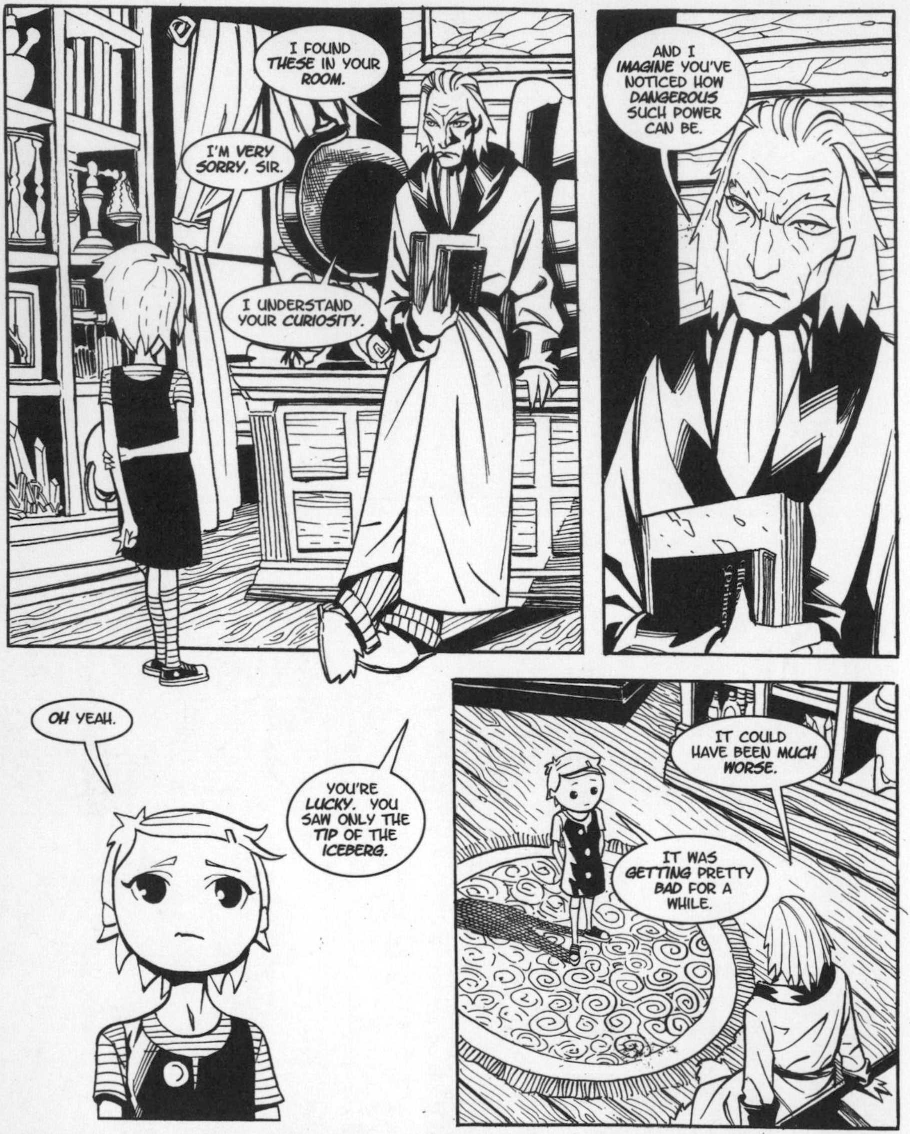
I FOUND THESE IN YOUR ROOM.
I'M VERY SORRY, SIR.
I UNDERSTAND YOUR CURIOSITY.
AND I IMAGINE YOU'VE NOTICED HOW DANGEROUS SUCH POWER CAN BE.
OH YEAH.
YOU'RE LUCKY. YOU SAW ONLY THE TIP OF THE ICEBERG.
IT COULD HAVE BEEN MUCH WORSE.
IT WAS GETTING PRETTY BAD FOR A WHILE.
YOU DID DRAW ATTENTION TO YOURSELF, SOMETHING AN INTELLIGENT WITCH TRIES TO AVOID.
WITCH?

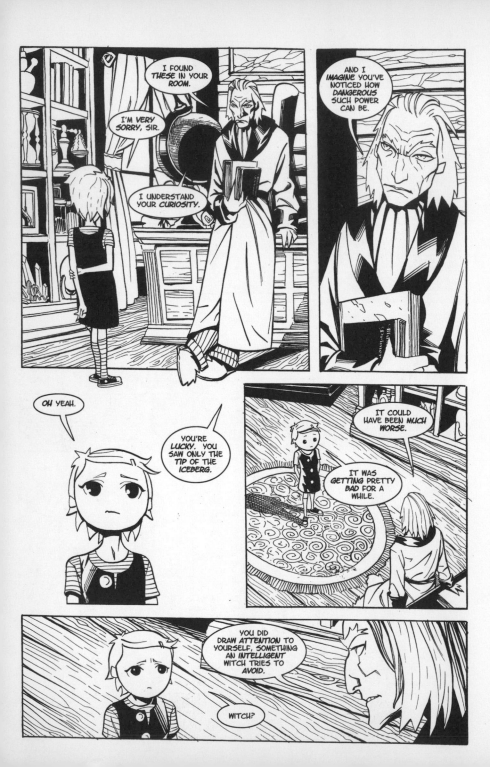

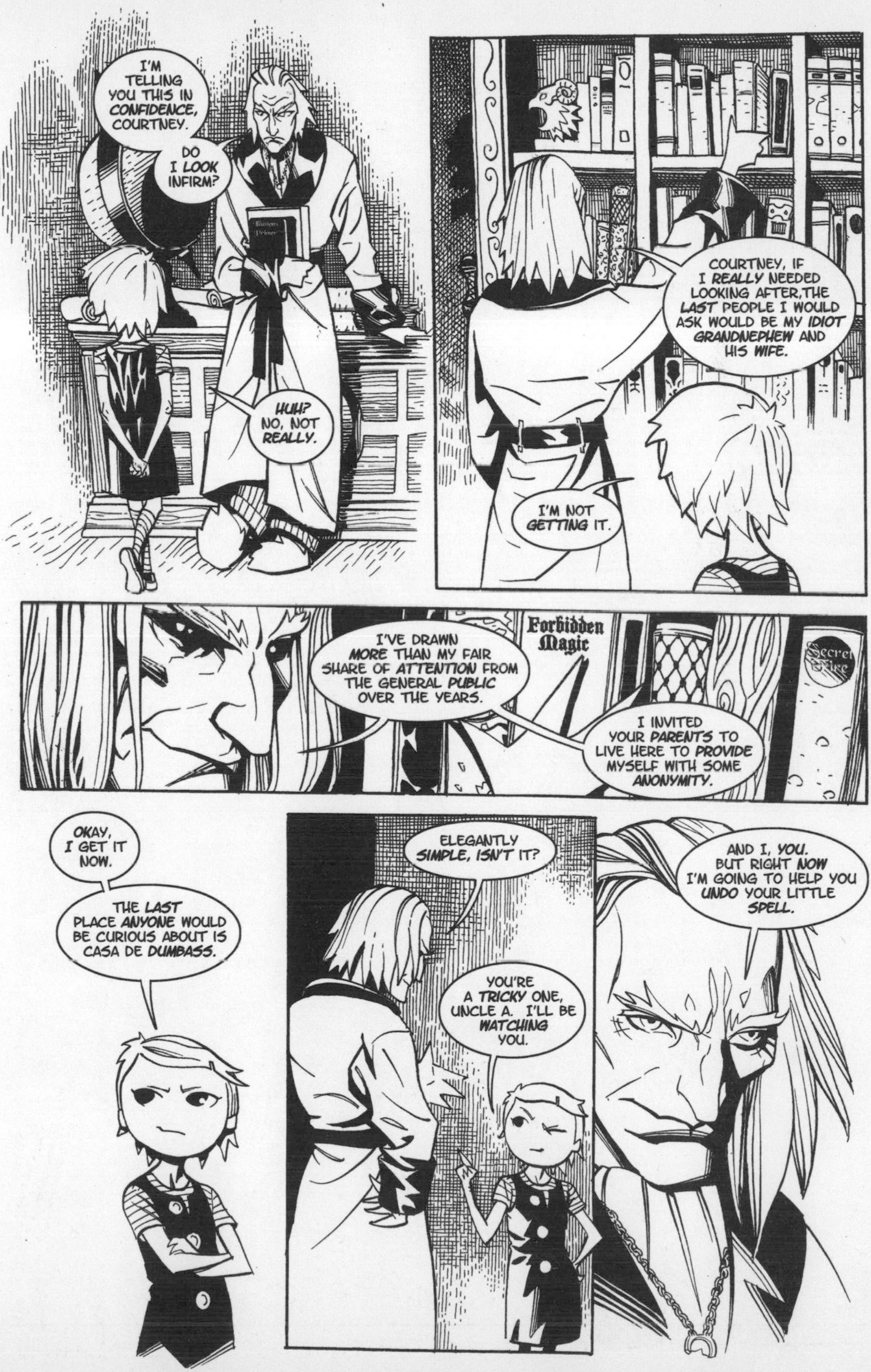
I'M TELLING YOU THIS IN CONFIDENCE, COURTNEY.
DO I LOOK INFIRM?
HUH? NO, NOT REALLY.
Illusions Primer
COURTNEY, IF I REALLY NEEDED LOOKING AFTER, THE LAST PEOPLE I WOULD ASK WOULD BE MY IDIOT GRANDNEPHEW AND HIS WIFE.
I'M NOT GETTING IT.
Forbidden Magic
Secret Fire
I'VE DRAWN MORE THAN MY FAIR SHARE OF ATTENTION FROM THE GENERAL PUBLIC OVER THE YEARS.
I INVITED YOUR PARENTS TO LIVE HERE TO PROVIDE MYSELF WITH SOME ANONYMITY.
OKAY, I GET IT NOW.
THE LAST PLACE ANYONE WOULD BE CURIOUS ABOUT IS CASA DE DUMBASS.
ELEGANTLY SIMPLE, ISN'T IT?
YOU'RE A TRICKY ONE, UNCLE A. I'LL BE WATCHING YOU.
AND I, YOU. BUT RIGHT NOW I'M GOING TO HELP YOU UNDO YOUR LITTLE SPELL.

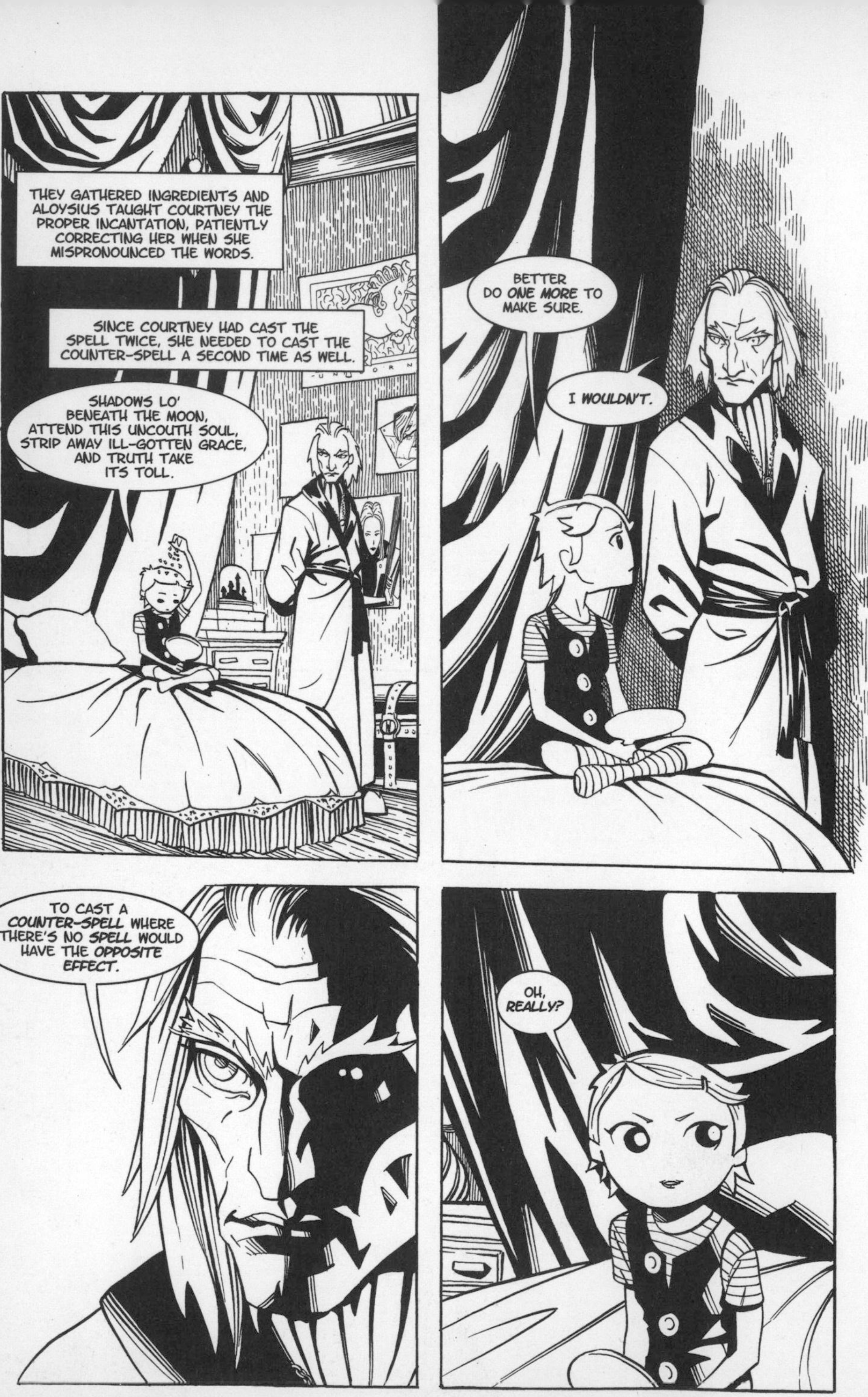
THEY GATHERED INGREDIENTS AND ALOYSIUS TAUGHT COURTNEY THE PROPER INCANTATION, PATIENTLY CORRECTING HER WHEN SHE MISPRONOUNCED THE WORDS.
SINCE COURTNEY HAD CAST THE SPELL TWICE, SHE NEEDED TO CAST THE COUNTER-SPELL A SECOND TIME AS WELL.
SHADOWS LO' BENEATH THE MOON, ATTEND THIS UNCOUTH SOUL, STRIP AWAY ILL-GOTTEN GRACE, AND TRUTH TAKE ITS TOLL.
BETTER DO ONE MORE TO MAKE SURE.
I WOULDN'T.
TO CAST A COUNTER-SPELL WHERE THERE'S NO SPELL WOULD HAVE THE OPPOSITE EFFECT.
OH, REALLY?

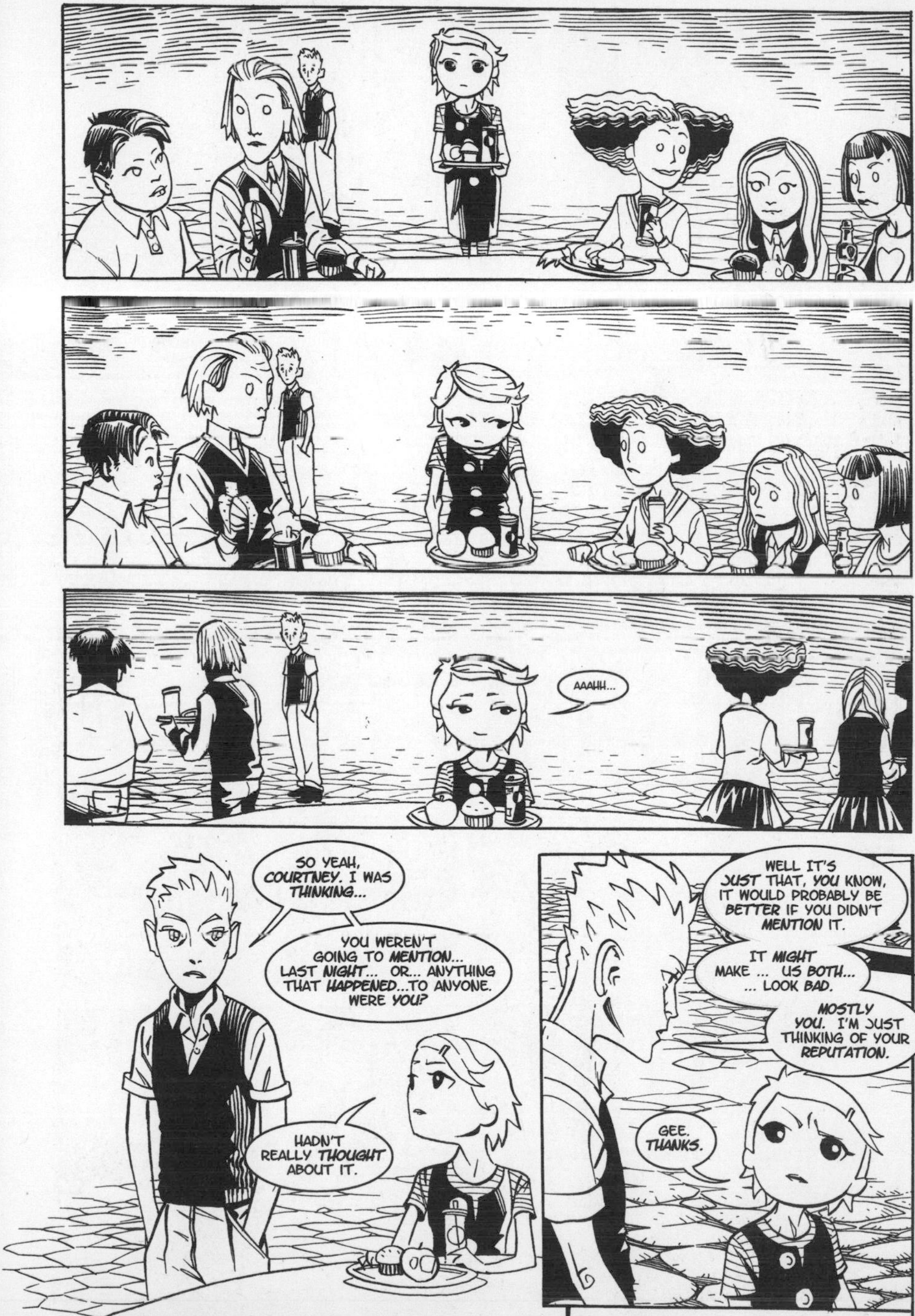
AAAHH...
SO YEAH, COURTNEY. I WAS THINKING...
YOU WEREN'T GOING TO MENTION... LAST NIGHT... OR... ANYTHING THAT HAPPENED...TO ANYONE. WERE YOU?
HADN'T REALLY THOUGHT ABOUT IT.
WELL IT'S JUST THAT, YOU KNOW, IT WOULD PROBABLY BE BETTER IF YOU DIDN'T MENTION IT.
IT MIGHT MAKE ... US BOTH... ... LOOK BAD.
MOSTLY YOU. I'M JUST THINKING OF YOUR REPUTATION.
GEE. THANKS.

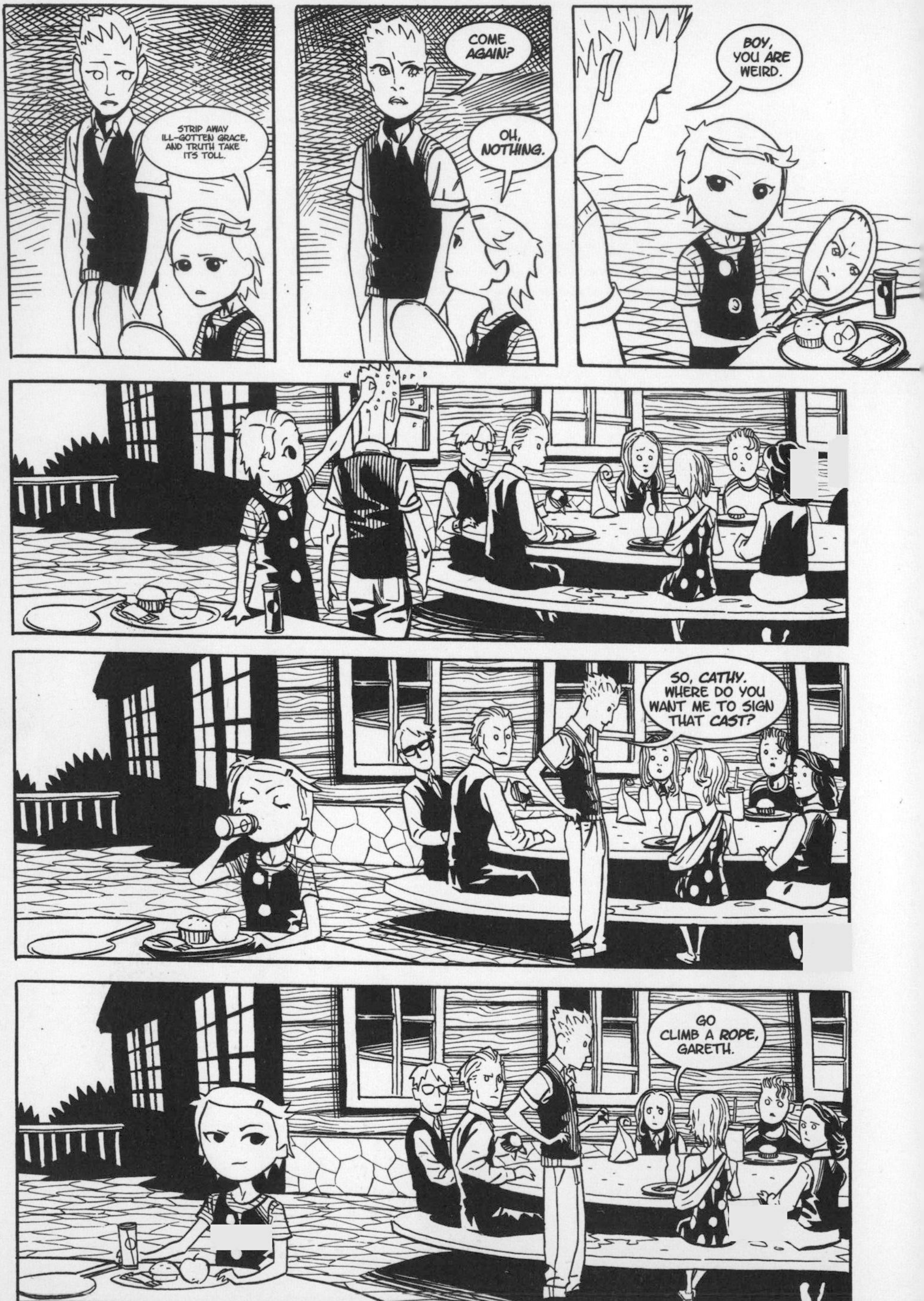
STRIP AWAY ILL-GOTTEN GRACE, AND TRUTH TAKE ITS TOLL.
COME AGAIN?
OH, NOTHING.
BOY, YOU ARE WEIRD.
SO, CATHY. WHERE DO YOU WANT ME TO SIGN THAT CAST?
GO CLIMB A ROPE, GARETH.

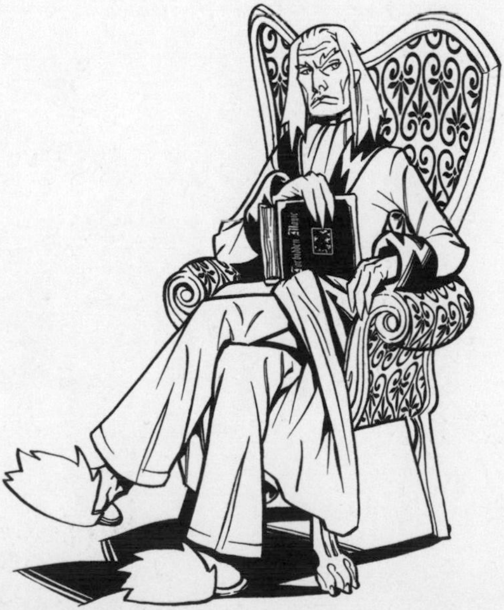
Forbidden Magic

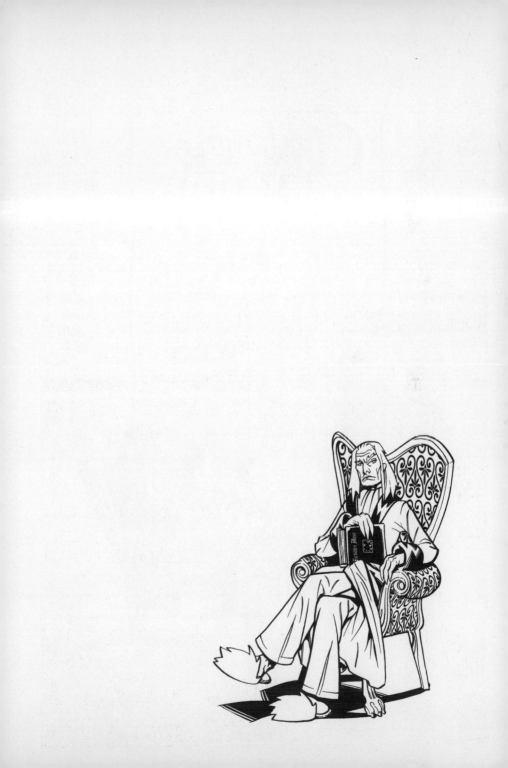

CHAPTER THREE

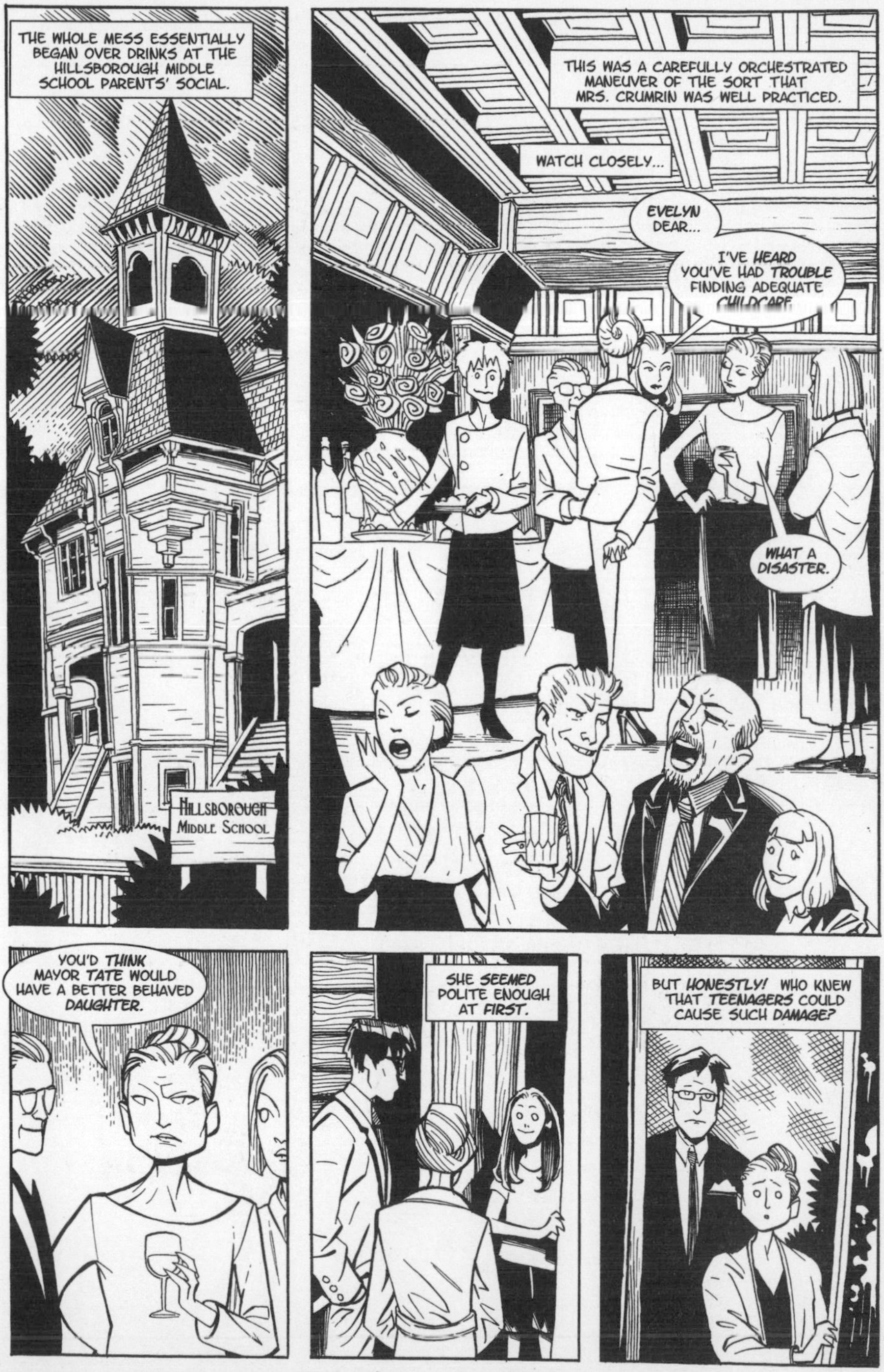
THE WHOLE MESS ESSENTIALLY BEGAN OVER DRINKS AT THE HILLSBOROUGH MIDDLE SCHOOL PARENTS' SOCIAL.
HILLSBOROUGH MIDDLE SCHOOL
THIS WAS A CAREFULLY ORCHESTRATED MANEUVER OF THE SORT THAT MRS. CRUMRIN WAS WELL PRACTICED.
WATCH CLOSELY...
EVELYN DEAR...
I'VE HEARD YOU'VE HAD TROUBLE FINDING ADEQUATE CHILDCARE.
WHAT A DISASTER.
YOU'D THINK MAYOR TATE WOULD HAVE A BETTER BEHAVED DAUGHTER.
SHE SEEMED POLITE ENOUGH AT FIRST.
BUT HONESTLY! WHO KNEW THAT TEENAGERS COULD CAUSE SUCH DAMAGE?

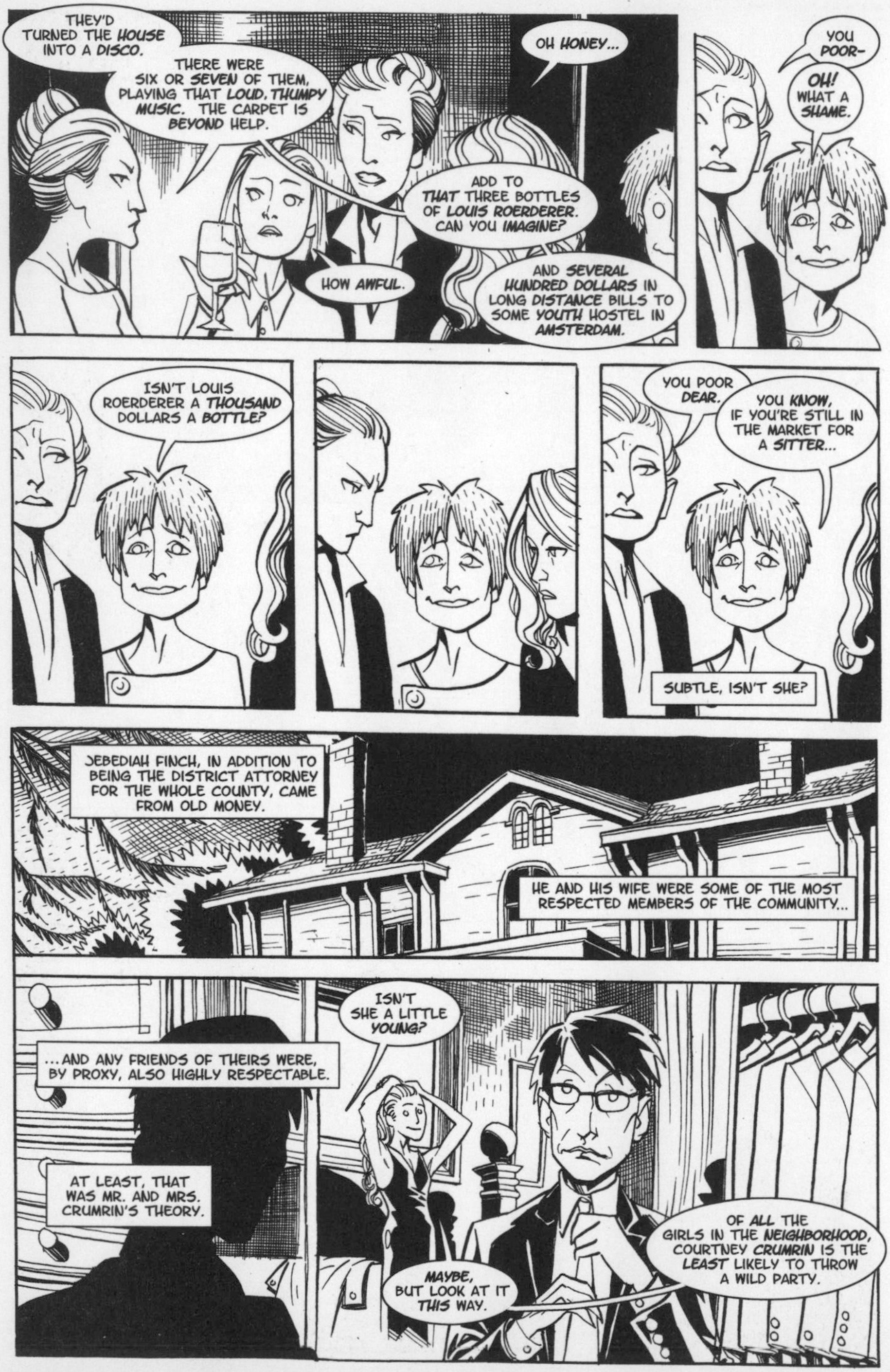
THEY'D TURNED THE HOUSE INTO A DISCO.
THERE WERE SIX OR SEVEN OF THEM, PLAYING THAT LOUD, THUMPY MUSIC. THE CARPET IS BEYOND HELP.
OH HONEY...
ADD TO THAT THREE BOTTLES OF LOUIS ROERDERER. CAN YOU IMAGINE?
HOW AWFUL.
AND SEVERAL HUNDRED DOLLARS IN LONG DISTANCE BILLS TO SOME YOUTH HOSTEL IN AMSTERDAM.
YOU POOR-
OH! WHAT A SHAME.
ISN'T LOUIS ROERDERER A THOUSAND DOLLARS A BOTTLE?
YOU POOR DEAR.
YOU KNOW, IF YOU'RE STILL IN THE MARKET FOR A SITTER...
SUBTLE, ISN'T SHE?
JEBEDIAH FINCH, IN ADDITION TO BEING THE DISTRICT ATTORNEY FOR THE WHOLE COUNTY, CAME FROM OLD MONEY.
HE AND HIS WIFE WERE SOME OF THE MOST RESPECTED MEMBERS OF THE COMMUNITY...
...AND ANY FRIENDS OF THEIRS WERE, BY PROXY, ALSO HIGHLY RESPECTABLE.
ISN'T SHE A LITTLE YOUNG?
AT LEAST, THAT WAS MR. AND MRS. CRUMRIN'S THEORY.
OF ALL THE GIRLS IN THE NEIGHBORHOOD, COURTNEY CRUMRIN IS THE LEAST LIKELY TO THROW A WILD PARTY.
MAYBE, BUT LOOK AT IT THIS WAY.

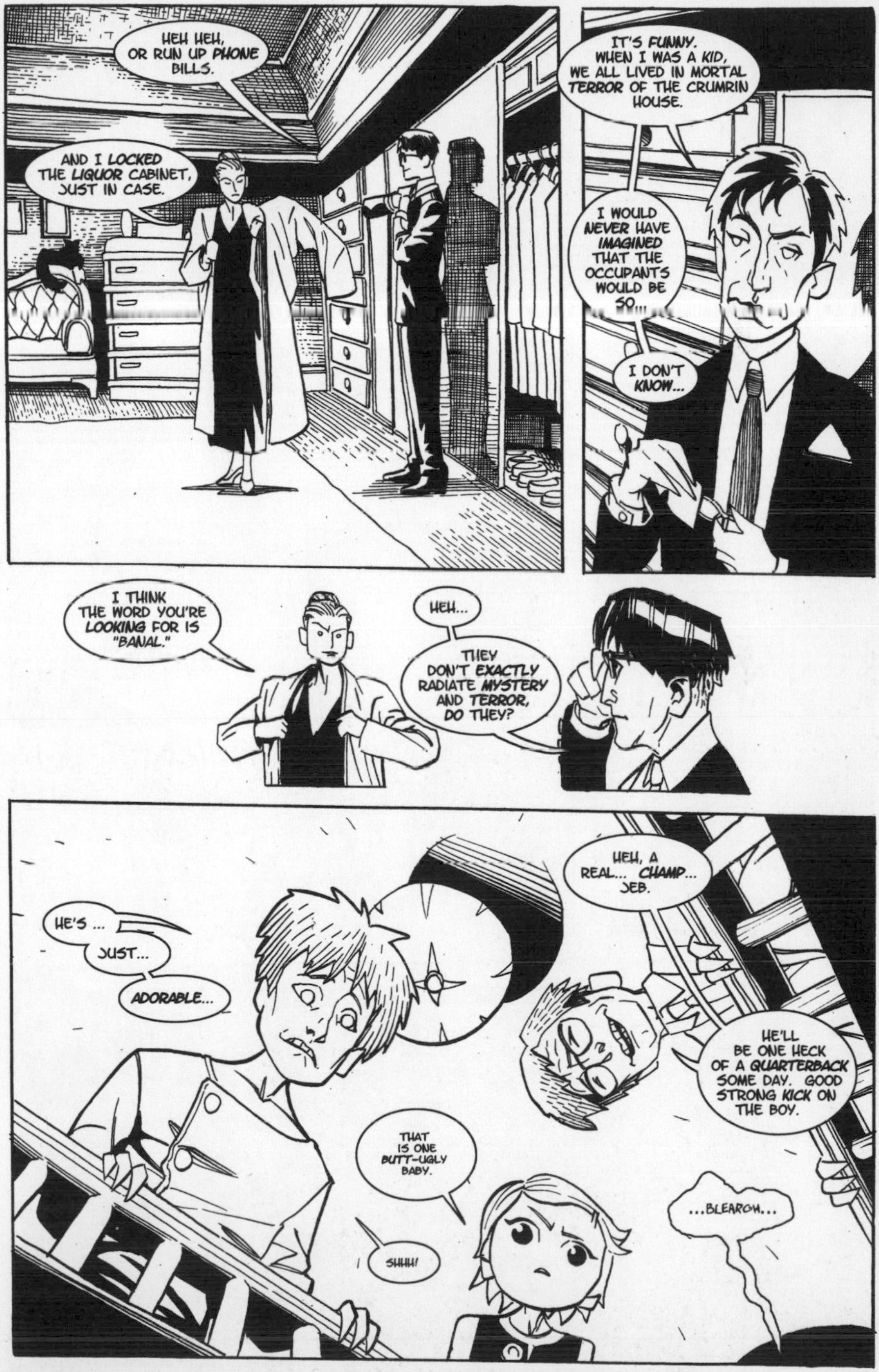
HEH HEH, OR RUN UP PHONE BILLS.
AND I LOCKED THE LIQUOR CABINET, JUST IN CASE.
IT'S FUNNY. WHEN I WAS A KID, WE ALL LIVED IN MORTAL TERROR OF THE CRUMRIN HOUSE.
I WOULD NEVER HAVE IMAGINED THAT THE OCCUPANTS WOULD BE SO...
I DON'T KNOW...
I THINK THE WORD YOU'RE LOOKING FOR IS "BANAL."
HEH...
THEY DON'T EXACTLY RADIATE MYSTERY AND TERROR, DO THEY?
HEH, A REAL... CHAMP... JEB.
HE'S ...
JUST...
ADORABLE...
HE'LL BE ONE HECK OF A QUARTERBACK SOME DAY. GOOD STRONG KICK ON THE BOY.
THAT IS ONE BUTT-UGLY BABY.
...BLEARGH...
SHHH!

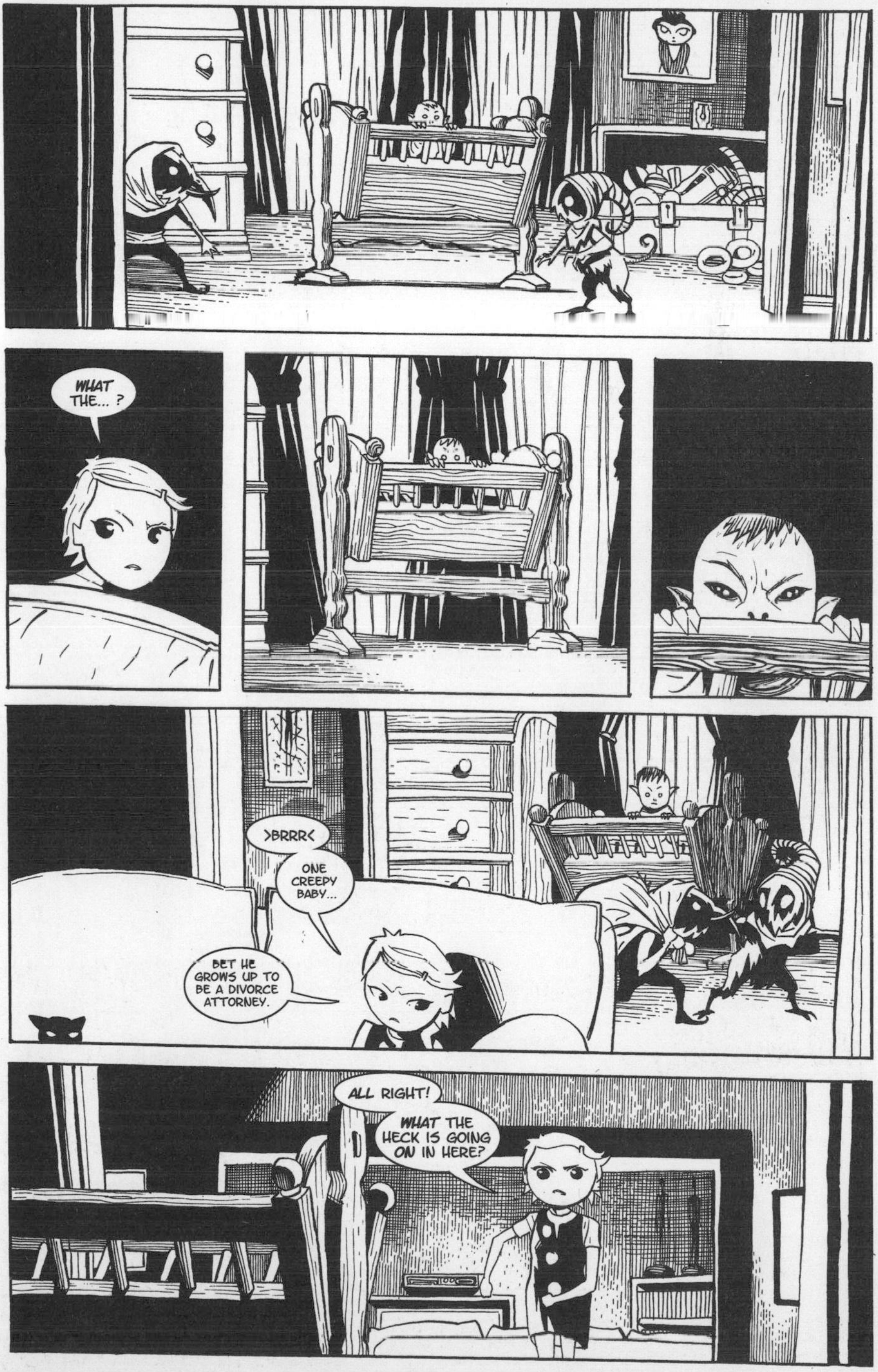
WHAT THE... ?
>BRRR<
ONE CREEPY BABY...
BET HE GROWS UP TO BE A DIVORCE ATTORNEY.
ALL RIGHT!
WHAT THE HECK IS GOING ON IN HERE?

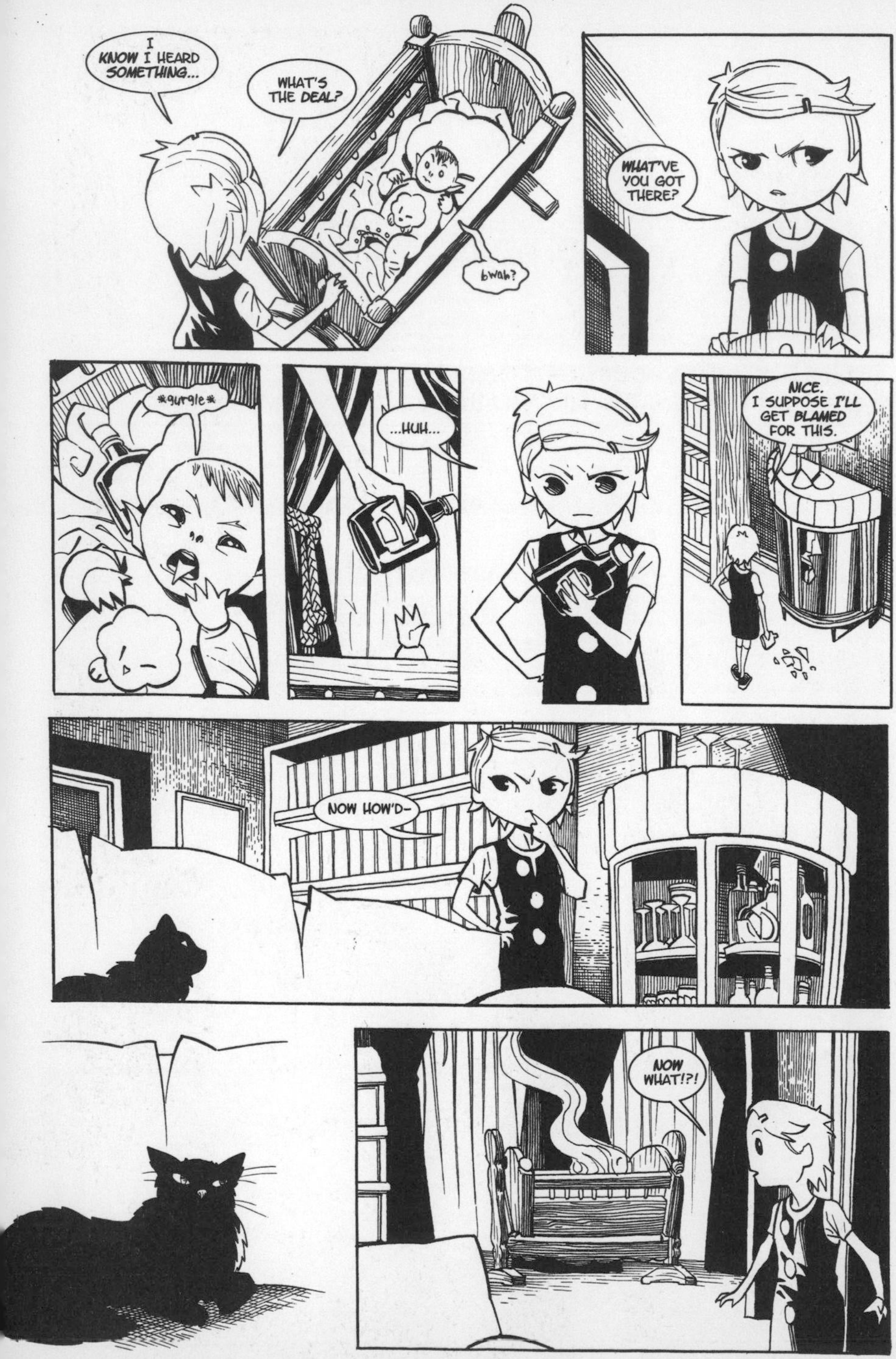
I KNOW I HEARD SOMETHING...
WHAT'S THE DEAL?
bwah?
WHAT'VE YOU GOT THERE?
gurgle
...HUH...
NICE. I SUPPOSE I'LL GET BLAMED FOR THIS.
NOW HOW'D-
NOW WHAT!?!

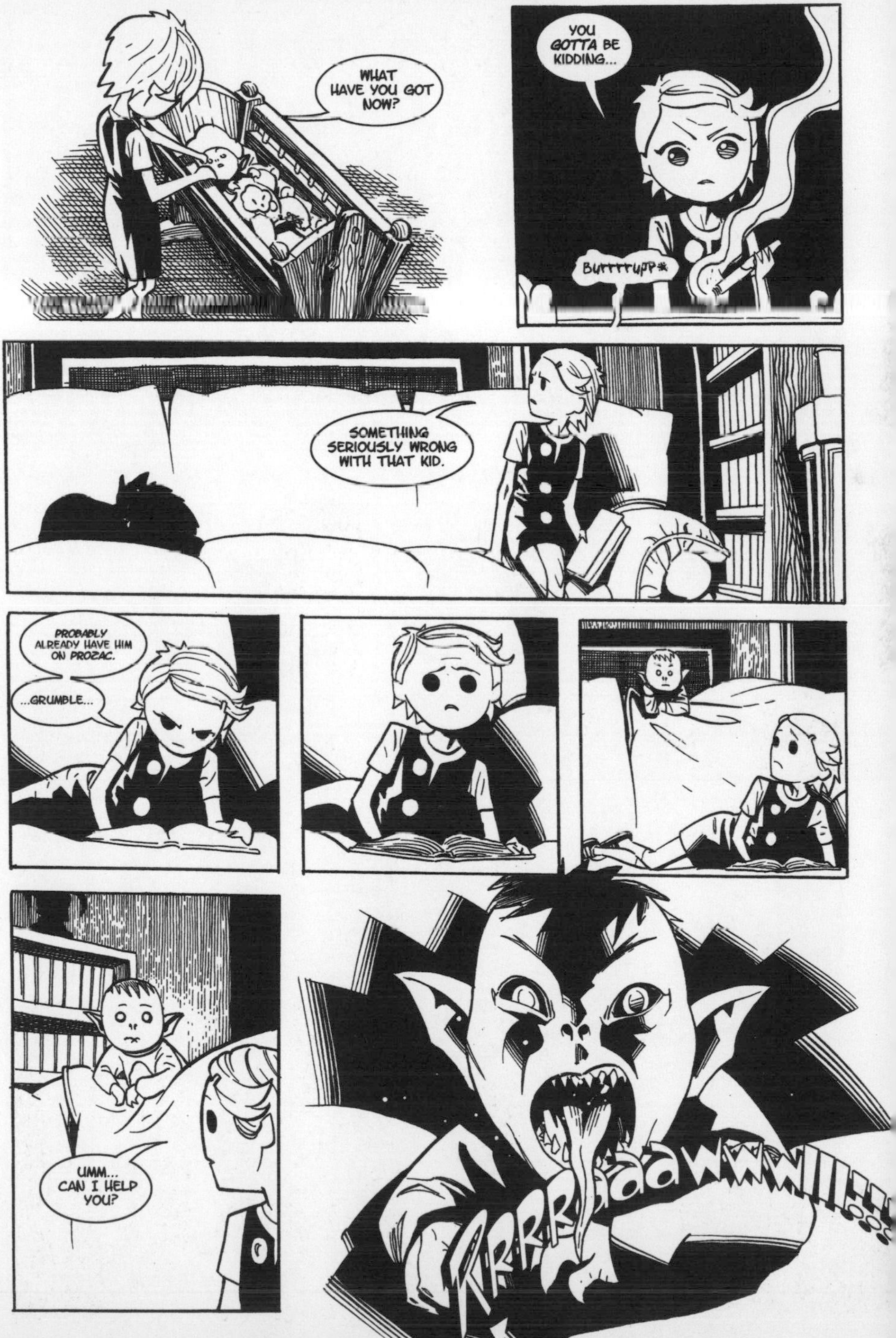
WHAT HAVE YOU GOT NOW?
YOU GOTTA BE KIDDING...
Burrrrupp*
SOMETHING SERIOUSLY WRONG WITH THAT KID.
PROBABLY ALREADY HAVE HIM ON PROZAC.
...GRUMBLE...
UMM... CAN I HELP YOU?
RRRRAAAWWWW!!!!

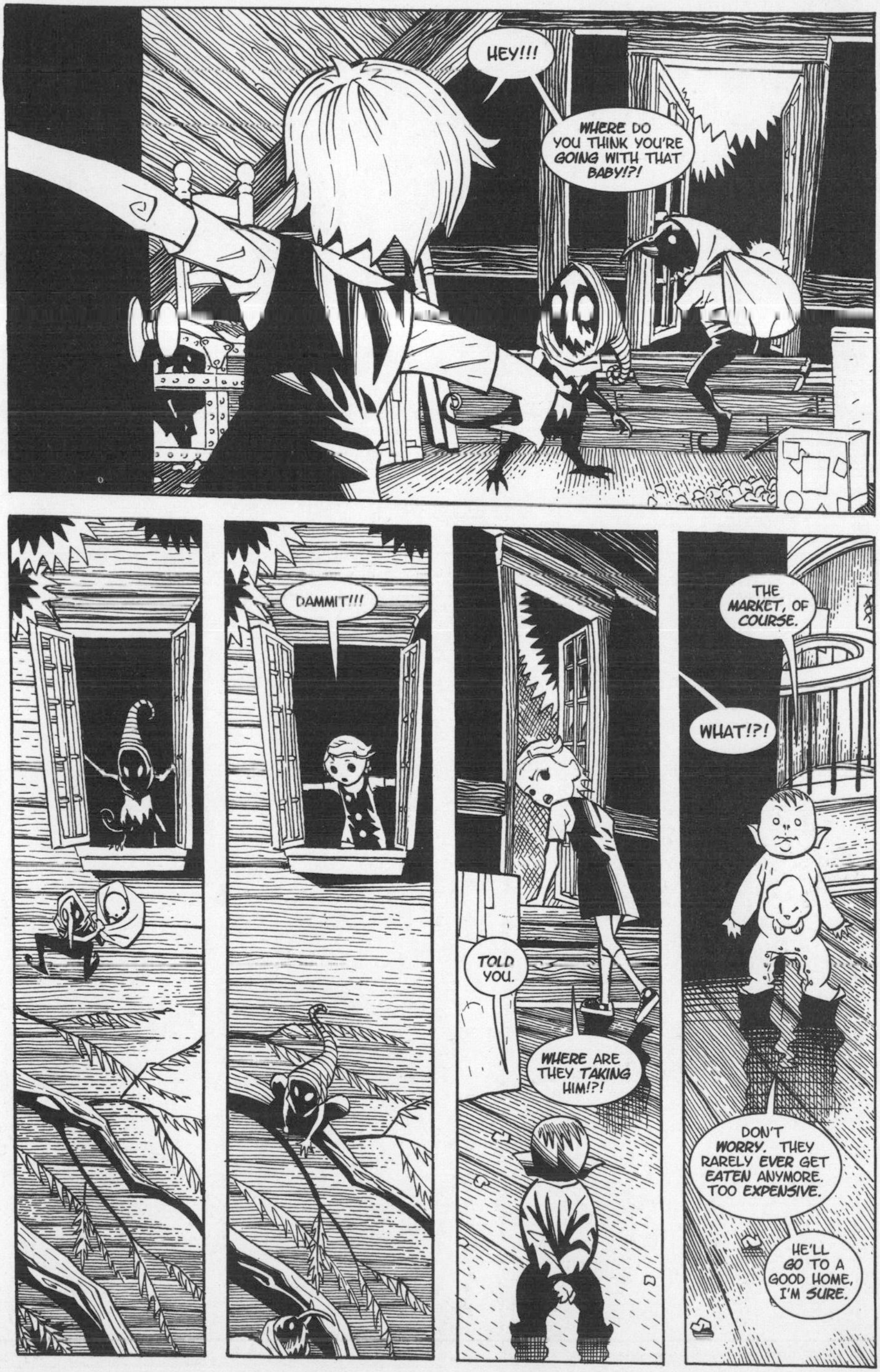
HEY!!!
WHERE DO YOU THINK YOU'RE GOING WITH THAT BABY!?!
DAMMIT!!!
TOLD YOU.
WHERE ARE THEY TAKING HIM!?!
WHAT!?!
THE MARKET, OF COURSE.
DON'T WORRY. THEY RARELY EVER GET EATEN ANYMORE. TOO EXPENSIVE.
HE'LL GO TO A GOOD HOME, I'M SURE.

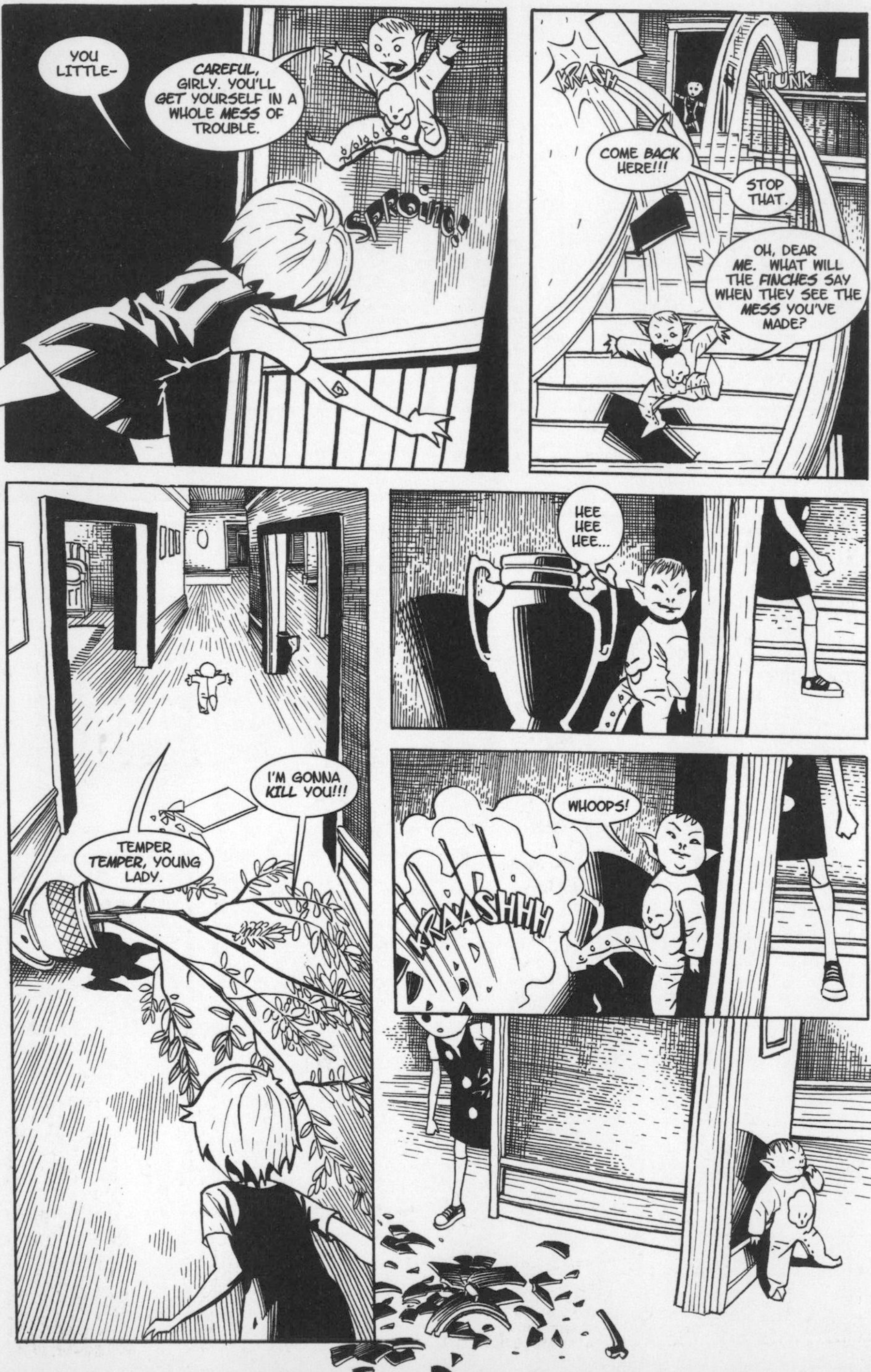
YOU LITTLE-
CAREFUL, GIRLY. YOU'LL GET YOURSELF IN A WHOLE MESS OF TROUBLE.
SPROING!
KRASH
THUNK
COME BACK HERE!!!
STOP THAT.
OH, DEAR ME. WHAT WILL THE FINCHES SAY WHEN THEY SEE THE MESS YOU'VE MADE?
I'M GONNA KILL YOU!!!
TEMPER TEMPER, YOUNG LADY.
HEE HEE HEE...
WHOOPS!
KRAASHHH

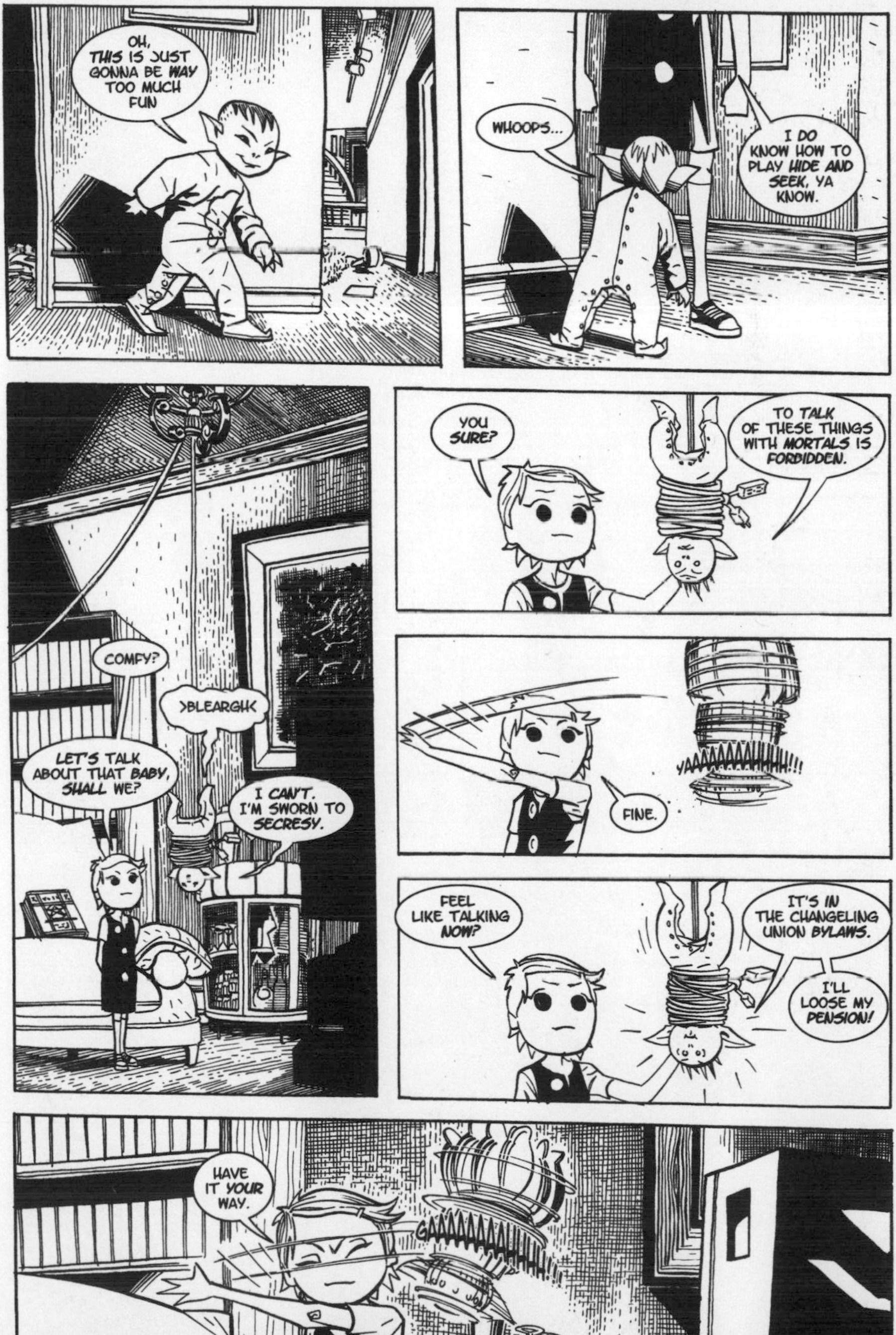
OH, THIS IS JUST GONNA BE WAY TOO MUCH FUN
WHOOPS...
I DO KNOW HOW TO PLAY HIDE AND SEEK, YA KNOW.
COMFY?
>BLEARGH<
LET'S TALK ABOUT THAT BABY, SHALL WE?
I CAN'T. I'M SWORN TO SECRESY.
YOU SURE?
TO TALK OF THESE THINGS WITH MORTALS IS FORBIDDEN.
FINE.
YAAAAAAAAHHH!!!
FEEL LIKE TALKING NOW?
IT'S IN THE CHANGELING UNION BYLAWS.
I'LL LOOSE MY PENSION!
HAVE IT YOUR WAY.
GAAAAAAAAAHH!

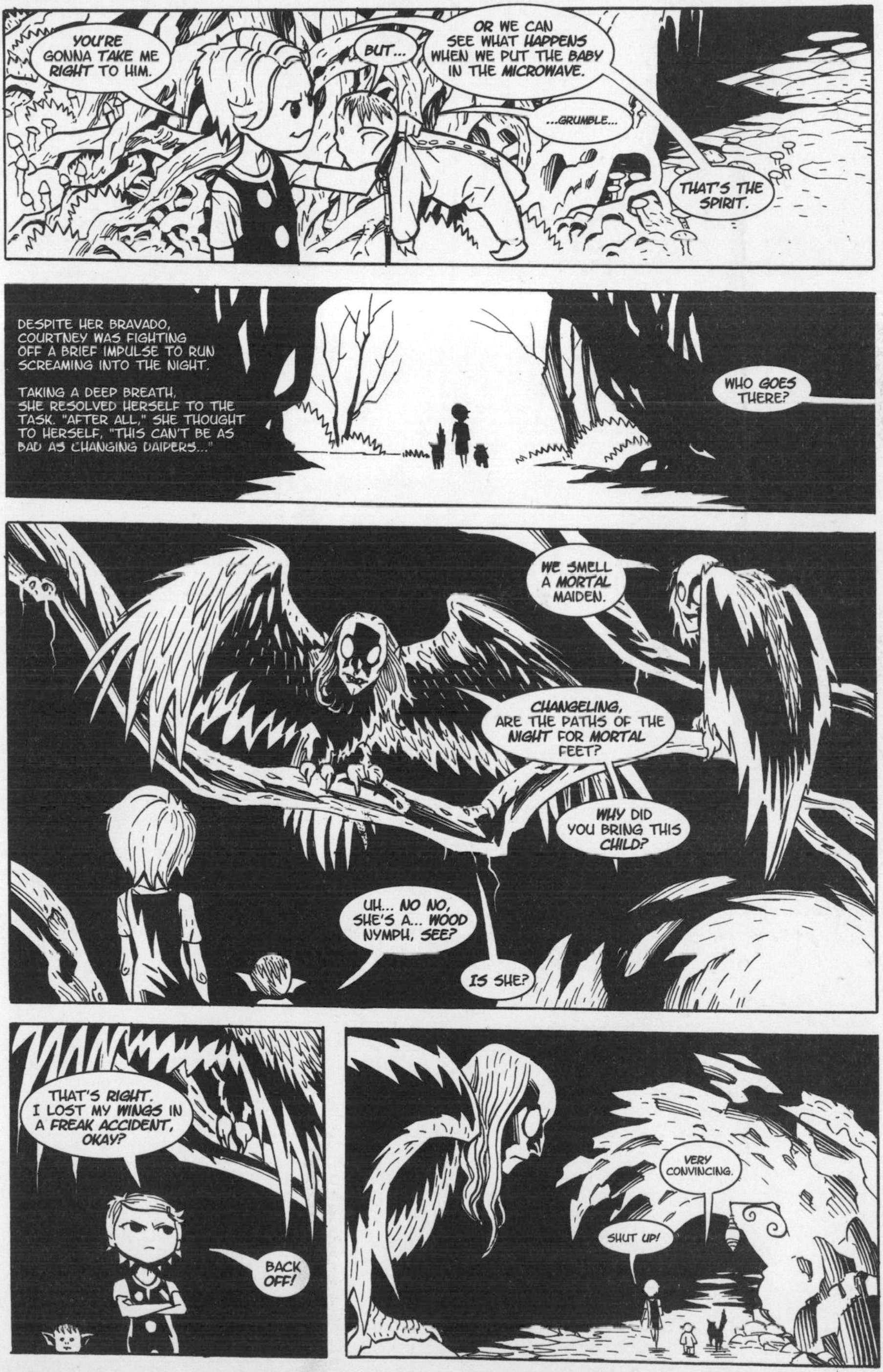
YOU'RE GONNA TAKE ME RIGHT TO HIM.
BUT...
OR WE CAN SEE WHAT HAPPENS WHEN WE PUT THE BABY IN THE MICROWAVE.
...GRUMBLE...
THAT'S THE SPIRIT.
DESPITE HER BRAVADO, COURTNEY WAS FIGHTING OFF A BRIEF IMPULSE TO RUN SCREAMING INTO THE NIGHT.
TAKING A DEEP BREATH, SHE RESOLVED HERSELF TO THE TASK. "AFTER ALL," SHE THOUGHT TO HERSELF, "THIS CAN'T BE AS BAD AS CHANGING DAIPERS..."
WHO GOES THERE?
WE SMELL A MORTAL MAIDEN.
CHANGELING, ARE THE PATHS OF THE NIGHT FOR MORTAL FEET?
WHY DID YOU BRING THIS CHILD?
UH... NO NO, SHE'S A... WOOD NYMPH, SEE?
IS SHE?
THAT'S RIGHT. I LOST MY WINGS IN A FREAK ACCIDENT, OKAY?
BACK OFF!
VERY CONVINCING.
SHUT UP!

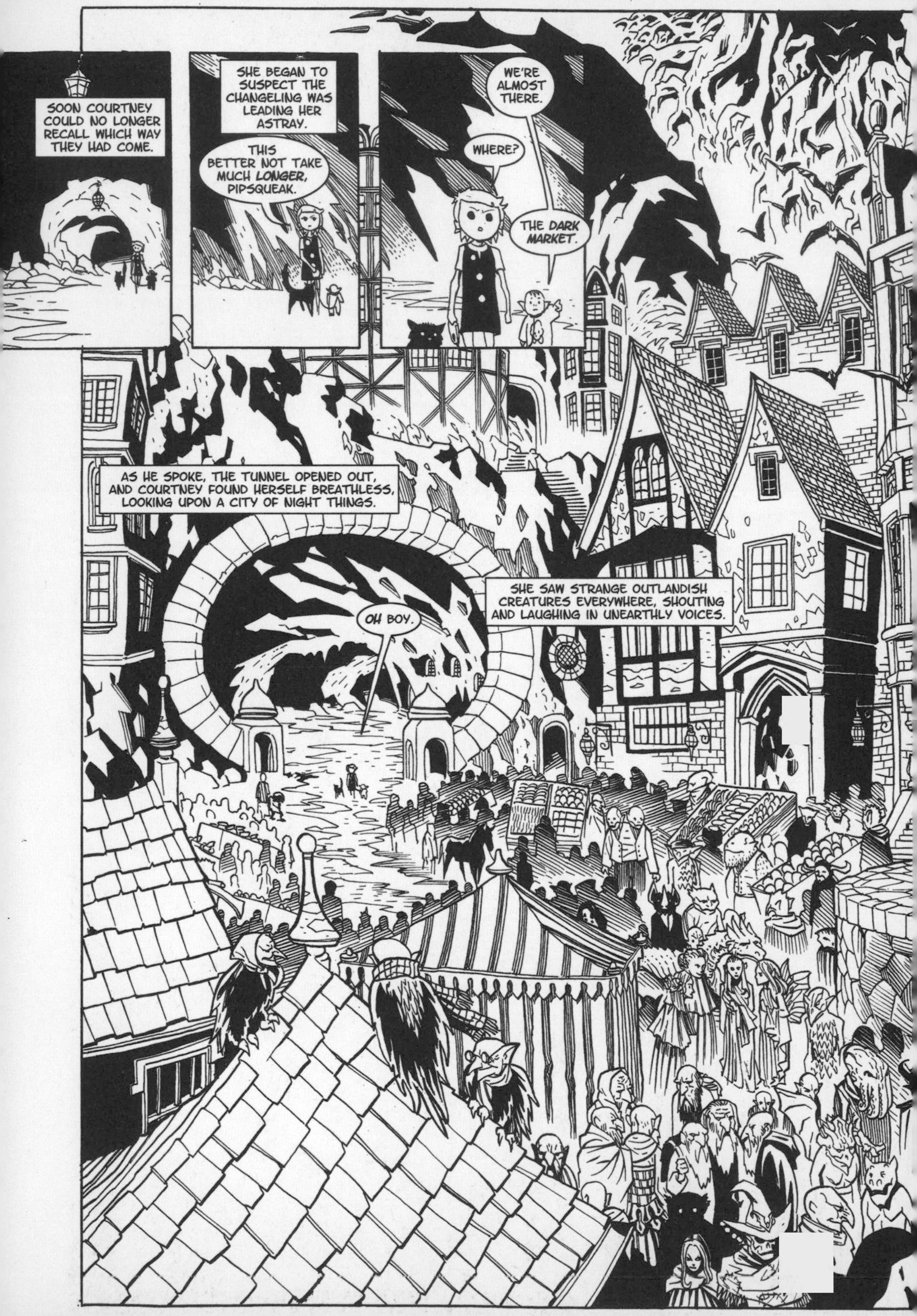
SOON COURTNEY COULD NO LONGER RECALL WHICH WAY THEY HAD COME.
SHE BEGAN TO SUSPECT THE CHANGELING WAS LEADING HER ASTRAY.
THIS BETTER NOT TAKE MUCH *LONGER*, PIPSQUEAK.
WE'RE ALMOST THERE.
WHERE?
THE *DARK MARKET*.
AS HE SPOKE, THE TUNNEL OPENED OUT, AND COURTNEY FOUND HERSELF BREATHLESS, LOOKING UPON A CITY OF NIGHT THINGS.
OH BOY.
SHE SAW STRANGE OUTLANDISH CREATURES EVERYWHERE, SHOUTING AND LAUGHING IN UNEARTHLY VOICES.

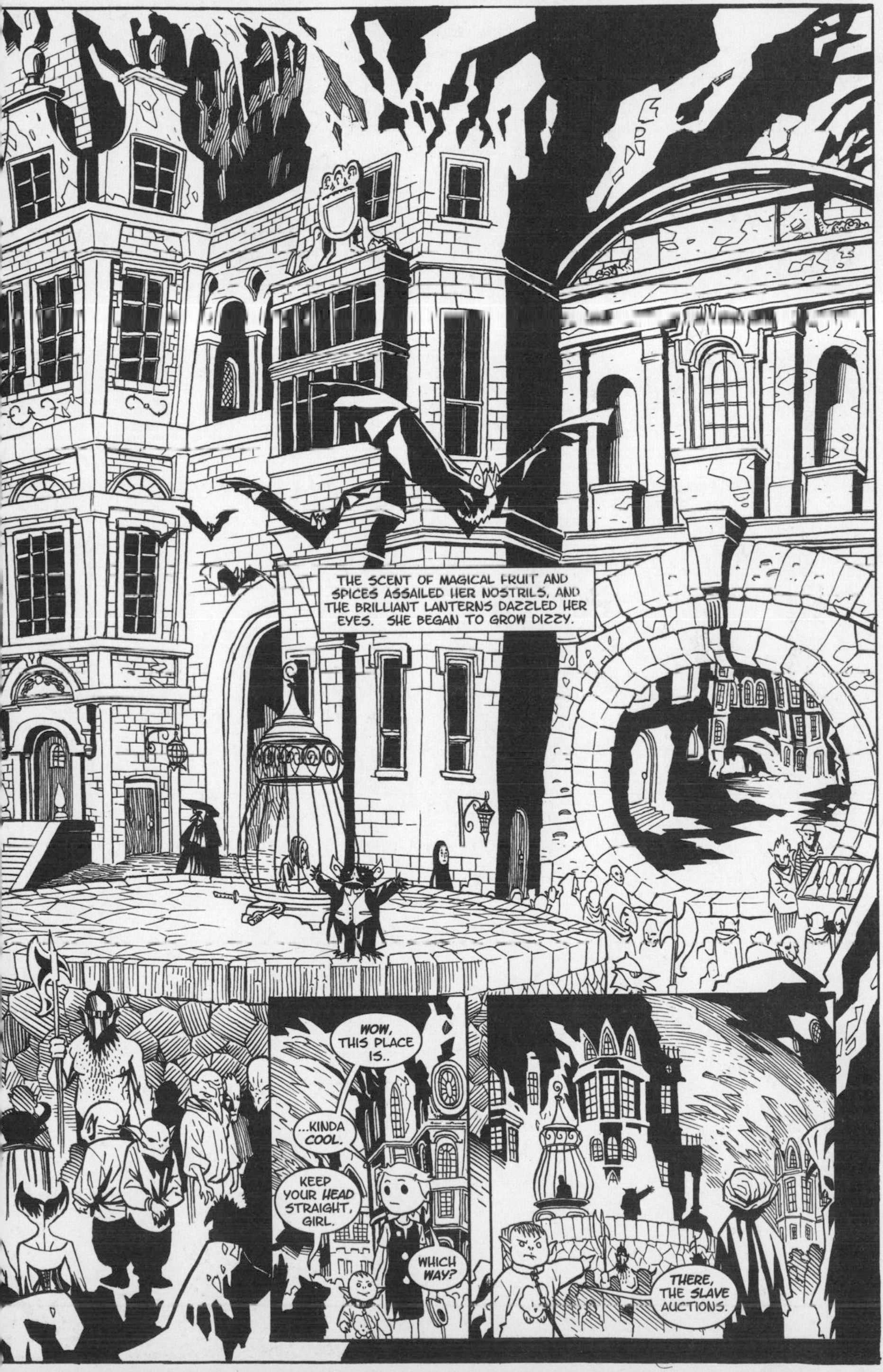
THE SCENT OF MAGICAL FRUIT AND SPICES ASSAILED HER NOSTRILS, AND THE BRILLIANT LANTERNS DAZZLED HER EYES. SHE BEGAN TO GROW DIZZY.
WOW, THIS PLACE IS..
...KINDA COOL.
KEEP YOUR HEAD STRAIGHT, GIRL.
WHICH WAY?
THERE, THE SLAVE AUCTIONS.

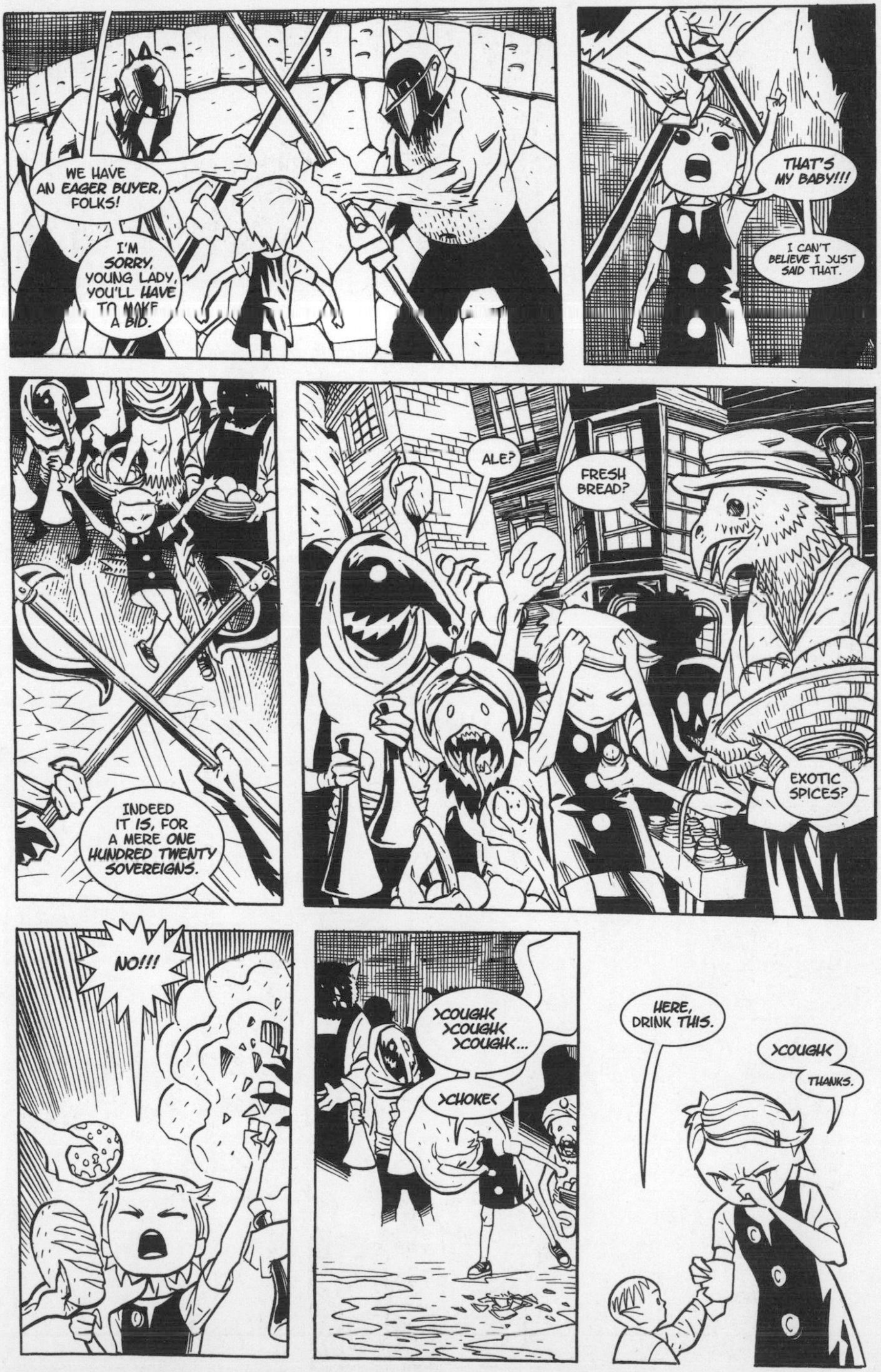
WE HAVE AN EAGER BUYER, FOLKS!
I'M SORRY, YOUNG LADY, YOU'LL HAVE TO MAKE A BID.
THAT'S MY BABY!!!
I CAN'T BELIEVE I JUST SAID THAT.
INDEED IT IS, FOR A MERE ONE HUNDRED TWENTY SOVEREIGNS.
ALE?
FRESH BREAD?
EXOTIC SPICES?
NO!!!
>COUGH< >COUGH< >COUGH<...
>CHOKE<
HERE, DRINK THIS.
>COUGH<
THANKS.

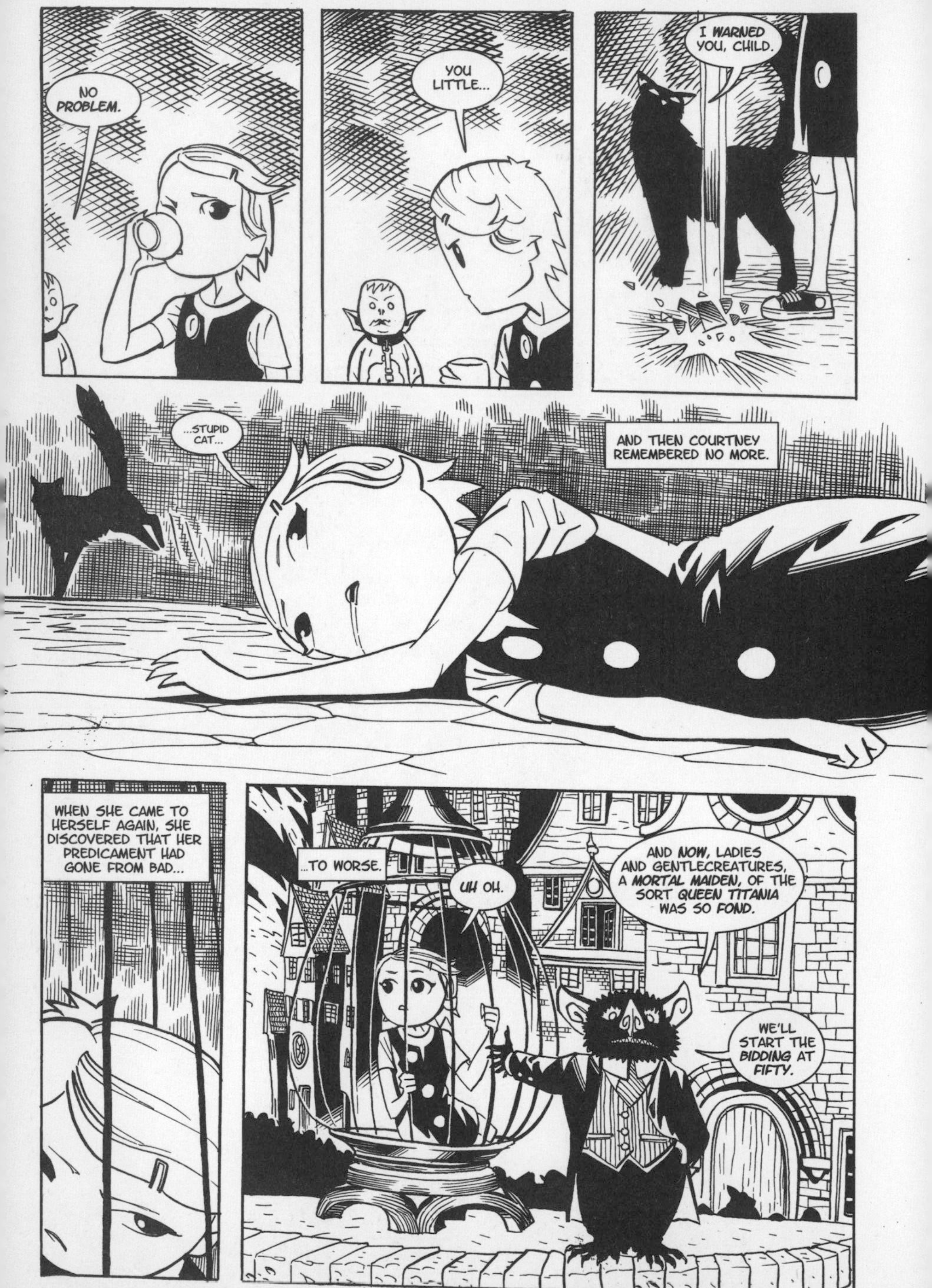
NO PROBLEM.
YOU LITTLE...
I WARNED YOU, CHILD.
...STUPID CAT...
AND THEN COURTNEY REMEMBERED NO MORE.
WHEN SHE CAME TO HERSELF AGAIN, SHE DISCOVERED THAT HER PREDICAMENT HAD GONE FROM BAD...
...TO WORSE.
UH OH.
AND NOW, LADIES AND GENTLECREATURES, A MORTAL MAIDEN, OF THE SORT QUEEN TITANIA WAS SO FOND.
WE'LL START THE BIDDING AT FIFTY.

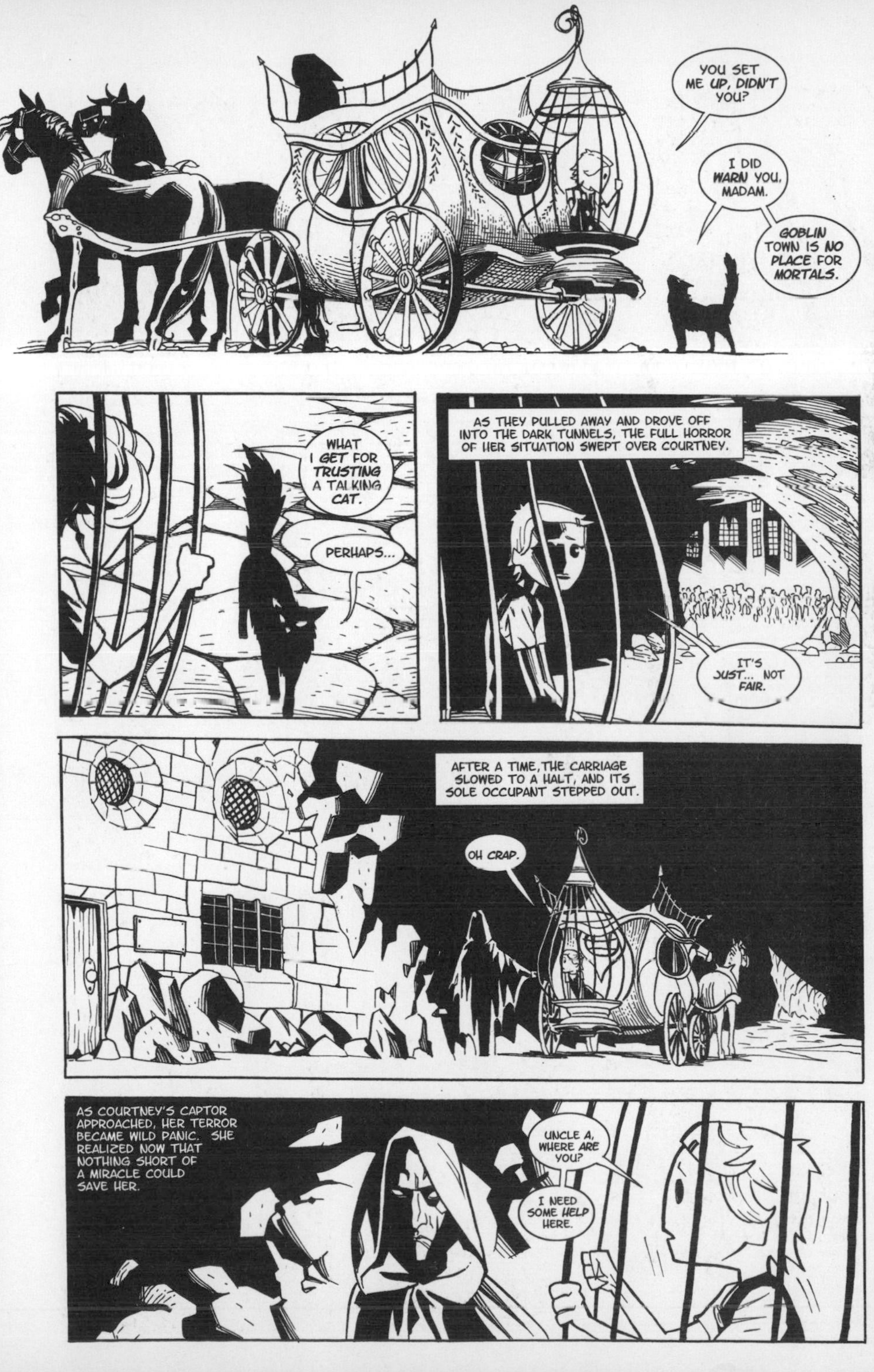
YOU SET ME UP, DIDN'T YOU?
I DID WARN YOU, MADAM.
GOBLIN TOWN IS NO PLACE FOR MORTALS.
WHAT I GET FOR TRUSTING A TALKING CAT.
PERHAPS...
AS THEY PULLED AWAY AND DROVE OFF INTO THE DARK TUNNELS, THE FULL HORROR OF HER SITUATION SWEPT OVER COURTNEY.
IT'S JUST... NOT FAIR.
AFTER A TIME, THE CARRIAGE SLOWED TO A HALT, AND ITS SOLE OCCUPANT STEPPED OUT.
OH CRAP.
AS COURTNEY'S CAPTOR APPROACHED, HER TERROR BECAME WILD PANIC. SHE REALIZED NOW THAT NOTHING SHORT OF A MIRACLE COULD SAVE HER.
UNCLE A, WHERE ARE YOU?
I NEED SOME HELP HERE.

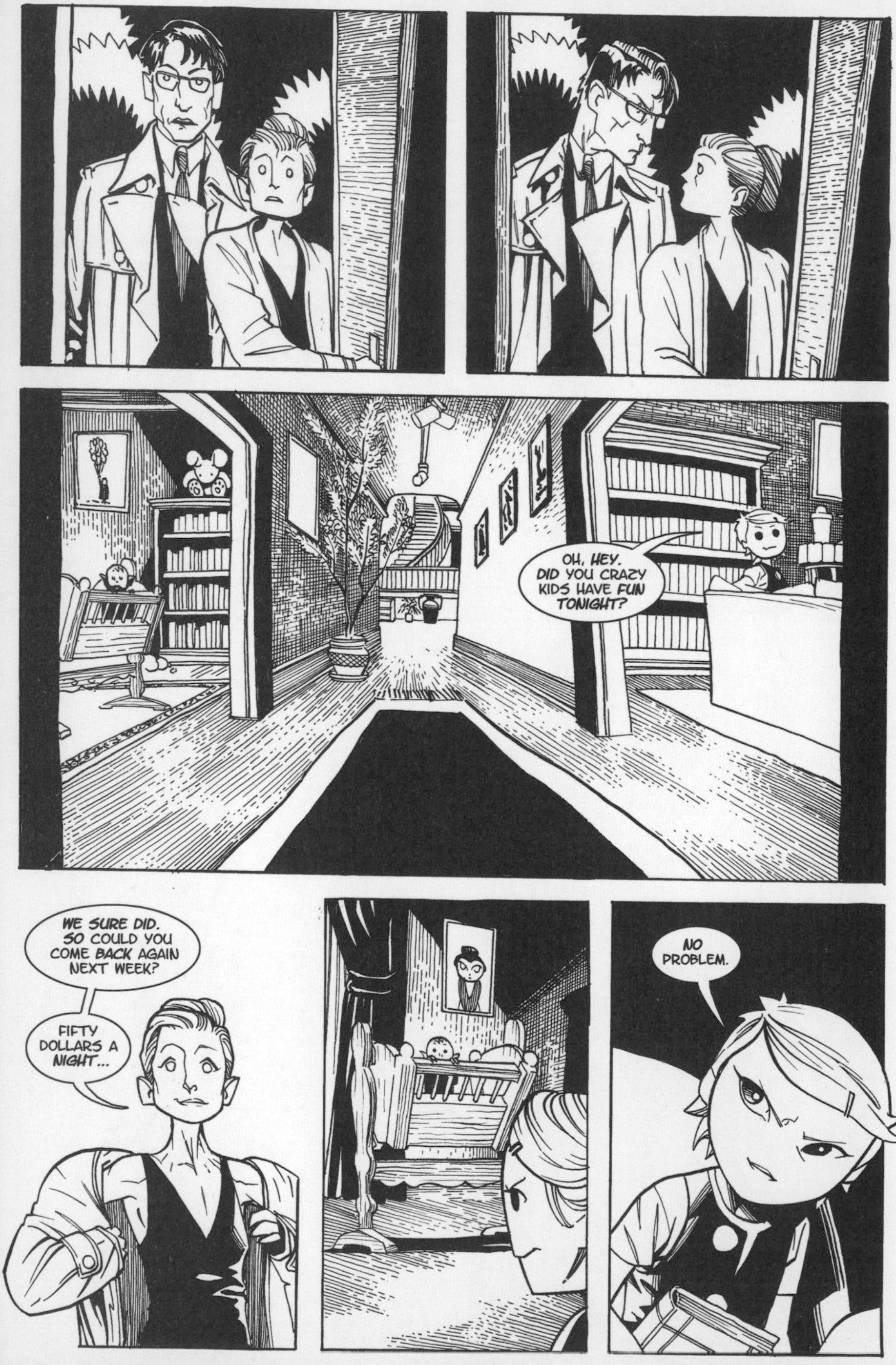
OH, HEY. DID YOU CRAZY KIDS HAVE FUN TONIGHT?
WE SURE DID. SO COULD YOU COME BACK AGAIN NEXT WEEK?
FIFTY DOLLARS A NIGHT...
NO PROBLEM.

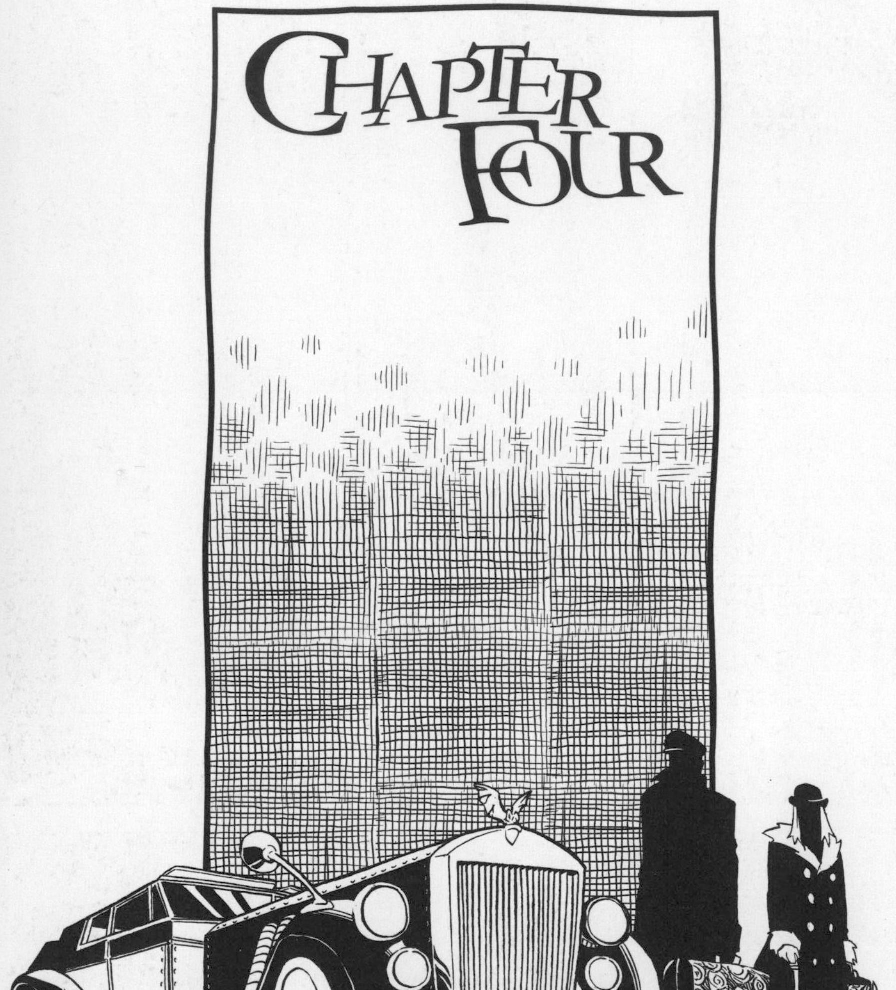
CHAPTER FOUR

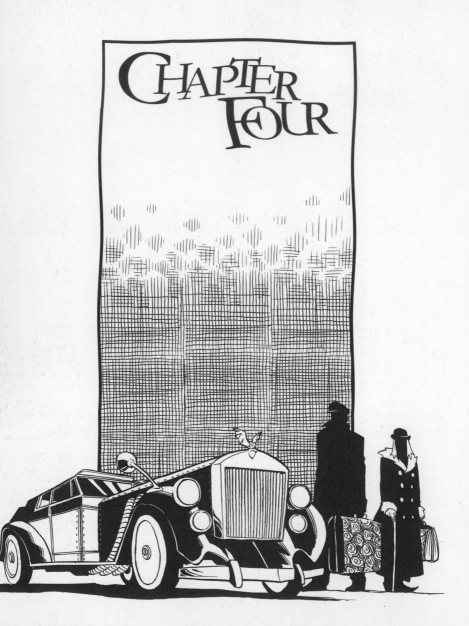

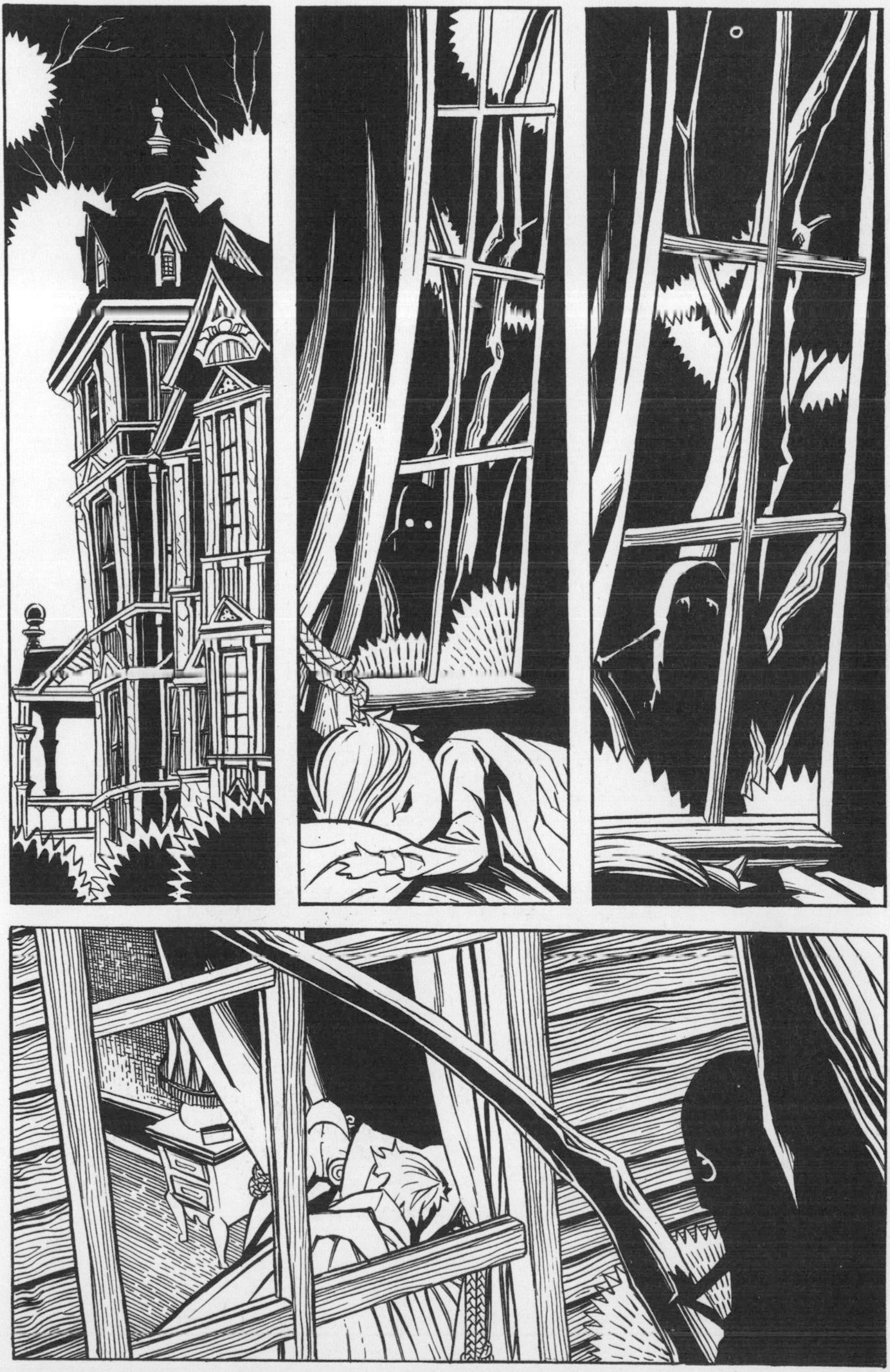

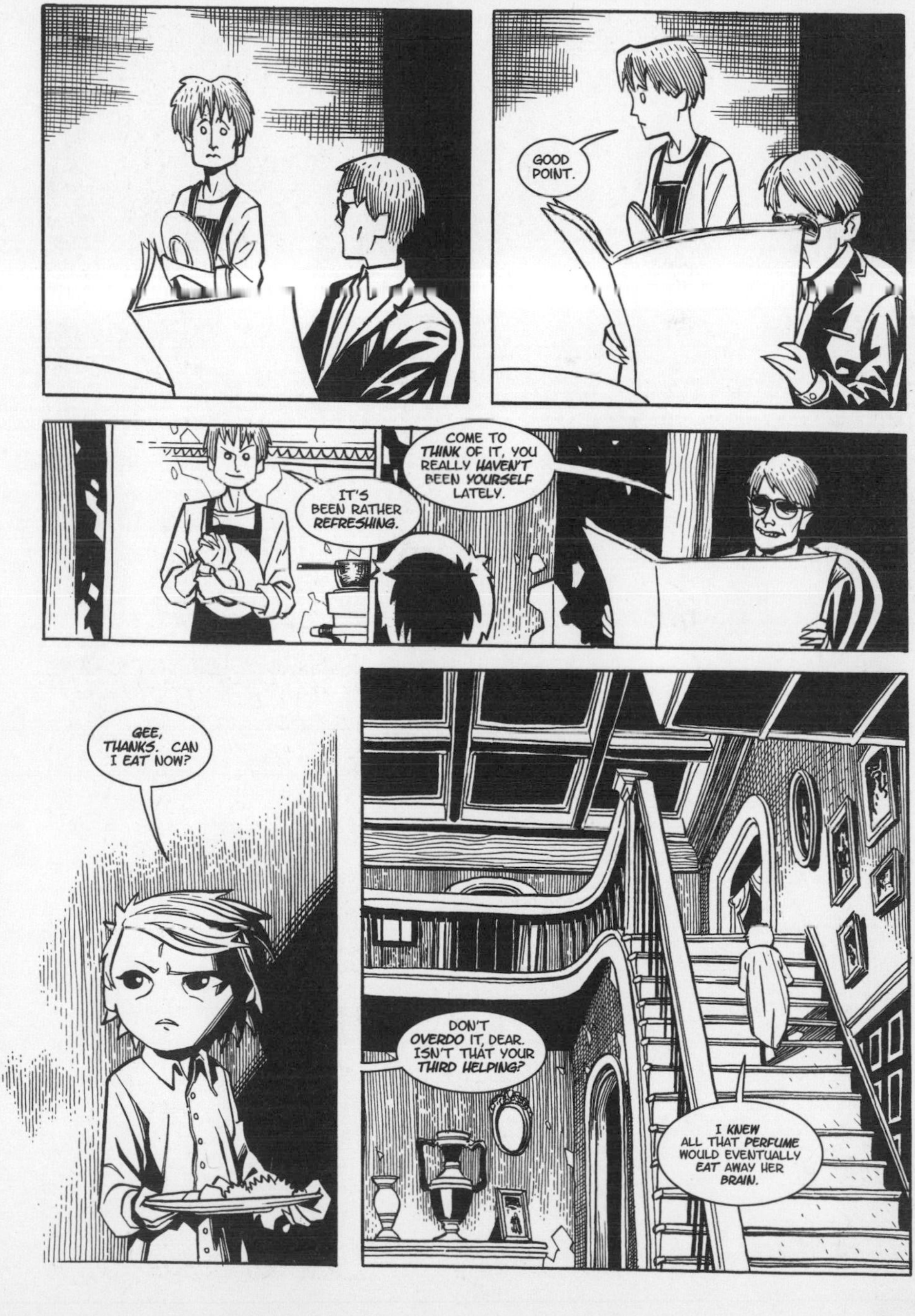
GOOD POINT.
IT'S BEEN RATHER REFRESHING.
COME TO THINK OF IT, YOU REALLY HAVEN'T BEEN YOURSELF LATELY.
GEE, THANKS. CAN I EAT NOW?
DON'T OVERDO IT, DEAR. ISN'T THAT YOUR THIRD HELPING?
I KNEW ALL THAT PERFUME WOULD EVENTUALLY EAT AWAY HER BRAIN.

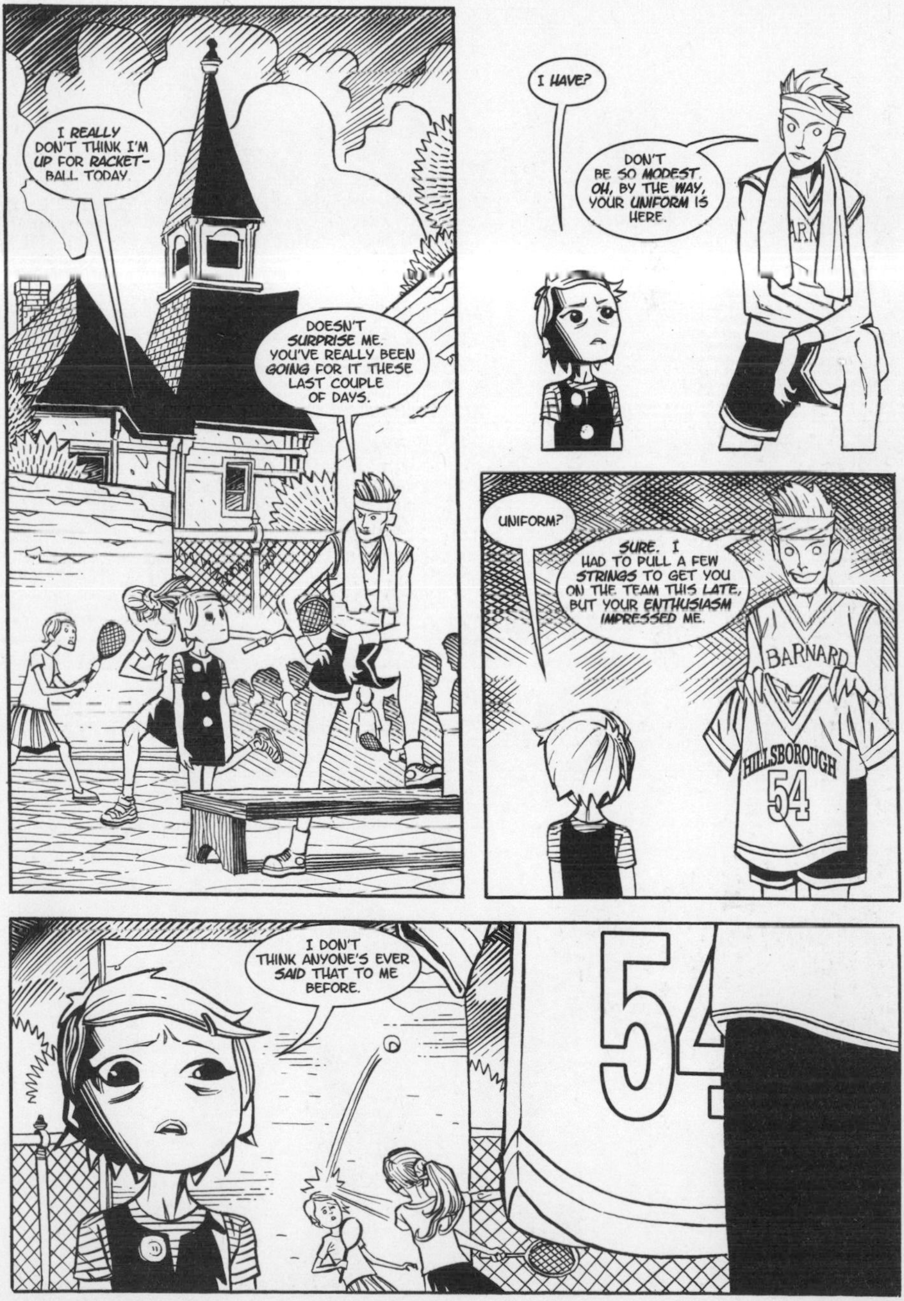
I REALLY DON'T THINK I'M UP FOR RACKET-BALL TODAY.
DOESN'T SURPRISE ME. YOU'VE REALLY BEEN GOING FOR IT THESE LAST COUPLE OF DAYS.
I HAVE?
DON'T BE SO MODEST. OH, BY THE WAY, YOUR UNIFORM IS HERE.
BARNARD
UNIFORM?
SURE. I HAD TO PULL A FEW STRINGS TO GET YOU ON THE TEAM THIS LATE, BUT YOUR ENTHUSIASM IMPRESSED ME.
BARNARD
HILLSBOROUGH
54
I DON'T THINK ANYONE'S EVER SAID THAT TO ME BEFORE.
54

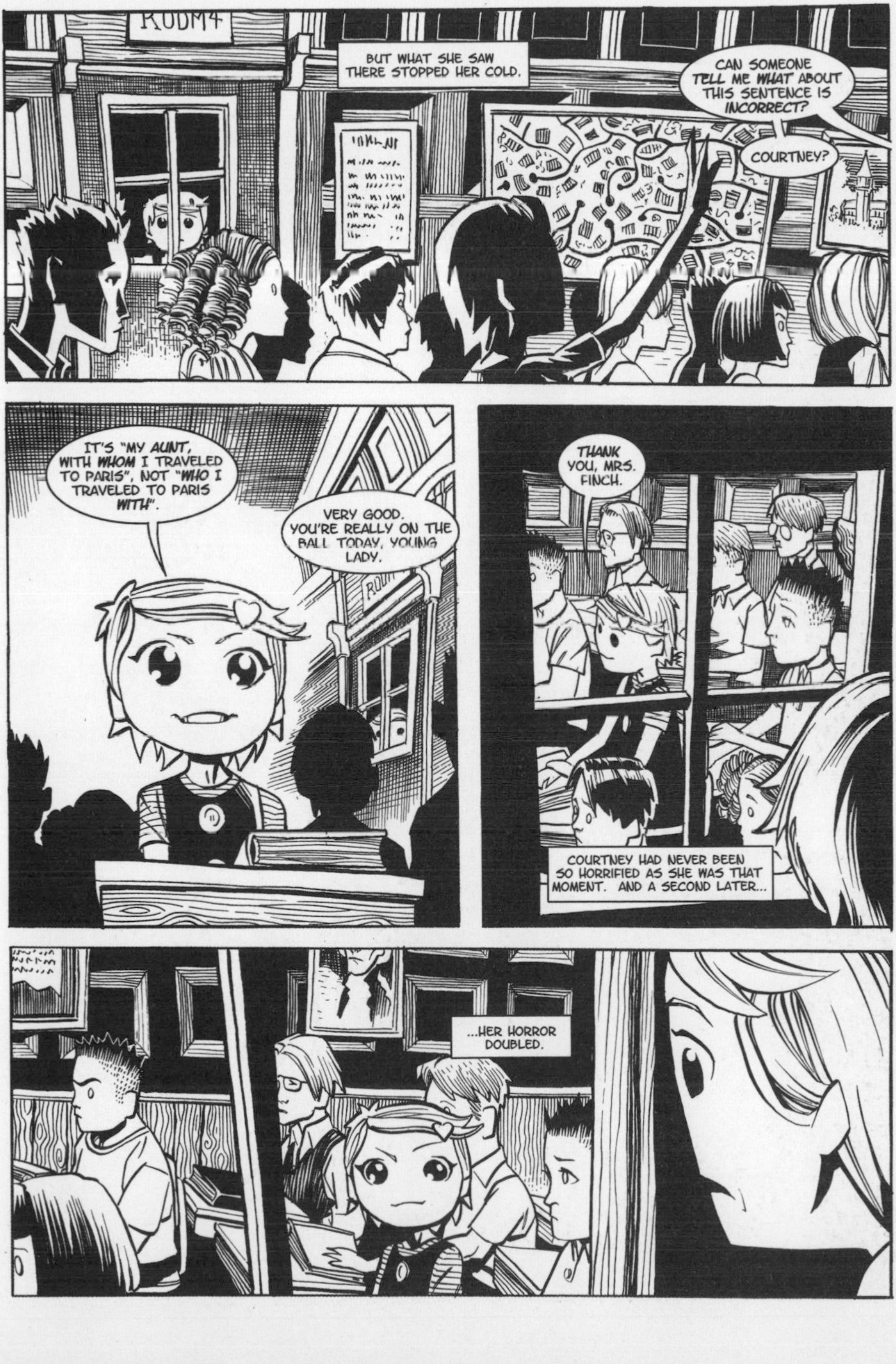
BUT WHAT SHE SAW THERE STOPPED HER COLD.
CAN SOMEONE TELL ME WHAT ABOUT THIS SENTENCE IS INCORRECT?
COURTNEY?
IT'S "MY AUNT, WITH WHOM I TRAVELED TO PARIS", NOT "WHO I TRAVELED TO PARIS WITH".
VERY GOOD. YOU'RE REALLY ON THE BALL TODAY, YOUNG LADY.
THANK YOU, MRS. FINCH.
COURTNEY HAD NEVER BEEN SO HORRIFIED AS SHE WAS THAT MOMENT. AND A SECOND LATER...
...HER HORROR DOUBLED.

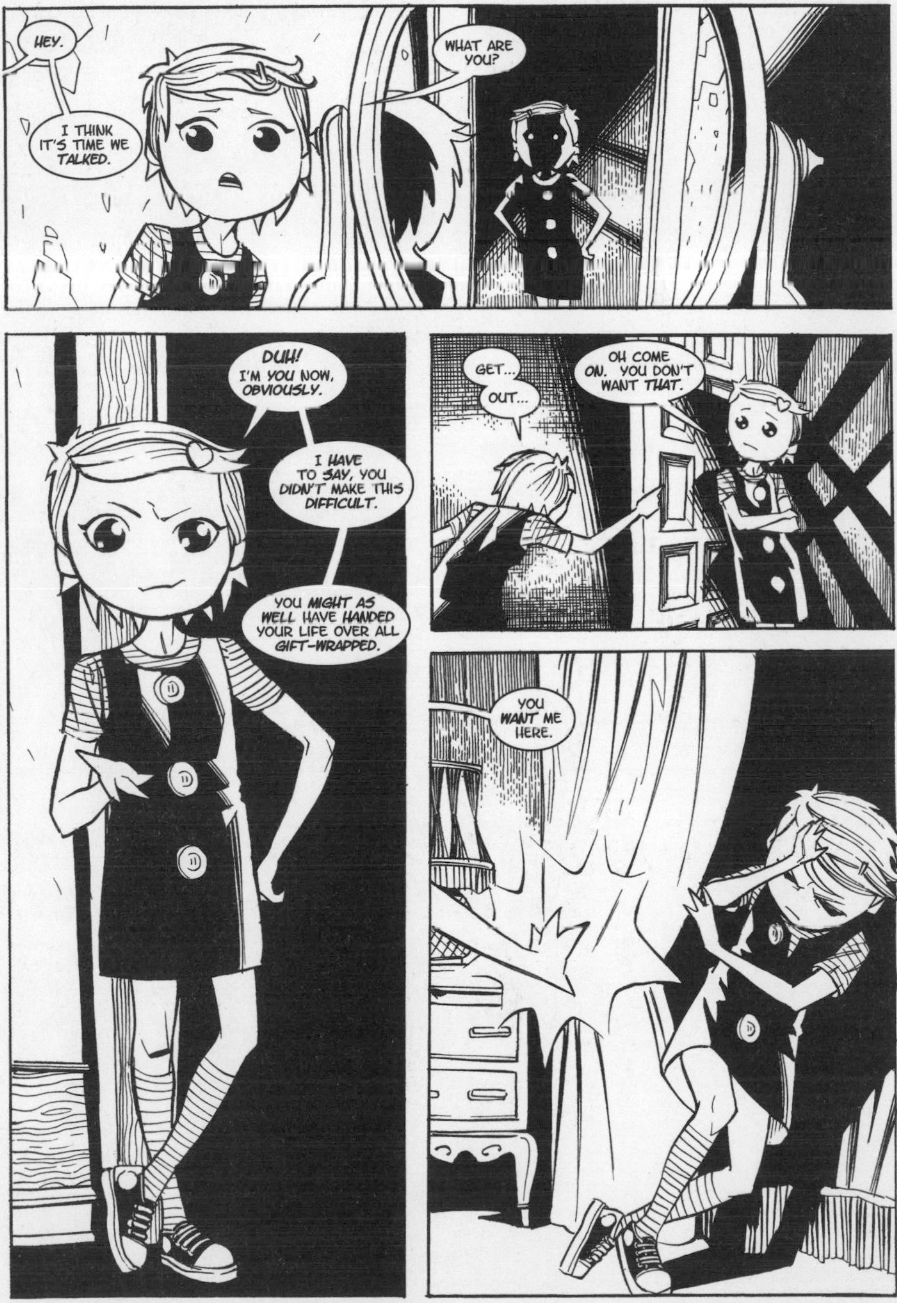
HEY.
I THINK IT'S TIME WE TALKED.
WHAT ARE YOU?
DUH! I'M YOU NOW, OBVIOUSLY.
I HAVE TO SAY, YOU DIDN'T MAKE THIS DIFFICULT.
YOU MIGHT AS WELL HAVE HANDED YOUR LIFE OVER ALL GIFT-WRAPPED.
GET...
OUT...
OH COME ON. YOU DON'T WANT THAT.
YOU WANT ME HERE.

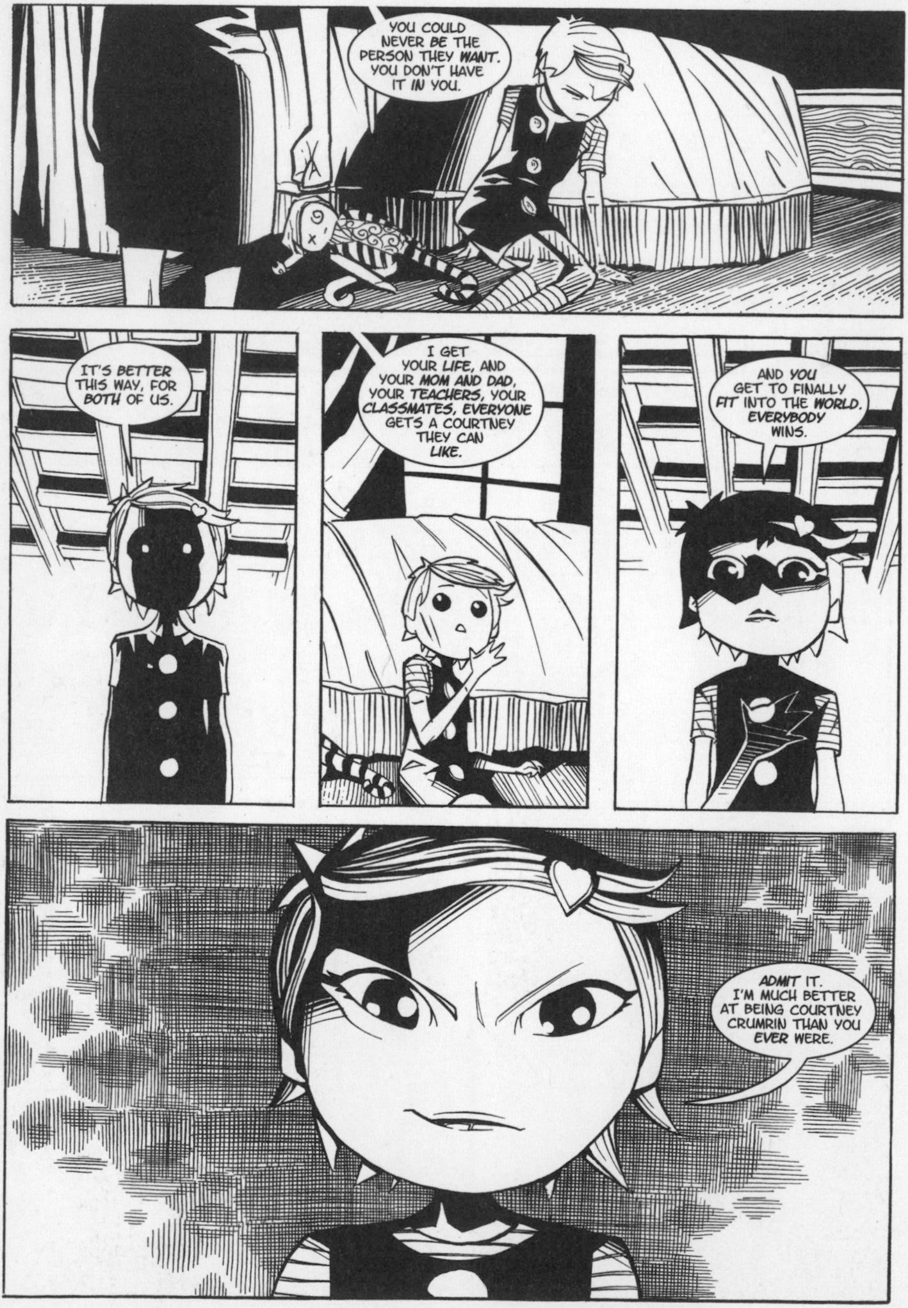
YOU COULD NEVER BE THE PERSON THEY WANT. YOU DON'T HAVE IT IN YOU.
IT'S BETTER THIS WAY, FOR BOTH OF US.
I GET YOUR LIFE, AND YOUR MOM AND DAD, YOUR TEACHERS, YOUR CLASSMATES, EVERYONE GETS A COURTNEY THEY CAN LIKE.
AND YOU GET TO FINALLY FIT INTO THE WORLD. EVERYBODY WINS.
ADMIT IT. I'M MUCH BETTER AT BEING COURTNEY CRUMRIN THAN YOU EVER WERE.

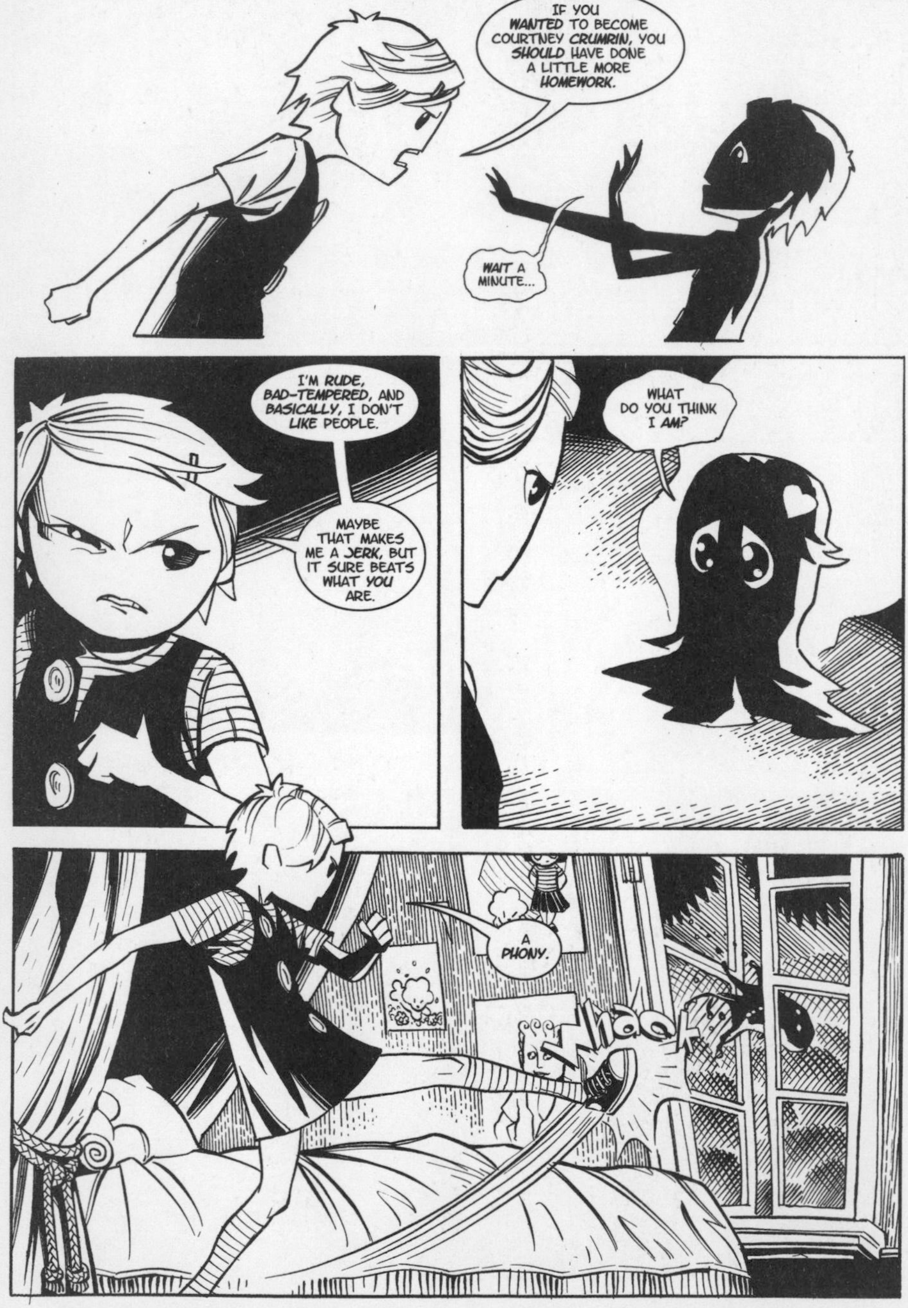
IF YOU WANTED TO BECOME COURTNEY CRUMRIN, YOU SHOULD HAVE DONE A LITTLE MORE HOMEWORK.
WAIT A MINUTE...
I'M RUDE, BAD-TEMPERED, AND BASICALLY, I DON'T LIKE PEOPLE.
MAYBE THAT MAKES ME A JERK, BUT IT SURE BEATS WHAT YOU ARE.
WHAT DO YOU THINK I AM?
A PHONY.
WHACK

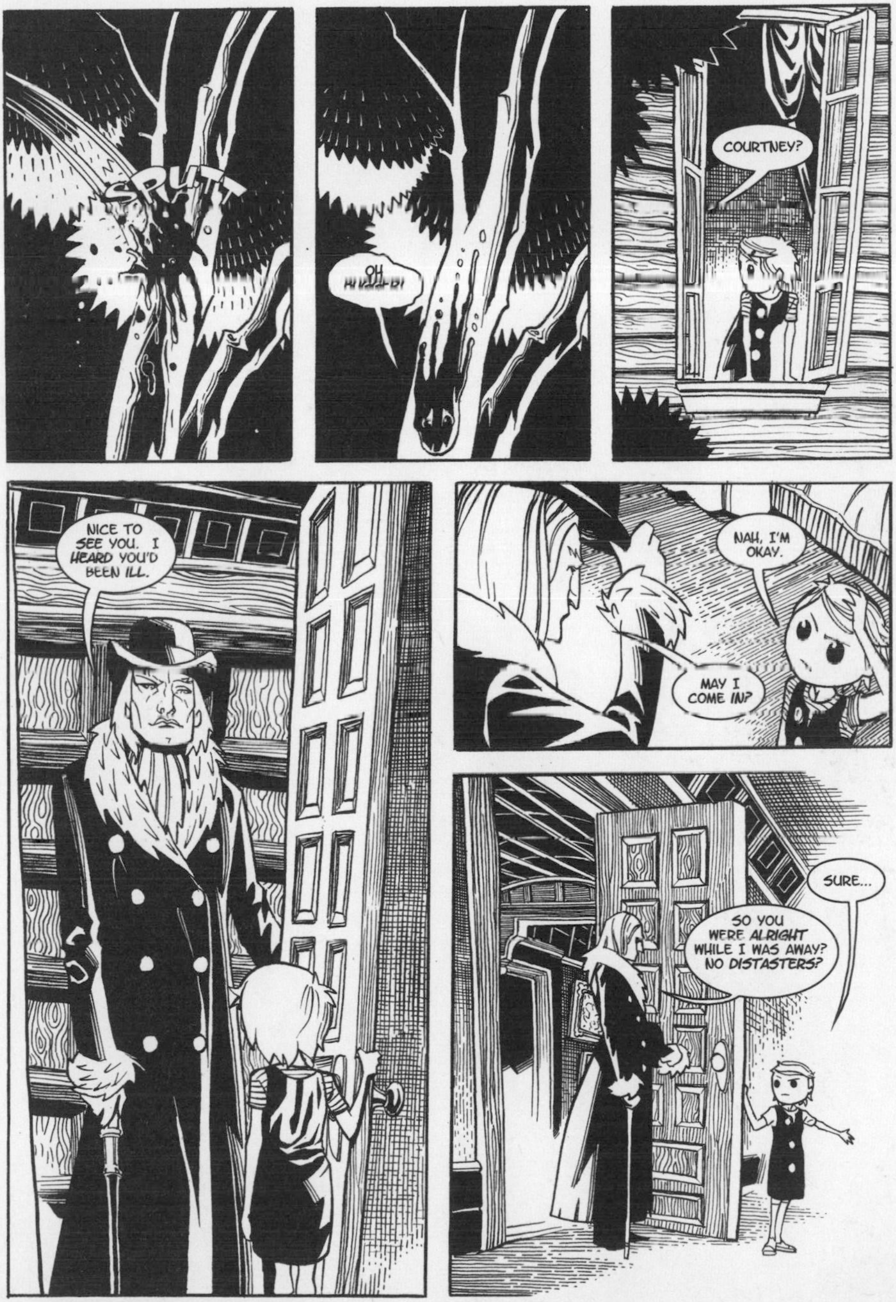
SPLITT
OH
COURTNEY?
NICE TO SEE YOU. I HEARD YOU'D BEEN ILL.
NAH, I'M OKAY.
MAY I COME IN?
SURE...
SO YOU WERE ALRIGHT WHILE I WAS AWAY? NO DISTASTERS?

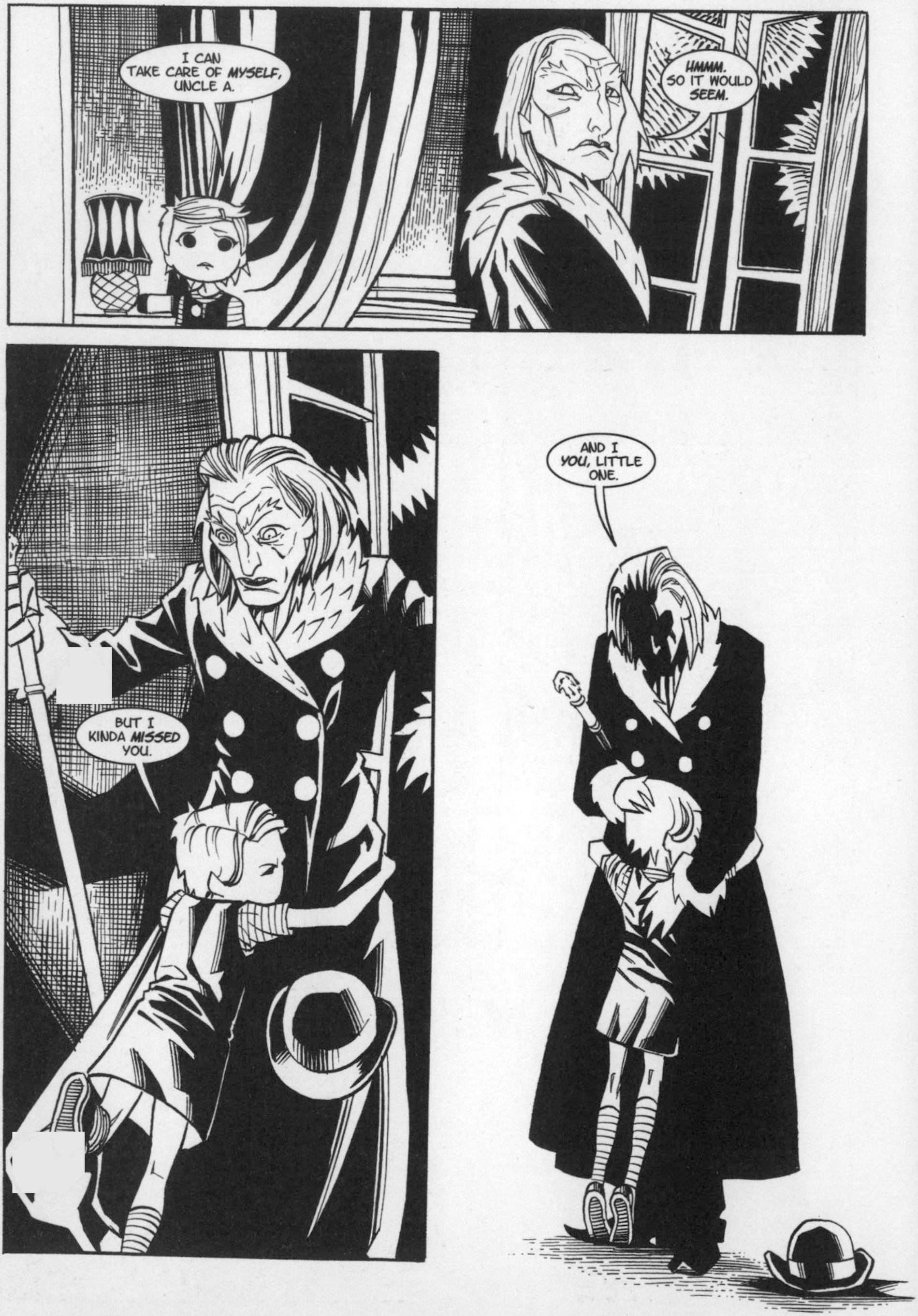
I CAN TAKE CARE OF MYSELF, UNCLE A.
HMMM. SO IT WOULD SEEM.
BUT I KINDA MISSED YOU.
AND I YOU, LITTLE ONE.

Ted Naifeh is a juicy, largish morsel, ahem, mortal just beginning his third decade in the waking world. He makes his home in San Francisco, where Night Things can no longer be distinguished from humans, and that's the way they like it. Ted has made his living carefully chronicling the lives of all manner of things both dark and beautiful in books such as *GloomCookie*, which he co-created with Serena Valentino; Dan Brereton's *Nocturnals* miniseries *Gunwitch: Outskirts of Doom*; and *How Loathsome*, which he is drawing and co-writing with Tristan Crane. If he can keep soul and body together long enough, he plans to launch a new series called *Eva: Iron Kitten* in the summer of 2003 through Oni Press, the world's only publishing company entirely owned and operated by Night Things.

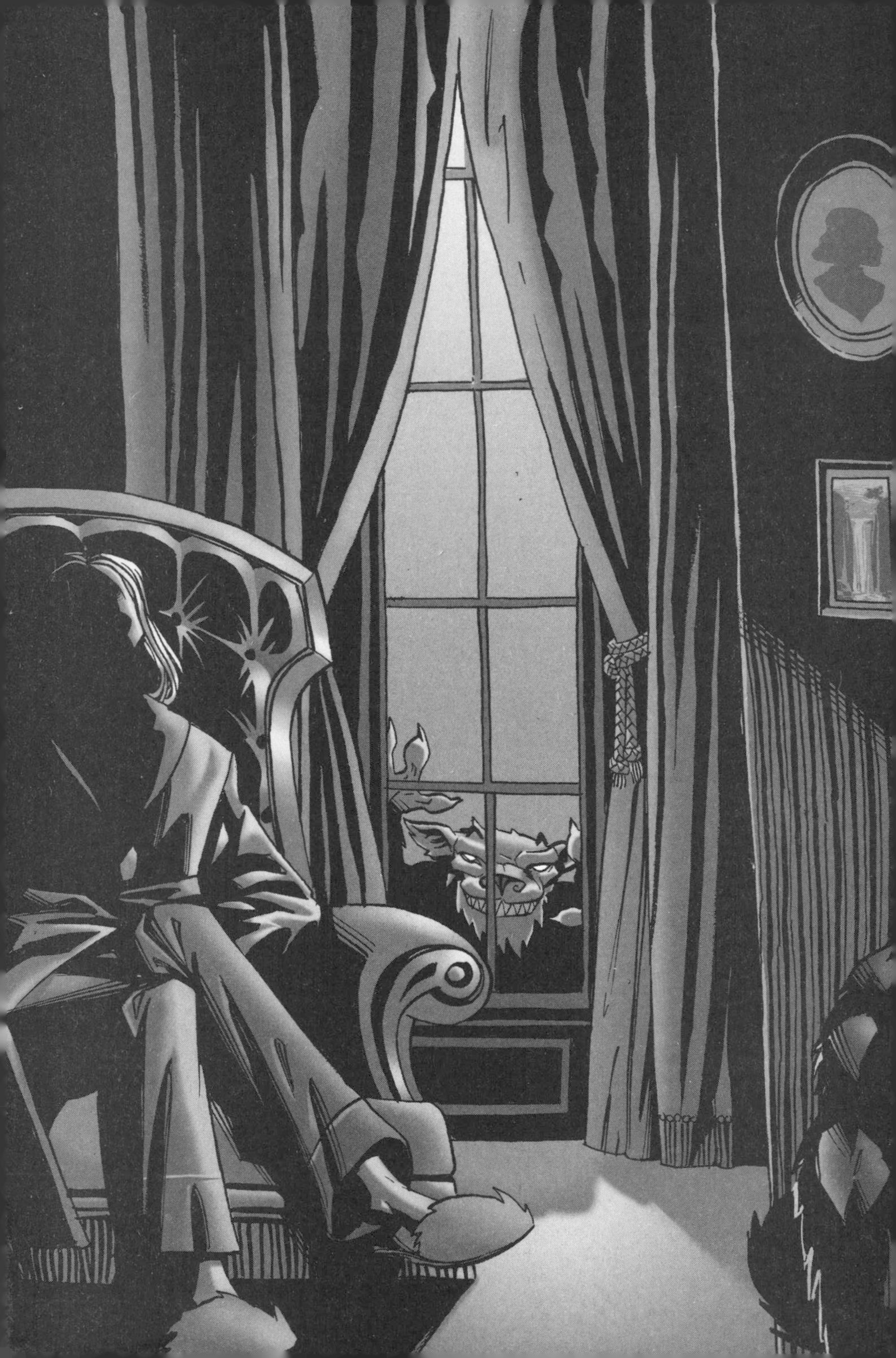

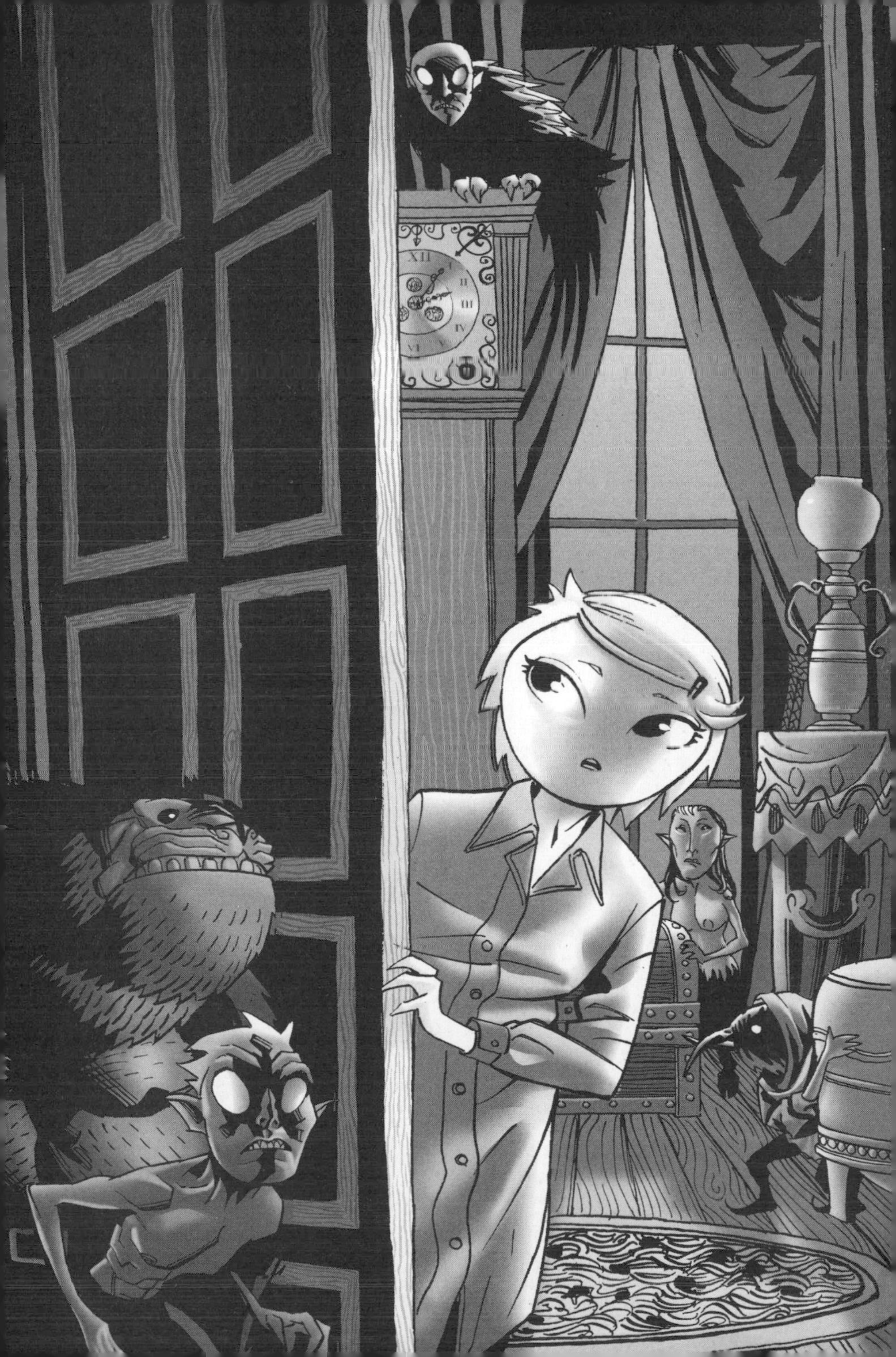

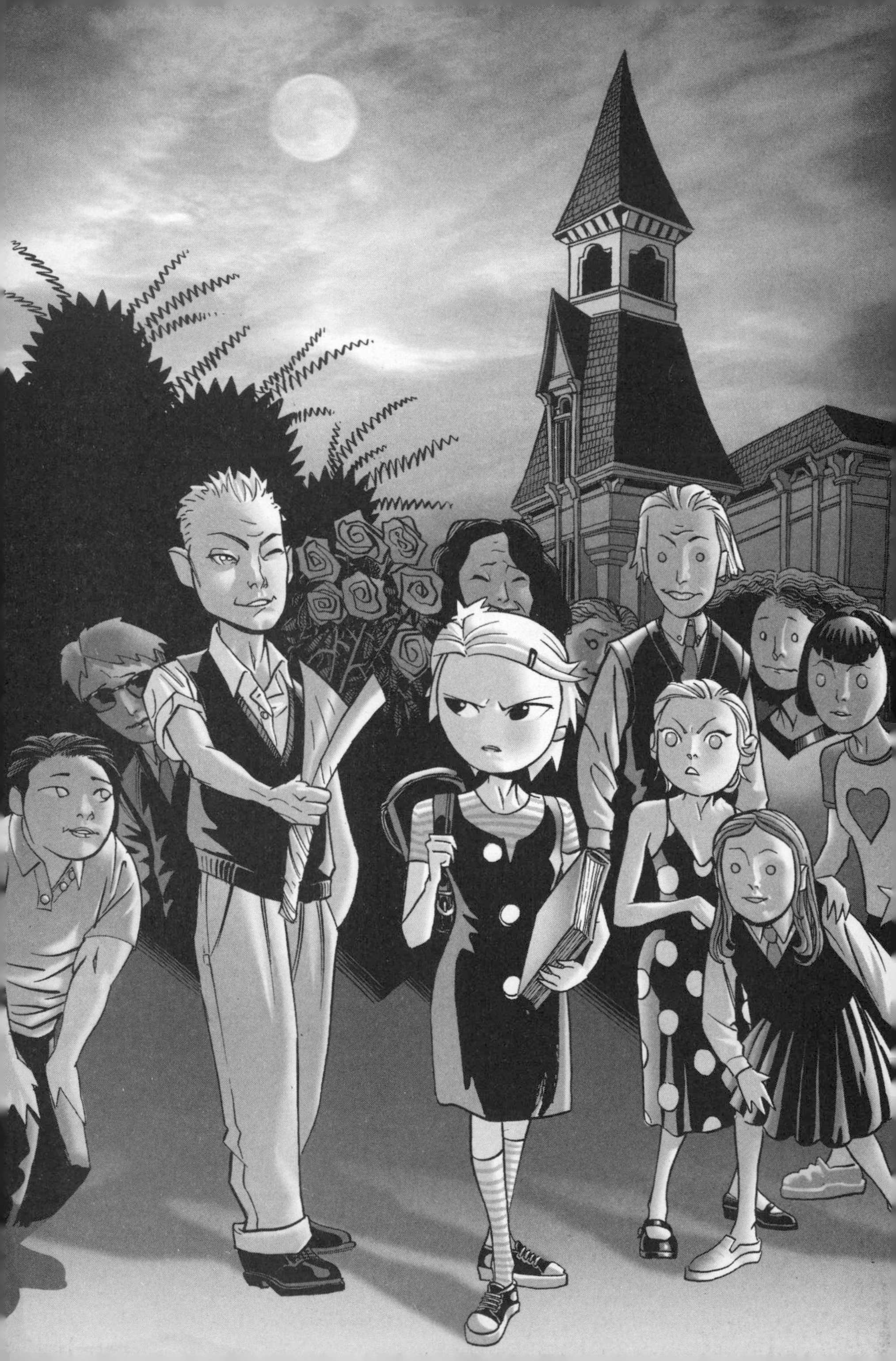

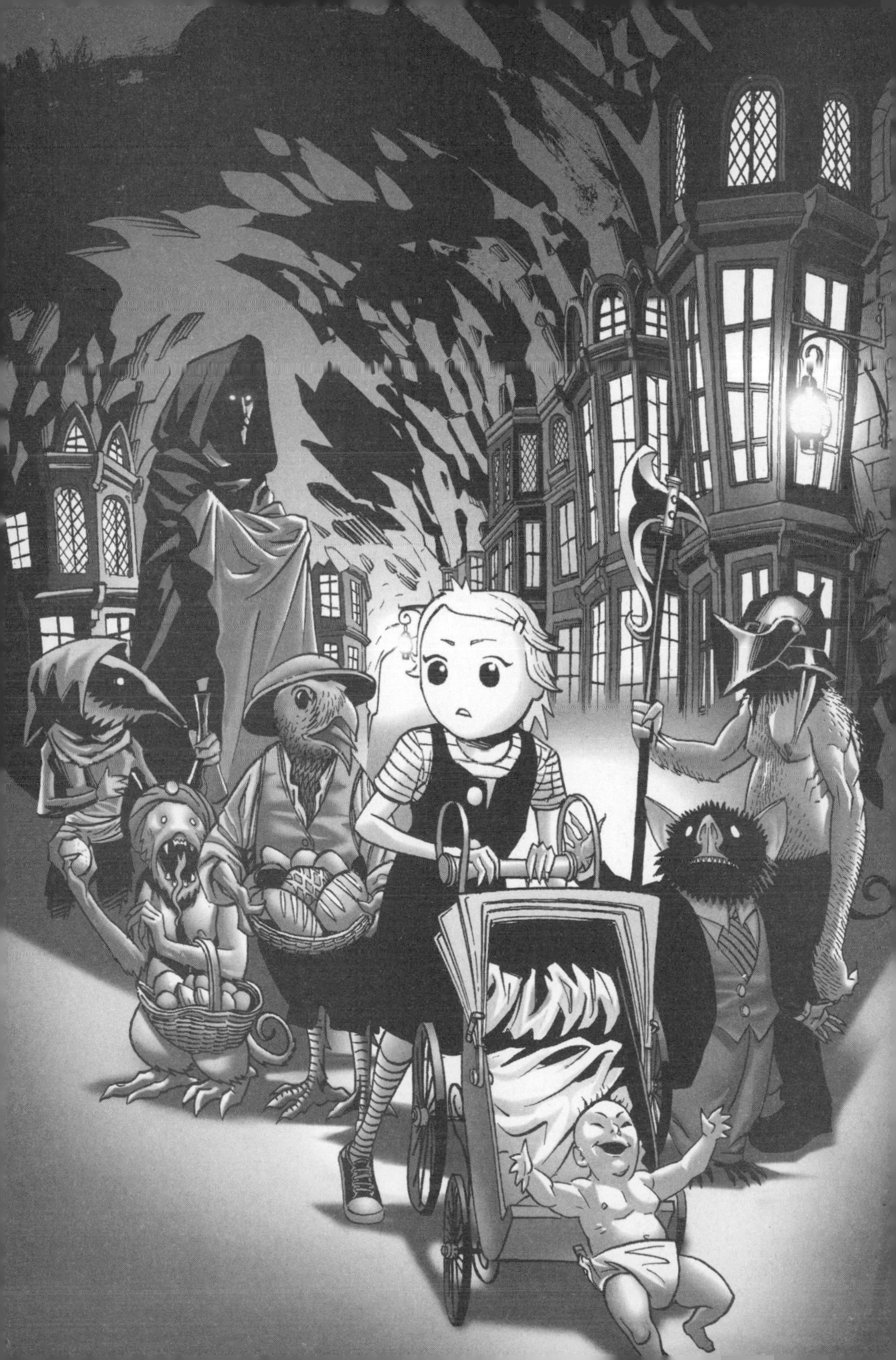

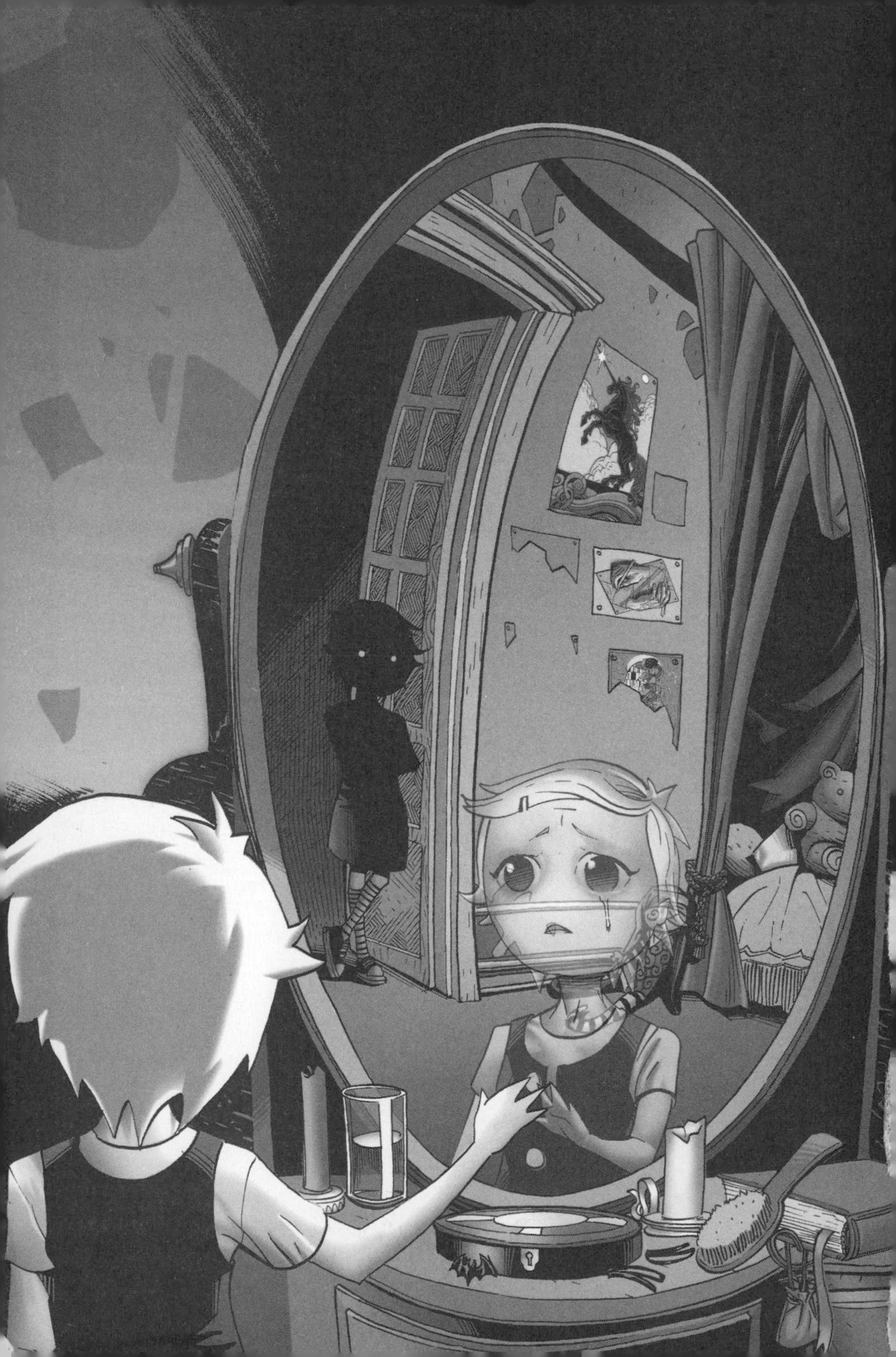

More great books from Oni Press:

**Courtney Crumrin
& the Coven of
Mystics**
by Ted Naifeh
128 pages
black-&-white interiors
$11.95 U.S.
ISBN 1-929998-59-7

**Courtney Crumrin
in the Twilight Kingdom**
by Ted Naifeh
136 pages
black-&-white interiors
$11.95 U.S.
ISBN 1-932664-01-7

Hopeless Savages Vol. 1
by Jen Van Meter
Christine Norrie
& Chynna Clugston-Major
136 pages
black-&-white interiors
$11.95 U.S.
ISBN 1-929998-75-9

**Hopeless Savages
Vol. 2: Ground Zero**
by Jen Van Meter & Bryan O'Malley
w/ Clugston-Major, Norrie, & Watson
128 pages
black-&-white interiors
$11.95 U.S.
ISBN 1-0200008-52-X

**Jason and the Argobots
Vol. 1: Birthquake**
by J. Torres & Mike Norton
112 pages
black-&-white interiors
$11.95 U.S.
ISBN 1-929998-55-4

**Jason and the Argobots
Vol. 2: Machina Ex Deus**
by J. Torres & Mike Norton
104 pages
black-&-white interiors
$11.95 U.S.
ISBN 1-929998-56-2

**Sidekicks Vol. 1:
The Transfer Student**
by J. Torres & Takeshi Miyazawa
144 pages
black-&-white interiors
$11.95 U.S.
ISBN 1-929998-76-7

**Mutant Texas:
Tales of Ida Red**
by Paul Dini & J. Bone
128 pages
black-&-white interiors
$11.95 U.S.
ISBN 1-929998-53-8

Available at
www.onipress.com
and finer comics shops
everywhere. For a comics
store near you, call
1-888-COMIC-BOOK
or visit
www.the-master-list.com.

For additional Oni Press
books and information
visit www.onipress.com.